ADVERTISING
STRATEGY

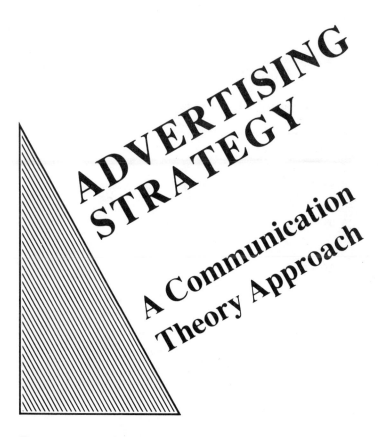

ADVERTISING STRATEGY

A Communication Theory Approach

Larry Percy
John R. Rossiter

PRAEGER SPECIAL STUDIES • PRAEGER SCIENTIFIC

Library of Congress Cataloging in Publication Data

Percy, Larry.
  Advertising strategy.

  Bibliography: p.
  1. Advertising. 2. Advertising media planning.
I. Rossiter, John R., joint author. II. Title.
HF5821.P43   659.1   79-25228
ISBN 0-03-055906-5

Published in 1980 by Praeger Publishers
CBS Educational and Professional Publishing
A Division of CBS, Inc.
521 Fifth Avenue, New York, New York 10017 U.S.A.

© 1980 by Praeger Publishers

0123456789   038   987654321

Printed in the United States of America

CONTENTS

1

INTRODUCTION

The business of developing advertising strategy is not a simple matter. Many people, including a number of marketing managers and advertising executives, feel there is little more involved in a good advertising strategy than agreeing upon a "great" creative idea that will either acquaint people with their product or service, or "sell" them that product or service, and then present that message to the greatest number of people. Sometimes they are lucky, and the product does sell. But what contribution has the advertising made? How did it help, if indeed it did (and product success was not the result of some other marketing factor), whom did it reach, and why did they respond?

More often, however, the product will not respond to such advertising. And yet the questions will remain. Why didn't it help; to whom should the message have been presented; what should have been said; how, and how often? This chapter introduces the reader to the ingredients of a successful advertising strategy, providing an overview, from a communication perspective, of the objectives one must consider for advertising, the responses one might expect to advertising, and these communication variables available to the advertiser that enable him to influence the outcome of his advertising efforts. In addition, an overview is provided of methods for evaluating advertising's success in meeting its objectives.

The remainder of the book treats in depth each of the five communication variables that influence advertising response, providing the reader with the necessary background to develop effective advertising strategies and evaluate their results—that is, to answer the major strategy questions confronting advertising management.

ADVERTISING RESPONSE

The success of an advertising strategy is evaluated in terms of the response the advertising gets from the target audience (or receivers, as we shall call them). Advertising response, however, is a multilevel phenomenon. At the first and narrowest level, advertising response begins with response to an individual advertisement: the target receivers must be exposed to the advertisement via media and the advertisement must be "processed" or understood as intended by the advertiser. At a broader level, advertising response comprises the ways in which a particular advertisement or series of advertisements contributes to the target audience members' awareness of, knowledge about, feelings toward, and intentions to act with regard to the advertised product (or service). These broader responses—to the product rather than to the individual advertisement—represent the second level of advertising response. Awareness, knowledge (or beliefs), feelings (or evaluations), and intentions to act (to buy, to look for, or to recommend the product) are *communication responses* that enter into the purchase or purchase-related decision. Thus, by instilling appropriate communication responses, advertising can have a causal impact on the target audience's buyer behavior.

It should be evident that communication responses can be achieved by factors other than advertising—word of mouth, for example, or other sources of marketing information. Consequently, communication responses to advertising must be compatible with communication responses obtained by the target audience through other sources (unless, of course, the purpose of the advertising is to counteract unfavorable communication responses derived from other sources). This introduces the important concept of the target audience member's or message receiver's communication status prior to receipt of the advertising—often called *initial attitude*. Initial attitude, a term we use generically to refer to the receiver's state of awareness, beliefs, evaluations, and intentions toward the product, is the critical component of advertising strategy from a communication standpoint. Advertising strategies will be quite different, according to: (1) whether the target receiver is aware or unaware of the product; (2) if aware, whether the receiver has particular beliefs about the product; (3) whether or not the receiver has to have positive feelings toward the product (which is not always necessary); and (4) what the receiver intends to do about the product—avoid it, try it, rebuy it, recommend it, and so on.

Consider the following typical scenarios. How many people in the United States are aware of Sansui hi-fi components? Relatively few. Of Pioneer hi-fi components? A great many. The two companies have, generally speaking, quite different tasks for advertising to perform. In Sansui's case, the company is probably addressing a vast potential market of unaware consumers. In Pioneer's case, the company is probably addressing an equally large market of consumers who are well aware of the brand. The advertising strategies will differ at the level

of the individual advertisement (different media exposure and message processing objectives) and at the broader level of communication objectives (awareness
as either absent or present as part of the receiver's "initial attitude"). Similar
scenarios could be constructed for the other three types of communication responses. Perhaps the typical belief necessary to induce purchase of Sansui is
service-related, for a foreign manufacturer, whereas for Pioneer, the belief may
be quality and price-related. Perhaps the attitudinal response necessary in
Sansui's case centers on favorable attitude formation; while in Pioneer's case it
may be favorable attitude maintenance or unfavorable attitude change. Similarly, intentions to purchase or visit dealerships may be differentially probable
for the two brands—Sansui requiring a great deal of convincing advertising information and Pioneer little other than an advertising-announced price reduction. These scenarios illustrate the importance of initial attitude (generically
considered as pertaining to any or all of the four types of communication
response) in the formulation of advertising strategy.

In summary, advertising response can also be viewed in terms of the ultimately desired behavioral outcome—usually purchase (or purchase-related) behavior. From
the firms' viewpoint, such behavior translates to sales and profit. In this book,
we will assume that advertising cannot achieve behavioral outcomes *without* first
achieving communication responses. In essence, advertising must communicate
to sell. Marketing research and *marketing strategy*, as contrasted with *advertising
strategy*, will have already indicated to the manager what needs to be communicated. The focus of advertising strategy, then, is on the communication
function.

In summary, advertising response is evaluated at two principal levels as a
contributor to purchase behavior:

- the individual advertisement level (media exposure and message processing)
- the product communication level (awareness, beliefs, evaluations, and intentions)

Advertising response (as the term is used in this book) is therefore distinguished
from market or buyer response: the former refers to "internal" communication
effects, whereas the latter refers to "external" behavioral outcomes caused in
part or in full by the communication effects of advertising.

Response at the Individual Advertisement Level

The receiver's response to advertising at the individual advertisement level
entails two steps: media exposure and message processing. The initial exposure
is rather straightforward; although as we shall see, it is difficult to measure. But,
even though exposure to advertising must necessarily precede processing of a

message and subsequent communication response to that advertising, in terms of advertising strategy development it will follow the creation of the actual message. This distinction is taken up in some depth in the Receiver Selection chapter. And, although message processing, too, is an obvious objective for advertising, it will rarely be dealt with directly in the formation of advertising strategy. Rather, message processing must be understood by the advertiser and his agency in order to affectively implement an advertising strategy, which will have as its goal a particular communication response.

Media Exposure

The first response that advertising must attain is exposure to the target receivers. If a potential buyer is not exposed to an advertising message, that advertising will obviously have no effect on his behavior. Essentially, exposure occurs when a receiver comes in sensory contact with the advertising. The sensory contact can be visual, in the case of print advertising, auditory in the case of radio commercials, or both visual and auditory in the case of television commercials.

However, sensory contact is rapid. Incoming information is held in sensory memory for approximately a second, during which time the receiver will react to the information stimulus (such as advertising) at a preattentive, subconscious level (Loftus and Loftus 1976). To measure exposure at this sensory level is obviously quite difficult, and, from a mass media standpoint, impossible. As a result, most advertisers have chosen to regard exposure as occurring if the receiver can be shown to have been exposed, not to the advertising, but to the media vehicle in which the advertising was placed. This has resulted in the widespread use of print vehicle readership, radio program listenership, and television program viewership reports as surrogate measures of advertising exposure.

There are a number of variations on these measures of advertising exposure, but most center on an opportunity for exposure as measured by media vehicle delivery. Yet, it should be clear to the reader that relying upon reported media behavior, as estimated by syndicated media surveys, is a rather poor indication of actual advertising exposure. While it is certainly an indication of *potential* exposure for advertising, there is no guarantee that everyone who reads a magazine or newspaper, listens to a radio show, or watches a television show makes sensory contact with a particular piece of advertising. And even more to the point, how can the advertiser be certain that particular media vehicles are providing the desired target receivers? This problem and some possible solutions are discussed in detail in chapter 5, "Media Selection."

Message Processing

Message processing defines that mechanism which links new (or repeated) information in the form of an advertising message with existing attitudes. One may think of this mechanism as encompassing three subprocesses: attention, decoding, and encoding. The receiver must pay attention to at least some aspect of the advertising message, decode and comprehend its meaning, and encode a personal interpretation of the meaning. Media exposure to advertising is necessary but not sufficient; the advertising must stimulate some cognitive activity on the part of the receiver if it is to have an impact on the receiver's communication response to the product. Attention, decoding, and encoding take place in what is generally referred to as short-term memory; although some favor a "depth of processing" explanation to this more traditional short-term versus long-term memory formulation (cf. Craik and Lockhart 1972). Either information processing explanation permits this three subprocess notion of message processing. We shall follow the more generally accepted short-term memory explanation.

Short-term memory has a limited capacity (a subject dealt with in considerable detail in later discussions of message construction). Sometimes this is not a problem, if the receiver deliberately seeks exposure to advertising and actively attends to the content. For example, Yellow Pages and retail newspaper advertising often receive active attention by consumers who are "in the market" for a particular product or service. More likely, however, in order for advertising to gain the receiver's attention, other competing thoughts must be screened out. This means that the advertising must be intrusive in order to displace other thoughts already in the receiver's short-term memory. Securing attention will obviously be enhanced by executions relevant to the receiver's interest.

But, even though a receiver attends to much of the advertising, not all of the points of the message may be communicated. Some may be simply ignored (not encoded); others misinterpreted (or encoded improperly); still others may be missed completely (never decoded). Nevertheless, in order for advertising to causally influence buyer behavior, some of the advertising's message points must be registered in the receiver's short-term memory. This could be as little as a brand name or as many message points as the advertising message presents. Moreover, if the purchase decision is not made immediately (that is, within a few seconds), then the advertising message points must also be registered in long-term memory for subsequent retrieval at the time of decision.

The study of psycholinguistics has provided a wealth of practical guidelines in evaluating just what a receiver will decode from a message. For example, consider the powerful effect verbs have in message comprehension. If one were to say "Modern homemakers *buy* frozen food," a receiver would probably understand this to mean that modern homemakers buy *some* or a *few* frozen foods. Positive verbs such as "buy" tend to elicit low implicit quantifier ratings. On the other hand, if one were to say "Traditional homemakers *avoid* frozen food," a receiver would understand this to mean traditional homemakers avoid *most* or *all* frozen foods. Negative verbs such as "avoid" tend to elicit high implicit quantifiers. The Message Strategy chapter elaborates upon this example, and provides many other illustrations of the importance of psycholinguistics in message processing.

Response at the Product Communication Level

Communication about the product is the purpose or objective of advertising strategy. Communication responses to advertising may be divided into four types:

Awareness: responses that allow a receiver to identify a product or service, on cue, in sufficient detail to consider it as a purchase option.

Cognitive: responses that associate a product or service with a characteristic or attribute that can positively influence purchase.

Affective: responses that represent the receiver's emotional evaluation of (or liking for) a product or service.

Conative: responses denoting the receiver's plans of action in relation to a product or service—such plans refer to purchase or purchase-related behavior.

While this approach to communication effects may seem to imply a hierarchy of effects, much in the manner of McGuire's (1972) information-processing paradigm, such a model is not required in order to appreciate the usefulness of communication objectives in determining advertising strategy. It is the purpose of advertising strategy to maximize the potential for achieving a desired communication effect through judicious control of the communication variables at the advertiser's disposal, regardless of how one may hypothesize such communication effects interact in choice or buyer behavior.

The hierarchy of effects class of model (cf. Robertson 1976) postulates exposure and message processing of various marketing stimuli over a period of time will generate awareness, which leads to belief formation (analogous to the awareness and cognitive objectives); these beliefs affect an evaluation of the product or service advertised (analogous to the affective objective), which in turn mediates intention (analogous to the conative objective). If this "learning" is maintained in the receiver's long-term memory, a buyer response will occur, such as purchasing a product or using a service.

However, suppose buyer response in a particular category appears better explained by some other model, such as Ehrenberg's "Awareness-Trial-Reinforcement" model (Ehrenberg 1974), Krugman's "Low Involvement" model, or Festinger's "Dissonance-Attribution" model (Ray 1973). In the case of Ehrenberg's model, initial exposure and processing of marketing stimuli generates awareness, leading to beliefs that are sufficient to motivate trial. If the usage experience is favorable, affect increases, reinforcing the behavior. Subsequent advertising then serves as a reinforcement reminder of the positive evaluation and intention to repurchase. It should be clear to the reader that, if this were an acceptable model of marketing communication impact upon buyer response in a particular situation, advertising strategy would still require attention to exposure and message processing; and the choice of specific awareness, cognitive, affective, or conative communication objectives would still be necessary to impact the buyer response. The affect of communication variables, such as receiver selection, source, message, media, and scheduling, on these objectives hold, regardless of how the communication effects may be thought to combine in buyer response.

The same would be true with the Krugman or Festinger model. Krugman's low involvement model suggests that exposure and message processing of marketing stimuli generate awareness and form latent beliefs in a subconscious meaning, which do not become consciously recovered until purchase occurs. After purchase, beliefs become salient and attitude toward the product or service is formed. If one were to accept this model for a particular marketing situation, advertising strategy would only be involved with awareness and cognitive objectives, though only the awareness objective would be measurable. But, even here, the influence of the communication variables on the advertising response would be critical. Following Festinger's dissonance-attribution model, once consumer behavior occurs in the market, for whatever reason (including previous advertising), dissonance arises over an unsure evaluation of the product. This could lead to deliberate exposure to, and message processing of, advertising that supports that choice—which in turn reinforces beliefs reducing dissonance. Assuming this model reflects buyer response in the market, advertising strategy would concern itself with attitude objectives (cognitive, affective, and conative), this time in expectation of post-purchase exposure.

So, although this book presents communication objectives in a traditional hierarchy of effects mode, this should not be understood as a *condition* for their acceptance and utility. The principles discussed hold, regardless of the buyer response model adopted for a particular marketing situation. Each of these communication response objectives are detailed below.

Communication Response Objectives

Awareness is a rather straightforward response. It must be achieved before behavioral effects can occur, even though it is generally not the sole communication objective. For example, awareness has been found to have a strong mediating or facilitating role in the formation of beliefs about and attitudes toward insurance companies. People prefer to deal with an agent from a company believed to be large and well known. This belief follows if awareness of the company is high—that is, if its visibility created through advertising makes it seem to be large and well known.

Frequently, more than one objective must be realized in order to satisfy a particular advertising strategy. And, while an advertiser may think he can accomplish his strategic objective with a single execution, more often multiple executions, each emphasizing a single communication response, will be necessary. An old-line railroad, which in recent years has diversified, decided to change its name in order to de-emphasize its railroad association. The first communication objective, of course, was to generate awareness of the new corporate name. But, at the same time, the company wished to instill diversification-oriented cognitions—in other words, an awareness and cognitively based advertising strategy. However, although awareness of the name was strong, this advertising wasn't enough to convince financial analysts (the target receivers) that the company really was more than just a railroad. Based upon the initial advertising, only an awareness response was realized; cognitive elicitation testing among financial analysts did not indicate an understanding that this company was well diversified. As a result, the strategy was altered to include a specific cognitive response. Advertising with a cognitive objective was created and supportive beliefs on behalf of the company's diversification were stimulated.

Beliefs about the product are the most common type of communication objective. These can have direct impact on buyer behavior. For example, research on the spray cooking lubricant category has indicated that there are two general classes of beliefs relevant to cooking spray: functional beliefs (for example, "costs less," "cholesterol-free") and usage beliefs (for example, "lightly coats surface," "odor free"). Multidimensional scaling analysis revealed that, while the usage beliefs tended to discriminate significantly among brands, the functional beliefs did not. This result suggests that message points for the advertising of cooking sprays should be restricted to the most positive usage beliefs. Functional beliefs, although believable, would not offer a unique brand advantage.

Evaluative or *affective* responses may also be a communication objective. Consider the dominant advertising strategy of early CB radios. After initial advertising written to "sell" the idea of CB radios, the primary message emphasis of most major manufacturers became "power." While power was not a bad attribute to promote, multidimensional scaling of characteristics that current and potential consumers preferred in a CB radio revealed that positive evaluations were more likely for radios regarded as "rugged and dependable." As a result, it would make sense to position a brand of CB radio as rugged and dependable rather than powerful. One CB advertiser who followed this strategy developed and maintained a strong number three position in the market while spending at a much lower rate than the two leading brands.

Another interesting example of an advertising execution's impact on an affective response involved the use of a visual versus verbal emphasis in print advertising (Rossiter and Percy 1978). Two rough ads were created for a (fictional) brand of beer positioned as a possible new import. Only the visual versus verbal emphasis differed in the two ads: one had a big picture with small copy; and the other large copy with a small picture. In each case, it was the same copy and picture. However, those seeing the big picture evaluated the beer *twice* as favorably as those seeing the smaller picture. This doesn't necessarily mean that one should always use large pictures in print advertising. But it does indicate that, if the desired communication response is attitudinal or evaluative, then an emphasis on visual content can help. Visual imagery created during message processing is an important and often overwhelming factor in generating favorable attitudes. Visual and verbal imaging are discussed in some depth in the Message Strategy chapter.

Finally, communication objectives very often include *intentions*. Intentions to behave generally have a strong influence on subsequent actual behavior. In a study of yogurt, it was discovered that consumers considered flavor, price, and brand the three most important attributes in a decision to buy. In attempts to determine which element to stress in advertising, a typical research procedure would be to ask which of these three is most important and which least important when buying yogurt. Asking that question revealed that flavor was considered most important, followed by price, with brand considered least important. However, this procedure ignores the fact that these three attributes will interact during the choice decision. When a research design was utilized that took this into account, and a conjoint measurement analysis completed, it showed that price was most important, followed by brand, then flavor. Using the traditional questioning procedure would have been misleading, underscoring the need for appropriate information in strategic planning. The importance of price in the consumers' choice to buy yogurt suggests advertising strategy should (a) create strong price-brand associations if one's brand is low priced; or (b) address price-value if one's brand is high priced.

MEASURING ADVERTISING RESPONSE

We have introduced the nature of advertising objectives from a marketing strategy viewpoint, and have pointed out the importance of exposure, message processing, and communication effects objectives in advertising strategy. While it is all well and good to establish specific objectives for advertising, how does one know if the objectives have been achieved. Obviously, some measurement of advertising objectives is in order; and numerous techniques and services are available to the advertiser for just that purpose. Detailed below are a few examples of consumer advertising response measures, but the list is by no means exhaustive.

Media Exposure: these measures are almost wholly based upon media vehicle audiences, and represent syndicated services available to any advertiser. While the exception of the well-known Nielsen, and less well-known Arbitron, television audience measures, which are based upon on-set recording devices, nearly all media vehicle audience measures are survey based. This would include Simmons survey of television viewership, Arbitron, Pulse Inc., and Simmons surveys of radio listenership, and Simmons surveys of print readership.

Message Processing: these measures are generally based upon laboratory experiments, although small-scale survey work is also conducted. While a number of commercially available "standardized" procedures are available, perhaps as often a custom-designed experiment is employed. In assessing immediate (that is, during exposure to the advertising) attention, physiological measures such as "brain waves" or pupil dilation are employed: postmeasures of attention include both recognition and general recall. Immediate measures of decoding involve the collection of descriptions or ratings of the advertising; postmeasures would include recall of the advertising. Immediate measures of encoding would involve elicited protocols (for example, "What are you thinking of now as you see this commercial?"); postmeasures would center on verbatim responses.

Communication Response: these measures are always independent of the actual advertising, but frequently employ a "pre-post" design (that is, one measure prior to the advertising's exposure, and one after a specified period of time). Cued name or package recognition provides a measure of awareness; cognitions are measured via direct scale judgements of appropriate attributes, or through multidimensional scaling of similarities judgements; affective reaction is measured directly by preference or indirectly through physiological or psychophysical product evaluations; and conations are indicated by expressed purchase behavior.

Buyer Behavior: perhaps the most common measure, generally comprising the primary research efforts of an advertiser's market research resource. Specifically, this would include custom-designed surveys at the individual buyer level, such as in-store observation, survey reports, and purchase diaries.

Sales: the most common measure, but owing to marketing considerations such as distribution and pipeline fill (the amount of product shipped but not yet at the retail level), perhaps one of the least exact. Aside from the advertiser's own shipment figures, syndicated store audits by Nielsen and ASI are available on a custom basis or for selected product categories; MRCA provides a household purchase diary; and SAMI reports warehouse withdrawals for selected product categories. All such measures provide a relative fix on sales volume and percentage market share.

Profit: measured by traditional accounting methods such as net pretax, net after-tax, return or investment, per share earnings, discounted present value or forgoing, etc.

As important as ultimate preference indicators may be, they are at best only descriptive of how well advertising has accomplished its objective. What is even more important to know is why the advertising has succeeded or failed. Only by moving to the level of explanation of communication effects can feedback be obtained to provide insight into how one's advertising can be modified to achieve better results.

Regardless of the desired response (with the possible exception of an awareness-only objective), evaluating advertising requires both a cognitive response and cognitive structure approach. Prior to seeing any advertising, people have a body of existing attitudes. It is important that an advertiser identify these. Usually this information is apparent after research has been conducted for the investigation of communication objectives. The resulting advertising is then presented to a sample of target receiver and their thoughts are elicited. To the extent a receiver plays back the intended message, reception of the message has been achieved. But, to insure an attitude change, whether at the belief, evaluation, or intention level, one must stimulate some kind of cognitive activity (or thinking)—something one may think of as the impact of the advertising response.

For example, suppose advertising says a food product is made with all natural ingredients. If the receivers play that point back, they certainly received the message. But if they embellish that point by saying "It's better because it's made with all natural ingredients," they have used the information in the message to infer that the product is better; this would be termed supportive arguing on behalf of the product—what we have referred to as impact.

As important as it is to understand the cognitive response to advertising, it is equally important to understand the resulting cognitive structure. It has been pointed out that receivers always have a head full of different attitudes. The question is: Have any beliefs, evaluations, or intentions changed as a result of the advertising, even if they weren't directly addressed in the message itself? Again, consider the "natural ingredients" claim. Suppose that, prior to exposure to the advertising, receivers felt a brand was moderately priced. After exposure to the advertising, however, they now perceive the product as expensive—not because the advertising said anything about price, but because the receiver inferred from the "natural ingredients" claim that the product would now be higher priced. It is critical that an advertiser understand the full impact of the message, including peripheral beliefs not directly addressed by the advertising (see Figure 1.1).

A multidimensional unfolding analysis of several frozen foods brands with a set of beliefs critical to frozen food preference revealed that although the advertiser's brand was associated highly with "quality" and "taste" (as well as "price"), it was not associated with such beliefs as "for whole family" and "for everyday use," which were beliefs associated with its major competitor. Given this, an advertising strategy was suggested, seeking a cognitive response objective. Six rough executions of three campaign approaches were created in an effort to move the brand's image closer to the "family" and "everyday use" beliefs, without sacrificing its association with "quality" and "taste." All but one of the executions communicated the desired strategy. But, when belief change was measured via another multidimensional unfolding, it was discovered that only three of the test ads achieved the desired goal; two others, although moving toward the desired new beliefs, unfortunately moved significantly away from the "quality" and "taste" beliefs. The sixth ad, the one in fact that failed to strongly communicate the strategy, only moved away from the "quality" and "taste" beliefs (Lautman, Percy, and Kordish 1978). As a result, the three successful test ads were finished and formed the basis for a new campaign.

Just as one measures the ability of one's own advertising to communicate a particular strategy, one can assess the ability of competitive advertising to com-

FIGURE 1.1

A Cognitive Response/Structure Procedure for Evaluating Advertising Response Effectiveness

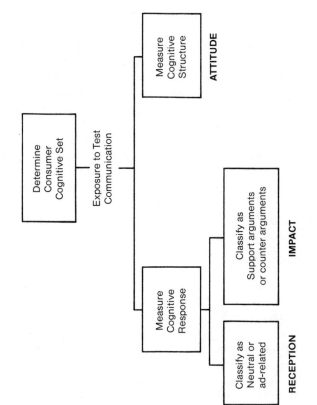

municate a particular strategy. This provides a reading of the relative strength of the advertising and its potential in the market. And even when this much effort doesn't seem warranted, a formal content analysis of competitive advertising is quite useful in gaining an understanding of just what is being said in the market.

ADVERTISING COMMUNICATION VARIABLES

In this section, each of the five communication variables important to the formation and implementation of advertising strategy are introduced. Each of these variables is treated in depth by the chapters comprising the remainder of this book. They are the variables the advertiser controls—the means of maximizing the potential for a buyer response stimulated by affective, well-targeted advertising.

Variable 1: Receiver Selection

Some people have a greater potential for responding to both advertising and other marketing stimuli. The importance of a sound receiver strategy is to identify those with the greatest attitudinal disposition toward the advertised category via a communication-oriented approach to market segmentation, and to uncover those receiver characteristics that will have the greatest affect on responsiveness to advertising. Three specific characteristics important to receiver strategy are: demographics, psychographics, and personality traits.

Demographics provide a description of market segments in terms of region, subculture, ethnicity, religion, age, sex, occupation, income, education, stage in family life cycle, and so on, and are used to select appropriate media vehicles. A demographic profile of a segment matched with the demographic profile of a vehicle's audience enables decisions to be made based upon the number of target receivers reached by a vehicle and thus (potentially) exposed to the advertisement.

Two of the more important demographic characteristics influencing advertising response are age and sex. Age, for example, tends to have a bimodal affect, for younger and older receivers exhibit lower attention and decoding ability. There also appears to be some evidence that women have greater verbal decoding ability than men, and as a result may be more likely to respond to advertising even though they are no more "persuadable" than men.

Psychographics is a rather nebulous term that covers such things as lifestyle or attitude, interest, and opinion (AIO) variables. Psychographic variables correlate with (but do not explain) buyer behavior. Their primary use is in providing a detailed description or "picture" of the target receiver, in order to more effectively design appropriate message content, particularly in selecting the types of people and settings shown in advertisements.

Personality traits reflect relatively stable individual difference variables that are explanatory or causal in that they mediate message processing and thus affect the response to advertising. Two personality traits explored in great depth in the personality literature are anxiety and extroversion, and each of these traits impacts advertising response. For example, anxiety in a receiver may either increase or reduce counter-arguing, depending upon the message appeal. Extroversion affects message conditioning; introverts tend to be more easily conditioned than extroverts. In addition to these specific individual difference characteristics, the initial attitude of a receiver is critical, not only to message processing (as we have already pointed out), but to maximizing the probability of achieving the desired communication response objective.

Variable 2: Source Factors

One must fully understand a target receiver's current disposition toward an intended communication source (or sources) *independently of the message* in order to appreciate the total impact of the message of an advertisement or commercial. The study of a source's affectiveness in this regard is greatly facilitated by the VisCap model of source effectiveness, which considers the visibility, credibility, attractiveness, and power of a perceived source. Each component of the model has a specific association with an advertising response. Visibility affects the awareness response, credibility the cognitive response, attractiveness the affective response, and power the conative response. Among the potential components within advertising that may be construed as sources, either singly or in combination for any one piece of advertising, are:

1. An *industry* as a perceived source: For example, the federal government, oil companies, commodities, the food industry. This could also include the advertising industry or media.

2. A *company* as a perceived source: For example, in corporate image campaigns, as well as company name associations.

3. The receiver's disposition toward the *product category* as a perceived source, including: (a) values served by the product class, (b) defining attributes, or (c) product space and market space.

4. The receivers' dispositions toward the *brand* as a perceived source, such as (a) buyer behavior status, or (b) communication status, including brand positioning in a joint space with other brands.

5. The receivers' dispositions toward broadcast or print *media* and specific media vehicles as a perceived source, especially (a) credibility-screening, and (b) the receiver's state during exposure.

6. The receivers' perceptions of *current users and personalities*, if any, associated with relevant sources (particularly the brand as source).

Variable 3: Message Strategy

The message in advertising provides the focal point for each of the other four communication variables. Whom one is talking to (the receiver) influences the message strategy; decisions as to execution rely heavily upon source factors; the message can, and frequently does, influence the selection of media; and what one has to say, and the objectives reflected in that message, dictate the scheduling strategy. The importance of the message in advertising strategy, while not transcendent, certainly requires careful attention. It is not enough to rely on "creative inspiration." Too much is involved.

There are three primary areas of concern in understanding an advertising message: appeal, structure, and content. Although you may think the kinds of appeals possible in advertising are endless, they may be classified according to Aristotle's typology of ethos, pathos, and logos. Ethos appeals concentrate on the source more than the actual words in the message, relying, for example, on a presenter's credentials as a reason for buying the product. Pathos defines emotional appeals. Here the message appeal might be based upon an emotional appeal surrounding the product or on an arousal of positive or negative emotions in the course of a logical, or logos appeal. A logos appeal reflects a rather straightforward reason for buying the product. Overall, most advertising will employ some combination of these appeals.

Message structure refers to the more macro view of advertising content. With a number of points to be made (usually) in any one message, concern must be focused on such things as the order in which the points are presented, or whether the receiver should be "set-up" or forewarned of the intended objective. Also, a number of styles in presentation offer potentially different responses. Should the message employ one versus two-sided arguments (comparison *within* brand) or use comparative arguments *between* brands (either explicit or implied)? Finally, since most advertising is made up of more than just one sentence, its grammatical structure can have a significant impact on potential response.

This leads directly to message content—the micro view of advertising content. Here, insights from the field of psycholinguistics add an extra dimension to the study of lexical structure as it applies to advertising messages. The meaning and use of words respond to various psychological processes, and a knowledge of these effects can have great impact on strategy decisions. This is particularly true of verb effects. Using one verb form rather than another may enhance interpretation, retard it, or even alter the intended meaning without the change being recognized by the copywriter.

The influence of words on a receiver's reasoning will obviously have an affect on his response to advertising. But, of equal, although less understood, importance is the impact of visual elements in the message. These, too, must be accounted for in evaluating the potential of a message achieving the desired response.

Variable 4: Media Selection

After a message has been created, it must be delivered to the target receivers. Once again, however, what on the surface appears to be a rather simple and straightforward process, in reality is quite complex. It is so complex, in fact, that most media planning is conducted with the barest of information, and with almost no regard for the advertising effects of a particular strategy. This occurs not because media professionals are indifferent, but because resources are not channeled to solve media problems or develop better information.

The effects of media variables on message processing suggest that broadcast media (especially television) tends to be more likely to stimulate attention because it requires very little effort on the part of the receiver. While this is "passive attention," to be sure, attention is achieved merely by the receiver presenting himself to the message. The next step, recognizing the advertising as a message through decoding and encoding a response, obviously requires involvement, and as a result, print media tends to be superior because the receiver has virtually all the time he needs to process and react to the advertising.

Determining specific media objectives and strategy requires an in depth understanding of one's target receivers, and some information about how often and how many may be reasonably reached within the constraints of a budget. While estimates of the potential "reach" and "frequency" for most media are available, what is generally missing is a strong link to the desired receivers. Without primary research specifically designed to establish this, one can never be sure of an efficient media plan.

Variable 5: Scheduling Strategy

Once the appropriate media vehicles have been selected to deliver the maximum number of target receivers coincident with the reach and frequency objective of the media strategy, the media must be scheduled. The "shape" of this schedule must reflect specific post communication affects known to be associated with particular advertising responses. For example, media must be scheduled closer together (that is, exhibit more "continuity") if the desired response is awareness. On the other hand, this becomes less of a concern when beliefs or attitude is the desired response. In that case, more attention may be given to increasing the pressure at specific intervals in order to raise the overall level of response. Since there is a finite amount of expenditure available for any particular time period, if one does not need to spread one's media expenditure evenly over the entire period to ensure continuous coverage, as the interval length between exposures (or "flighting") increases, more media pressure may be expended at those times. This will increase the reach and frequency potential during those periods, and hence the potential for response.

SUMMARY

It is the job of those creating advertising to utilize all of the communication variables at their disposal to maximize a positive response to their advertising. Much of what is presented in the following chapters is aimed at providing the background necessary to achieve media exposure and to postively affect message processing in a manner consistent with the advertiser's desired communication response objectives.

2

RECEIVER SELECTION

Typically, when one talks of receiver variables, the concern is with those characteristics of the person to whom a communication is directed: and, more specifically, with that person's state upon receiving the message of the communication. We will be concerned with how these characteristics correlate with product usage (for example, in media considerations), but, more important, how they correlate with the receiver's response to advertising.

In the usual advertising context, the advertiser seeks to describe the target audience in terms of some behavioral criteria (such as heavy category users—a post-decision response) or demographic profile (generally decocted from certain inferred behavioral notions and correlated either with the advertising presentation or post-decision responses) he feels will be persuasible. From a practical standpoint, this is frequently predicted more on the fact that these data are both intuitively satisfying and easily understood, as well as readily available through syndicated research for use in developing media schedules. But, as we shall see, this ignores an understanding of those factors particular to the persuasibility of advertising. It views the problem only as one of "matching" profiles of people currently behaving in a manner thought to be compatible with the advertiser's product or service to similar receivers in a global target audience. This, in effect, assumes a product orientation to strategy development, rather than an advertising or communication orientation.

In this chapter we shall begin by discussing the need to identify the target receivers through a market segmentation based upon communication objectives. Then we will discuss the importance of those characteristics that mediate the receiver's response to advertising. This process of selecting receivers based upon advertising objectives within an understanding of how their individual characteristics (attitude, trait-variables, and state-variables) will affect an advertising response places the advertiser in a better position to maximize the impact of his message.

Part I
Receiver Identification
and Classification

Janis and Hovland (1959) have dealt with such individual differences among receivers (or, as they referred to them, audience variables) as general persuasibility, initial opinions, intelligence, self-esteem, cognitive complexity, and various personality traits. Fishbein and Ajzen (1975) have remarked that receiver variables are generally viewed as influencing people's confidence in their own beliefs (consistent, of course, with their own notions of attitude and attitude change), and they categorize them as *relatively stable individual difference variables*, such as general persuasibility, chronic anxiety, self-esteem, sex, and intelligence, as well as *situational and topic factors* such as anxiety, involvement, extremity of one's own position, and the receiver's information or knowledge of the communication topic. McGuire (1969a, 1973) too, sees this dichotomy, discussing receiver variables having to do with a given social-influence situation (namely, the degree to which a person is actively involved with the communication) and more general and enduring individual difference variables that persist outside a specific communication situation. In other words, receiver variables may be viewed as (a) what kinds of people tend to be more persuasible—trait-variables; and (b) in what state is a given individual most persuasible—state-variables.

IDENTIFYING TARGET RECEIVERS
WITH MARKET SEGMENTATION

On the surface, there does not seem to be anything particularly difficult about segmenting a market. One is usually thinking about little more than subdividing a market into homogeneous groups in which each group represents a specific potential target market for the company's product or service (Kotler 1976). The appeal of market segmentation follows from the feeling that no one company or product can satisfy everyone. As a result, it just seems to be good business sense to concentrate on those groups in a market where actual or potential buyer behavior is reasonably homogeneous, or where the within-group response variance is less than the between-group response variance. Selecting a target market segment could then follow from a belief that one of the segments is less well-attended by mass marketing strategies or because it is thought to be more highly disposed toward a company's offering. The problem, of course, comes in deciding how to segment a market.

Bases for Market Segmentation

Almost any receiver characteristic can be considered (and probably has been) as a basis for segmenting a market. The usefulness of any particular characteristic as a segmentation basis, however, may be thought of as a function of certain conditions (Kotler 1976). First, it must be memorable in such a way that one may readily determine whether the within-segment response variance is indeed less than the between segment response variance. If the receiver characteristic chosen for segmenting a market is something like aggressiveness, perhaps because it is felt aggressive people may be more interested in a new competitive outdoor sports product, one may find it difficult to obtain a reliable measure of a receiver's aggressiveness.

Second, the accessibility of the receivers who make up a segment must be considered. This is obviously important if advertising is to efficiently ready the receiver, and is critically affected by the media variables (discussed in chapter 5). Continuing with our example, even if one were able to measure a receiver's aggressiveness, how can one effectively focus advertising efforts on more aggressive people. Special measures of media behavior correlates would be required. While this is certainly not impossible to acquire, the media habits of aggressive receivers may not be particularly distinct from nonaggressive receivers. Finally, the profitability of the resulting segments must be considered. A segment must be sufficiently large, and potentially profitable, to justify the expense of specifically targeted market and advertising efforts. While the potential for the desired advertising response could indeed be greater among aggressive receivers, if there are only a few sufficiently aggressive receivers, from a marketing or communication standpoint the response would not be worthwhile. For example, suppose potential response among aggressive receivers was 80 percent, but they only constitute 20 percent of the market—an effective response of 16 percent. If the potential among nonaggressive receivers was only slightly more than 20 percent, it would still constitute a more effective response (since a 20 percent share of 80 percent of a market would also equal an effective response of 16 percent). It follows, then, that the better one's segmentation basis meets these conditions, the more likely one will be able to achieve the desired advertising response from the targeted segment of receivers.

The more traditional bases of market segmentation include: analysis of buyer behavior, demographic, and geographic variables. These variables provide an intuitively sound basis for looking at a market at a discrete level, and, in fact, occasionally provide reasonable marketing evidence for their use as segmentation criteria. Certain products or services just naturally skew toward such things as product category use, buyer roles, or situational usage. Geographic area or receiver trait variables, such as demographics (for example, age, income, occupation, or social class), also offer convenient a priori market segment bases. While they clearly offer convenient correlates for media behavior data and hence a strong probability for successful presentation of the advertising to those types of receivers, many researchers have found that receiver demographic characteristics generally fail to be efficient discriminators (cf. Frank 1968; Percy 1976). Psychographics, also a consumer trait variable, occasionally differentiate market segments along life-style variables, which are usually inferred from a receiver's activities. Frank, Massy, and Wind (1972) offer a detailed discussion of these traditional bases of market segmentation and FitzRoy (1976) reviews a number of segmentation methods utilizing these variables.

Each of these variables, however, tend to have one point in common when used as a basis for market segmentation—a product orientation. Even the so-called "benefit segmentation" approach (Haley 1968), in which receivers are grouped according to the benefits they are seeking from a particular product, deals with features or attributes of a product. The marketer may seek to relate these benefits to consumer motivation, but the segmentation basis remains product oriented.

Important as product objectives are to successful marketing, implementation of marketing strategies perforce rely on communicating those strategies effectively to the consumer; and this usually entails some form of advertising. It follows, then, that for purposes of a truly effective market segmentation strategy, one's segmentation basis should reflect a communication or advertising orientation. Although each of the product-oriented approaches to market segmentation mentioned above may indeed correlate with buyer response to advertising, they are not within the power of the advertiser to control or effect. An advertising orientation is best realized through an attitudinal segmentation of a market, in which the basis of segmentation is consumer attitude, especially as it relates to the environment in which a product is used.

It is fundamental to such an approach that one's efforts are centered on the usage environment and only incidentally on a brand or product. In competition for the consumer dollar, it is critical to understand exactly where any specific purchase will fit. Emphasis on the usage environment permits the evaluation of a product, among homogeneous attitude segments, within the broader parameters of use, where it and the alternatives to use are weighted in the general context of a consumer's routines and experiences. If the attitude object of interest is a power tool, or a toothpaste, or a laundry product, background data for an attitudinal segmentation would be concerned more with the situational context of use than the product itself. This understanding of the environment in which a product will be used permits the advertiser a broader range in developing and evaluating strategic alternatives than an understanding of only his product's use would allow.

The usual product orientation segmentation variables, as we have noted, are only descriptive and cannot tell one how to influence behavior or buyer response through advertising. However useful these variables are in defining the overall market structure and in correlating with other advertising communication variables, one is quickly led to the conclusion that the basis for receiver selection segmentation must lie with attitude. This assumption is necessary, given the context within which communication oriented market segmentation is considered. One investigates the environment in which a product is used, and determines receiver attitude(s) toward that environment. These attitudes bear directly on strategy development, because they influence advertising response and buyer behavior. Understanding how best to position a product in order to positively reflect an attitudinal disposition permits the development of more effective strategy; for example, if certain negative attitudes or saliences mitigate trial, understanding what they are permits strategy development aimed at positive modification or attitude change (a task well suited to advertising).

Thus considered, market segmentation is a method aimed at isolating those groups of receivers who hold similar attitudes about the usage situation for a particular brand or product class. Once these groups have been determined, they are studied in depth, along the more traditional and product-oriented segmentation variables, in order to best understand the cognitive, affective, and conative judgments (that is, beliefs, evaluations, and intentions) of the receiver. One determines for each attitude segment uncovered:

1. What these particular receivers' behavior and motivations are, especially as they relate to the brand and product class under study.

2. How the perceptions of the brand and product class among these receivers relate to the benefits they seek.

The understanding derived from this profiling of the attitude segments permits a review of the segments in order to select a target market of "prime receivers." They are prime receivers because they are attitudinally disposed toward a positive buyer response. Marketing and advertising efforts are then channeled toward these more promising segments after determining how the particular brand or its image may be positioned or modified to produce the greatest belief compatibility with the prime receivers selected.

A Methodology for Advertising Oriented Market Segmentation

The usual practice, as detailed by Percy (1976), in conducting a segmentation study of this nature is to attempt to develop as complete but compact a list as possible of all category and product benefits that might be important to consumers, and to successfully identify where the product fits in the routines of the consumer. Typically, this leads to a three-phase segmentation program. The first phase is made up of small scale qualitative work in both behavioral and motivational areas. Depth interviews or group sessions or both are utilized in order to help generate a comprehensive list of all conceivable attitudes or beliefs associated with consumer behavior and desires with respect to the product class, in order to supply some initial hypotheses as to the relationships and combinations of various influences.

Since the list generated is almost always filled with latent redundancies, and is too unwieldly to be effectively administered in a large-scale survey, a second phase based on personal interviews in each of several important product oriented subgroupings (perhaps user or brand groups, demographic groups, or others suggested by the first phase) are used for data reduction. Here, as many as several hundred items are factor analyzed, eliminating overlap and synonymity among the many variables resulting in an understanding of what beliefs are important and how they relate to product alternatives. Additionally, exhaustive cognitive and perceptual probing is done. The net effect of this phase is a managable-sized list of relatively independent and pertinent items that may be used in the final phase, instead of the long and redundant list of the first phase.

The final phase is a comprehensive look at the market and potential receivers. Utilizing all the significant items suggested from the earlier phases, a highly structured and projectable behavior and attitude study is conducted, resulting in receiver segments based upon common attitude and profiled over product-oriented variables. This "funnel" approach, in which a broad area is initially studied, and successively refined, is illustrated in Figure 2.1.

Essentially, the first phase of the study adds to one's present storehouse of knowledge; the second phase orders it; and, in the third phase, the actual attitudinal segmentation is conducted, along with a determination of how the real world measures up to one's view of it. An illustration of how this methodology aids in receiver selection is provided in the following example, based upon results from a proprietary study of an analogous product category.

Example: Consider a hypothetical product category of male interest. Ownership is known to be widely distributed over a number of different products, with individual consumers likely to own none, one, a few, or many items, each item available in a broad range of price, quality, and sophistication—say, stereo and high fidelity components.

An attitudinal segmentation study is conducted to better understand the basic attitudinal structure of the stereo and high fidelity market, and to isolate those groups of potential receivers who "think alike." The results of this research indicate that there are five dimensions of attitude that tend to discriminate men's attitudes toward stereo and high fidelity components: a prepurchase decision factor, and a specific use factor. The actual segmentation results in five groups representing distinct attitudinal segments. These groups of potential receivers are summarized below:

FIGURE 2.1

Three Phase Study Paradigm

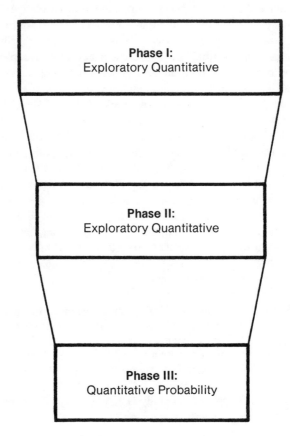

Phase I:
Exploratory Quantitative

Phase II:
Exploratory Quantitative

Phase III:
Quantitative Probability

Q_1: UNSOPHISTICATED (33 percent) who feel strongly there are many items in the category too sophisticated for them, and who are alone in feeling that higher price does not mean higher quality.

Q_2: NOTHING-BUT-THE-BEST (23 percent) who strongly feel only the best will do and nothing is too sophisticated, and who know what they want before they go shopping.

Q_3: NOVICE (18 percent) who in distinct contrast to the second group feel no need at all for the best, yet strongly believe you get what you pay for.

Q_4: UNINTERESTED (15 percent) who feel strongly there are many items they would never buy, that better components do cost more, and who feel one does not buy components for specific uses.

Q_5: EXPERT (11 percent) who strongly feel they know what they want before shopping and that most brands offer a good selection, and who definitely feel you get what you pay for.

Having isolated these five groups of receivers with similar attitudes, extensive profile data is provided in order to identify any perceptual, behavioral, or demographic differences. With these extensive profiles available, the advertiser has the responsibility of selecting those to be considered prime receivers for the advertising, and establishing a foundation for strategy compatible with those prime receivers and his marketing goals. Taking this available information, and assuming one is marketing a line of high-quality components, each of the attitude groups can be "graded" or judged in a fashion similar to that shown in Table 2.1.

TABLE 2.1

Attitudinal Group Profiles for Determining Target Receivers

	General Attitude	Self-Image	Ownership	Usage	Intention
Q_1: Unsophisticated (33 percent)	Fair	Fair	Poor	Fair	Fair
Q_2: Nothing-but-the-best (23 percent)	Good	Good	Good	Good	Good
Q_3: Novice (18 percent)	Fair	Fair	Good	Fair	Fair
Q_4: Uninterested (15 percent)	Poor	Poor	Poor	Fair	Poor
Q_5: Expert (11 percent)	Good	Good	Good	Good	Good

In so assessing the market, it is clear that the NOTHING-BUT-THE-BEST and EXPERT segments should form a core of one's target receivers. Not only are their existing attitudes and beliefs compatible with high-quality stereo components, indicating a higher probability of receiver response to the brand's advertising, but their behavior and intentions also indicate a more active potential. These two groups would account for approximately one-third of the market.

However, with a more general substrategy, one could hope to include both the novice and unsophisticated within an overall potential for buyer response. This would add an additional 52 percent of the market, indicating a gross potential of about 85 percent of all men. Only the uninterested are to be ignored in receiver selection.

With a specific strategy directed to the "prime segments" accounting for one-third of the market, along with the potential of some response (if correctly addressed) among an additional one-half of the market, the advertiser is in a good position to maximize advertising efforts; the best receivers have been selected for the message. For example, with a strategy that emphasized a recognizable brand image for strong association with the "prime segments's" preshopping decision making, coupled with a sales message underscoring the company's full line of products, one should find reasonable success in buyer response. This type of message strategy, geared to these receivers, could be thought of in terms of: A product for everything you want to hear. Such a strategy can be easily adapted beyond the prime receivers to the more general audience, addressing the various levels of sophistication of these receivers.

It should be pointed out, however, that this selection of receivers and the accompanying strategy assumes the brand is (or the company wishes it to be) a line of high-quality stereo and high fidelity components. If the company's marketing goals center around a line of low-priced products, the grading of the five receivers' in terms of their attitude would change (but not in terms of the other measures). Under these circumstances, the UNSOPHISTICATED, who aren't looking for sophisticated equipment and don't feel they need to pay a lot for quality, and the NOVICE, who don't want the best, would be selected as the prime receivers. While this would account for about one-half of the market, little potential would exist among those in the other half. They are either not interested in stereo and high fidelity components at all, or are only in the market for more expensive, higher quality products.

With a good knowledge of the attitudinal structure of a market, along with a practical understanding of behavior, intentions, and demography among the various attitude groups, the advertiser is in an excellent position to identify receivers with attitudes compatible with the product to be sold, leading to strategies tending to increase the probability of the desired buyer response to the advertising. Such knowledge of the selected receivers also contributes to more effective message development and media selection, again increasing the probability of successful advertising response.

INDIVIDUAL-DIFFERENCE CHARACTERISTICS

In order to better acquaint ourselves with the relationship between a receiver and his influenceability, we shall not review how personal characteristics of the receiver may correlate with persuasibility. A great many individual-difference correlates with persuasibility have been reported in the literature, but no attempt shall be made to review them all here. Rather, some representative examples from three general areas highly important to advertising will be discussed: demographic characteristics, ability levels, and personality traits. In addition, personality as a receiver state variable will be discussed, and contrasted with personality as a trait.

Demographic Characteristics

Perhaps the two most frequently studied demographic characteristics in communication are sex and age. The effect of a receiver's sex on persuasibility seems clear: women tend to be more persuasible than men (McGuire 1973). There has been a tendency to assume that this difference may, in part, be due to a greater propensity on the part of women to yield, perhaps as a result of cultural training in conformity (Hovland and Janis 1959). McGuire (1969a) suggests that, if this were the case, one should expect the difference due to sex to be most pronounced in suggestibility situations (in which the net influenceability relationships are dominated by persuasion mediators into advertising), and least pronounced in persuasibility situations (in which the persuasion response is counteracted by the reception response).

However, the opposite tends to be true. In the more subtle and complex persuasibility situations, women are indeed more likely to be influenced. In answer to this seeming contradiction, McGuire suggests that the greater influenceability of women may be due to their more effective message reception rather than to their greater yielding. In fact, there seems to be some evidence that females are, in general, more verbal, more likely to attend to and comprehend the spoken and written word (a point that would seem to suggest the desirability of a female target audience in advertising whenever possible, minimizing male participation in dual audience situations). It should follow that sex differences in influenceability would be more pronounced as the communication situation becomes more complex and requires greater verbal interest and skill for adequate reception of the message. To the extent that this is true, one would be less likely to develop involved and complex copy in male-oriented print advertising.

Turning next to age, we shall concern ourselves only with chronological age (deferring a discussion of mental age to the next section on ability levels). McGuire (1973) reports that there appears to be a rapid rise in persuasibility from infancy to the age of five or six, presumably reflecting greater motivation and ability for attention and comprehension of persuasive communication messages. Barber and Calverley (1964), among others, conclude that maximum suggestibility is generally found later, at about eight or nine years of age. The evidence is clearer that after one reaches the age of about nine, there is a decided decline in ease of suggestibility until adolescence (cf. Hull 1933; Stukat 1958; Weitzenhoffer 1953), at which time the curve levels off until senility once again causes a decline through lessened exposure, attention, and comprehension (see Figure 2.2). This nonmonotomic relationship is precisely what one would expect if, as McGuire (1969a) reminds us, we interpret chronological age as positively related to message reception and negatively related to persuasion, both fairly plausible assumptions. Some additional support for this notion is offered by the cross-experimental interpretations of Hovland and Janis (1959), which suggest that persuasibility declines with age more for boys than for girls.

While there appears to be a definite relationship between the two demographic characteristics of sex and age and persuasibility, for most advertising communication situations, only sex seems relevant. Only in the case of advertising directed toward children or adolescents would chronological age seem to be a factor. In research on other demographic characteristics, such as race, socioeconomic class, and religion, no significant relationships to persuasibility have been uncovered (McGuire 1973); and even when they are found, the relation-

FIGURE 2.2

Effects of Age on Persuasibility

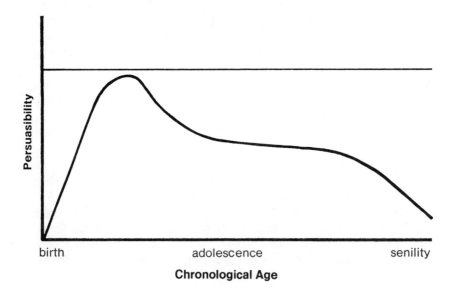

ships lend themselves to many interpretations. This would suggest that in terms of the persuasibility of an advertisement (basically an attitudinal objective, affective or conative), with the exception of sex, demographic characteristics are of little importance. Nevertheless, for some behavioral concerns, demographic considerations may be somewhat useful in identifying target receivers—for example, when the product or service being advertised is clearly marketed to a specific age or socioeconomic group.

Ability Levels

Considering now the relationship between intelligence (one's mental age) and persuasibility, the usual or intuitive expectation is that the more intelligent a receiver, the more resistant to a persuasive communication. One would conjecture that the more intelligent a receiver is, the harder to persuade, because the receiver has more arguments in support of beliefs, will be better able to detect the flaws in the persuasive arguments of advertising, should have more confidence, and, as a result, be better able to endure a discrepancy between held beliefs and those of the advertising message, and so on. Additionally, research by Greenwald (1968) and Wright (1974a) indicate that more intelligent individuals might be more likely to counter-argue than less intelligent individuals, and as such be more difficult to persuade.

While these and other studies have occasionally found such commonsense notions of a negative relationship between intelligence and persuasibility to hold, as many more have found the opposite. Early communication research on susceptibility to persuasion reviewed by Murphy, Murphy, and Newcomb (1937) led to the conclusion that there was no consistent relationship between intelligence and susceptibility to persuasion. Later work reported by Hovland and Janis (1959) also failed to show any appreciable relationship between susceptibility to persuasion and intelligence. So where does this seeming incongruity leave one in assessing the effect of a receiver's intelligence on the likelihood of being persuaded by an advertising communication? The answer lies in understanding how intelligence mediates an advertising response, particularly the persuasion versus reception objective phases.

McGuire (1969a) points out that this rather confusing situation should be expected on the basis of principles inherent in information processing, since they would position intelligence to be positively related to influenceability via the processing steps associated with exposure and decoding of the message while negatively related via the encoding of a response. In terms of an advertising communication, one would expect the more intelligent receiver to more adequately attend to and comprehend the message. These receivers usually have a wider range of interests and concerns, so a greater variety of message subjects should attract their attention; they should also have a longer attention span. And even more obvious, the more intelligent the receivers, the greater the likelihood that they will adequately and correctly comprehend and encode the point of the advertisement and the arguments used in its support (McGuire 1972). It now appears a commonsense argument might be made for both the positive and negative relationships observed through the years in studies of receiver influence-ability and intelligence.

But, in the creation of advertising, which is more likely? With simple and repetitive message formulations (such as constitute the vast majority of all advertising copy) the mediational role of message reception is unimportant for most normal adults, all of whom are pretty much at the asymptote regarding the receipt of an advertising communication. In other words, most advertising communications are not created at such a level that factors of intelligence play a part in attention or comprehension. Almost everyone who attends to an advertising message will comprehend it completely. As a result, there is little individual difference in message comprehension, and one would expect the net negative relationship mediated by the encoding stage of message processing to manifest itself in the intelligence-persuasibility relationship of the receiver, suggesting that for most advertising communications more intelligent receivers will be more difficult to persuade.

On the other hand, this same reasoning would lead one to expect that, in the relatively few cases in which advertising communication requires detailed and subtle argumentation, a more complex relationship between intelligence and susceptibility to persuasion would obtain. A great deal of individual-difference variance in message receptivity should be expected among potential receivers, leading to a more influential role for the positive relationship between intelligence and receptivity in determining the net impact of intelligence on the desired advertising. Hence, when a persuasive message has an element of subtlety or involves fairly complex material, one would expect a more intelligent receiver to be more likely persuaded. McGuire (1969a) reviews a number of empirical results supporting this conclusion.

Although the impact of a receiver's intelligence on response to advertising is discussed in more detail in the next chapter, one can see that, for any receiver representing any segment of the total range of intelligence, the relationship between intelligence and the likelihood of being persuaded by an advertising message may be positive or negative, depending upon whether the formulation of the message content leaves more room for individual differences in message reception or persuasion in response to the advertising. An interesting footnote to this conclusion with regard to advertising measurement would suggest that recall measures (which are primarily measures of reception carry-over effects) should be higher for more intelligent receivers than for less intelligent receivers.

One final consideration in discussing ability levels, although not specifically applicable to advertising communication, would include the relationship between a receiver's mental health and persuasibility. The same concern for the information processing steps mediating advertising response noted in the discussion of intelligence and persuasibility once again apply. While the mentally ill are likely to have a low level of self-confidence, and as such be more likely to yield to a persuasive message, mental illness also tends to be characterized by a withdrawal tendency that would interfere with reception of the advertising messages (McGuire 1973). Their withdrawal symptoms seem to protect the severely mentally ill from persuasion owing to a low probability of reception even more than their low self-image exposes them to yielding.

Personality Traits

Of all the possible correlates of persuasibility, personality traits have probably been studied more than any other. Unfortunately, the results of these studies have proved even more complex and contradictory than those we have already discussed for demographic characteristics and ability levels. The confusion can perhaps be illustrated by considering a personality trait such as self-esteem. Research by Janis (1955) found a negative relationship between self-esteem and capability of being persuaded, while at the same time McGuire and Ryan (1955) discovered a positive relationship. As work continued over the next few years, the question became more ambiguous. A nonmonotonic inverted-U relationship between the two variables was found by Cox and Bauer (1964). Here susceptibility to persuasion was highest at intermediate levels of self-esteem. In the same year, Silverman (1964) also reported a nonmonotonic relationship. However, his was in the reverse direction, with susceptibility to persuasion lowest at intermediate levels of self-esteem (see Figure 2.3).

The most satisfactory theory attempting to account for these varied results is offered by McGuire's (1968a) theory of personality-persuasibility relationships, which he bases on five postulates underlying these complex obtained relationships. In reviewing each of these five postulates, attention will be drawn to the importance of message processing objectives in applying this theory to advertising strategy. It should also be pointed out that, although these principles were developed in connection with the personality-persuasibility relationship, they are generally applicable to all relationships between individual-differences and susceptibility to persuasion.

The mediational principle

In this first postulate it is assumed that the receiver's persuasibility characteristics, like other aspects of the communication situation, affect attitude and behavioral change through advertising response. Nevertheless, this fact is frequently overlooked in discussions of the relationship between personality traits and susceptibility to influence. Too often, the conceptual analysis is confined to

FIGURE 2.3

Contradictory Relationship between
Self-esteem and Influenceability

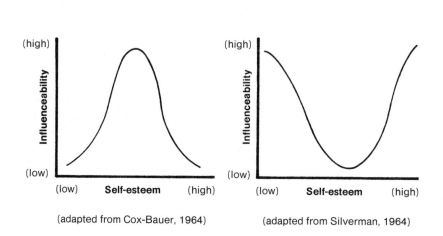

(adapted from Cox-Bauer, 1964)   (adapted from Silverman, 1964)

the persuasion responses, much as we saw in our discussion of intelligence in the section on ability levels. For example, a receiver with a higher level of self-esteem would be thought better able to tolerate disagreement between himself and the source of a communication. As a result, conjecture regarding the relationship between self-esteem and persuasibility tends to assume a negative relationship owing to this negative impact on attitude change and intention objectives. Following from this, one might conclude that self-esteem must be negatively related to persuasibility. While this may be correct as it stands, it completely ignores other potential objectives in advertising response.

The mediational principle, then, implies that one can only fully understand the relationship between a personality trait and persuasibility to the extent that one considers the impact of that personality trait on specific advertising responses. As McGuire (1969a) points out, this principle in itself does not allow us to make any confident predictions, but simply calls our attention to the complexity of the undertaking.

The compensation principle

This second postulate takes into account the tendency of personality traits (as well as other individual-difference characteristics) to have opposite effects on susceptibility to influence via different advertising responses. In other words, it is assumed that the reciprocal relationships observed above for self-esteem (and earlier for intelligence) are the usual case rather than the exception. For example, anxiety, which will be discussed in greater detail below, tends to make a receiver more susceptible to advertising through increased persuasibility, but at the same time less likely to be persuaded because of lower message reception.

Two corollaries to this principle are also suggested by McGuire (1968b, 1969a). The first states that the overall relationship between an individual-difference variable and susceptibility to influence tends to be nonmonotonic, with some intermediate level of the variable being optional for the ability to be influenced. The basic idea subsumed in this corollary is that when two determinants of a relationship go in opposite directions, the resultant relationship tends to be nonmonotonic under a wide range of parametric conditions (see Figure 2.4). A number of empirical studies support this conclusion (McGuire 1969a).

A second corollary states that a receiver's level of susceptibility may be manipulated up or down, depending on the initial status of the personality trait in question. Such manipulations actually occasion a personality state. If a receiver's self-esteem state is raised, for example, the susceptibility to persuasion will also rise if the initial state was quite low; if the initial state was quite high,

FIGURE 2.4

Compensation Principle: Corollary One

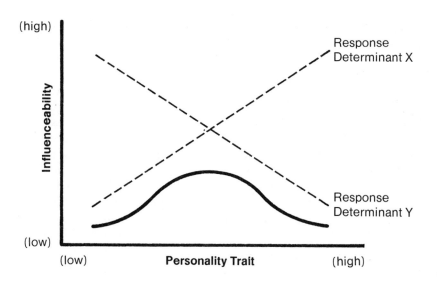

further increase would tend to lower susceptibility to persuasion. This, of course, follows from the first corollary and helps account for apparently discrepant results of identical manipulations of such personality traits as self-esteem and anxiety. This trait-state distinction is treated in more detail later.

The situational-weighting principle

The third postulate states that the relationship of a given personality variable to persuasibility will depend on how widely the different mediating steps can vary in a given situation, especially on a within receiver segment basis. It is restrictive in the sense that it specifies some of the conditions under which one might expect certain relationships to hold, or at least the situation in which it is more likely to occur.

We have already discussed several cases in which this principle has been operating. For example, when a persuasive communication is extremely simple and repetitious (such as, we have remarked, is true for much advertising), one would expect the normal range of the population to show very little variation in the attention to or comprehension of a message. As a result, the receiver's personality traits would be related to persuasive impact via something beyond message reception. If the communication message was complex and such that one would expect a great deal of variance over the population in the extent of reception, then the relationship of the receiver's personality traits to the desired advertising response would tend to have more influence in determining its impact.

The confounding principle

The fourth postulate concerns the tendency of most personality traits to cluster into syndromes. In other words, one personality trait will frequently be embedded in a group of other personality characteristics that facilitate the receiver's coping with the opportunities and weaknesses afforded by that trait. As a result, a trait such as self-esteem has a net relationship to susceptibility to influence that is determined not only by its own impact on a response to advertising, as we have noted, but also by the interaction in message processing of other personality variables that tend to be correlated with self-esteem. For example, self-esteem tends to be related to depression and withdrawal (Bennis and Peabody 1962). A receiver with lower self-esteem would, as we have seen, lack resistance to persuasive communication and be highly susceptible. However, this same receiver would also be depressed and show a high degree of withdrawal, thus avoiding exposure to persuasive communication by becoming a poor receiver.

In a corollary to this principle, an important difference is noted between chronic (or trait) and acute (or state) levels of personality characteristics. The assumption that chronic personality characteristics become embedded in compensatory tendencies means that the relationship of a trait such as self-esteem will tend to relate to susceptibility to influence in ways somewhat different from an acute level on that same characteristic due to some momentary factor (McGuire 1973). While this may be considered largely a methodological distinction in experimentation, one should still expect certain systematic differences in how a given personality characteristic will relate to persuasibility, depending on whether one is considering the characteristic's chronic or acute level. The chronic level of a personality characteristic is the usual syndrome of confounding tendencies; an acute level has been manipulated, and one must remember to make the distinction.

The interaction principle

This final postulate concerns the interaction of a receiver's personality traits with other aspects of the communication situation (such as source and message) in determining the overall impact on persuasibility. For example, one can alter the relationship between personality traits and persuasibility to a certain extent by varying the source characteristics. McGuire (1968a) has shown that the relationship between authoritarianism and persuasibility depends to a large extent on the characteristics of the source. Work has been done in the area of interactions with message factors and the relationship between ego-defensiveness and susceptibility to influence (cf. Katz, Sarnoff, and McClintock 1956; Stotland, Katz, and Patchen 1959), or when the relationship between personality traits and persuasibility is shown to be dependent upon the issues argued in the message (Leventhal and Perloe 1962), and with media variables and the relationship of sex to susceptibility to influence (Knower 1935). One might even consider receiver-receiver interactions where the receiver's sex moderates the relationship between personality characteristics and persuasibility. Hilgard, Lauer, and Melie (1965) have shown this relationship to be more sizable to men than women.

Perhaps now the reader is better able to understand the mediating effects of a receiver's personality traits on the susceptibility to persuasion. At any rate, the reader should be able to account for many of the seemingly contradictory relationships discussed below by one or more of the above principles.

Self-esteem

We shall now concentrate our discussion on a specific personality trait, looking at self-esteem and its potential mediating role in advertising. Self-esteem is perhaps the most studied personality trait in connection with susceptibility to influence. And, as we have seen, significant positive, negative, and nonmonotonic relationships have been found by various researchers between self-esteem and persuasibility. Yet, despite this array of conflicting results, a coherent framework exists when approached within the parameters of McGuire's five postulates. For example, the numerous studies reporting, on the one hand, negative relationships between self-esteem and persuasibility and on the other positive or nonmonotonic results seem explicable only in terms of an overall inverted-U relationship between self-esteem and susceptibility to influence, consistent with the principles discussed above (see McGuire [1969a] for a review of these many conflicting studies). According to the situational weighting principle, the relationship between self-esteem and susceptibility to influence will more likely be negative when the persuasive communication is simple, and nonmonotonic and positive when the communication is more complex or specific, allowing for more individual-difference variance in message reception (that is, attention to and comprehension of the communication message).

This is an important, if not somewhat uncontrollable, consideration in the development of advertising communications. To the extent that one's target audience is comprised of receivers with low self-esteem (as might be the case in marketing self-help products), the message copy formulation should be as simple as possible and repeated as often as possible to ensure up to at least an affective objective in advertising response. If the target audience is comprised largely of receivers with high self-esteem (as might be the case with high-fashion clothing), a more detailed and unique message would be called for to take advantage of the positive relationship suggested by the situational-weighting principle. The rub, of course, comes in determining the level of self-esteem in your target audience.

Personality as a Receiver State Variable

In contrasting personality states with personality traits, one may regard a state as a temporal look at a receiver during a given moment in time and at a particular level of intensity (Thorne 1966), while a trait is relatively enduring. Although a personality state is not permanent, it can recur when evoked by an appropriate stimulus (for example, through specific advertising messages) and may even persist as long as the evoking condition continues. Emotional reactions, for example, may be viewed as expressions of personality states (such as when a particular piece of advertising arouses "warm" feelings). Personality traits, on the other hand, would reflect the receiver's individual differences in the frequency and intensity with which those emotional states had occurred in the past, and the probability that they would be experienced in the future. This means that when one understands a receiver's personality traits and the states evoked by particular advertising stimuli, one may reasonably predict simular reactions from future advertising. The effect of receiver personality state and trait characteristics on advertising response is shown in Figure 2.5.

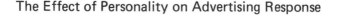

FIGURE 2.5

The Effect of Personality on Advertising Response

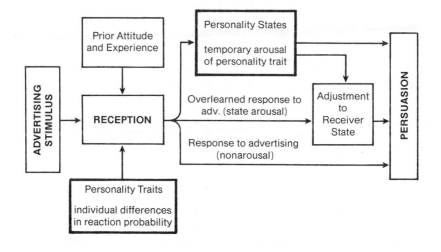

As one might expect, the stronger a particular personality trait, the more likely it is that a receiver will experience the emotional state that corresponds to that trait, and the greater the probability that the receiver will exhibit the behavior associated with it. In fact, the stronger the personality trait, the more likely these reactions will be experienced at much higher levels of intensity (Spielberger, Lushene, and McAdoo 1977). One can see how the level of a personality trait may be used to predict a response to advertising. Looking at Figure 2.5, suppose we know that our target receivers possess high levels of personality traits such as succorance, abasement, and nurturance (traits reflective of a "mothering" nature). If advertising reflected a highly nurturant message, such as the need for a product or service to better care for one's family, one would expect the receiver's high trait levels to intensify a nurturant state, which in turn would greatly increase the probability of message persuasion. However, the extent to which a particular personality trait effects receiver response to the advertising will also depend upon the receiver's perception of the advertising stimuli, especially the source and message variables.

Anxiety

Anxiety is traditionally regarded as a two-factor personality characteristic, with both a trait and state value (sometimes, in the case of anxiety, referred to as a drive and a cue value). As a trait, anxiety might be thought of as a multiplier of whatever behavioral inclinations may be operative at a particular moment, in much the same way as hunger acts as a drive. In its trait aspects, anxiety tends to increase the likelihood of preexisting response tendencies. So, in receivers with a high trait-level of anxiety, anxiety state reactions will be common under a real or even perceived stress situation. When such anxiety-provoking stimuli are absent, even receivers with a high level of trait anxiety will be unlikely to experience an anxiety state.

As a state, or cue as it is sometimes called, anxiety is conceptualized as an independent condition to which specific responses are likely to be associated, evoking distinctive response tendencies. For example, one might think of anxiety as a state warning the receiver to avoid the present situation (for example, through flight, withdrawal, repression) because it is perceived as threatening in some way. This avoidance reaction becomes conditioned to the extent that it has proven successful in the past in terminating the threatening stimulus that brought on the original anxiety state.

The implication here for advertising communication is significant. In general, the successful characteristic response elicited by anxiety as a state will affect the advertising response. Almost always, it will tend to interfere with both the attention to and comprehension of a persuasive advertising message. Avoidance reactions, whether by actually leaving the room, turning off the radio or television, putting down the magazine, or merely employing repression and avoidance of thinking, certainly interfere with the receiver's ability to concentrate on advertising and to assimilate rationally the contents of the arguments used in the message. The same would be true if one desired an affective or conative response (if the message is, in fact, attended to). In general, to the extent that a high anxiety state is created by the advertising message, the less likely it will influence or persuade the receiver. For example, in public service advertising stressing the dangers of drugs, smoking, or alcohol, if a high enough level of anxiety is reached through a fear appeal, it will become increasingly likely that, when these subjects come up, the receiver will repress the whole matter rather than consider appropriate behavior.

While high levels of anxiety are certainly detrimental to the reception of advertising, it is likely to have a facilitating effect on its persuasibility. One explanation for this is found in the confounding principle: high levels of anxiety tend to be clustered with lower levels of personality traits, such as self-esteem and self-confidence. These response tendencies should make the receiver more compliant; yet the likelihood of correctly encoding the message to an eventual attitudinal or behavioral change response is slight when anxiety state is high.

But what of anxiety as a trait? If one assumes that for any advertising communication there is some initial tendency for the average receiver to pay at least some attention, try to comprehend the message, and so forth, anxiety as a trait should tend to multiply all these initial tendencies, making them more likely to occur. Assuming this happens, the personality trait of anxiety would tend to enhance the persuasive impact of the advertising's message.

This contradicts what one would expect considering anxiety as a state. What is to be made of a situation in which a single personality characteristic would predict different changes in attitude or behavior via a response to an advertising message, not only depending upon the desired response, but also upon the state of the trait considered? Considering each aspect of anxiety independently leads one to conclude that the overall relationship between the level of anxiety and potential change through the response to advertising would be the by now familiar nonmonotonic, inverted-U. But, considering the two aspects together would suggest an even more complex nonmonotonic relationship of multimodal form, perhaps an M-shaped one. Is the theory so complicated that any outcome may be accommodated within its framework, obviating prediction; and provide no guidance in the creation of a persuasive advertising communication?

McGuire (1972) points out that, although this theory of mediating independent variables (such as source and message) cannot predict at just what point inflections will occur in the relationships between complex individual-difference variables (such as anxiety) and attitude or behavior change, it does at least say how the inflection points should move as certain other independent variables are varied orthogonally (that is, independently). Although one may not be able to specify exactly what level of anxiety in a receiver will be optimal in producing attitude or behavior change for any given level of another independent variable, one can say that, for example, as the message complexity of an advertising message increases, the maximal point will move to the left, so that with increasing message complexity lower and lower levels of anxiety will prove most effective in producing maximum attitude or behavior change. Much the same could be said for any of these seemingly complex relationships, assuming one understands the interaction of the independent variables with a receiver's response to advertising. This understanding, of course, is one of the goals of this book.

A Personality-Attitude-Behavior Link

Implicit in the discussion of personality as an individual difference characteristic of a receiver, either as a trait or state variable, is the notion that, in some fashion, the receiver's personality will affect the likely response to advertising. Unfortunately, empirical evidence has traditionally been slight. Typically, only about five or ten percent of the total variance in buyer behavior has been accounted for by personality construct measures, and as Kotler (1976) points out, even when stronger evidence of individual personality differences in purchase behavior is found, the implications for marketing strategy are far from clear.

Yet, personality as a predictor or mediator in communication theory persists, despite this apparent lack of success in empirical explanation. Surely, if personality traits or states mediate the reception of a communication message, and affect the ability of advertising to generate the desired response, personality must correlate with subsequent behavior. If not, as an individual difference characteristic of receivers, personality should not attract the attention of the advertising or marketing manager in his efforts to maximize advertising response.

Percy (1975, 1976b) has suggested that the reasons for the low accountability and conflicting results to date of research in personality and behavior are (a) reliance on individual personality traits as opposed to profiles of personality traits, and (b) a failure to recognize the importance of attitude or disposition as a mediator of specific behavior. He points out that personality implies a whole, not a string of independent personality traits. Why should it be surprising that a single personality trait, which may covary in a multitude of ways with other traits, fails to contribute much on its own to the prediction of a specific consumer behavior, such as a buyer response to a brand or product. It makes far better sense to consider a profile of personality traits that reflects the interactions of various personality traits. Any chronic personality trait that tends to make an individual extremely resistant (for example) or extremely receptive to a particular influence probably becomes embedded over a period of time in a matrix of other traits that serve as correctives in moving the person toward an intermediate level of behavior (McGuire 1972).

Sparks and Tucker (1971), after noting essentially weak or spotty relationships between specific personality traits and the use of particular products, went on to demonstrate significant relationships between profiles of these same traits and bundles of various product usage. Building on these results, Alpert (1972) studied the relationship between personality structure and product attributes. Although he cited a few limitations, he nonetheless found strong relationships in matching personality profiles of product attributes' determinance.

In a study of banking behavior (Percy 1976b), a very interesting set of profiles contrasting those who have savings accounts but no checking accounts versus those who have checking accounts but no savings accounts was uncovered. As detailed in Figure 2.6, one sees that the two groups exhibit almost completely opposite personality profiles. The importance of this finding would be critical to the development of advertising copy. In talking to the saver who doesn't check, the creative tone should be soft and the message coddled in a sort of "we know what's best" manner. Quite the contrary, of course, would apply to the checker who doesn't save; the checker would be uninterested in any soft-selling copy. As Engel et al. (1973) suggest, advertising copy can be much more effective if the artists and writers have a rich understanding of the total life-style of those to whom they are writing. But, even more important, here is data suggesting that the receivers of such advertising should be more likley to respond.

Percy (1975, 1976b) has hypothesized a Personality-Attitude-Behavior

FIGURE 2.6

Personality Profiles of Savers Who Don't Check versus Checkers Who Don't Save

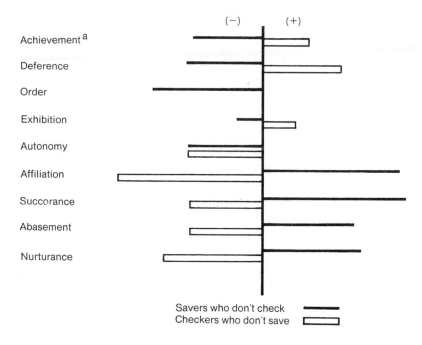

^{a}Scales derived from modified EPPS.

link of personality (expressed as a profile), as a common denominator among receivers who tend to hold similar attitudes toward a product-market, and, in relating them through these commonly held attitudes to specific behavior. Personality is considered a mediator of behavior, but only through an underlying attitudinal construct. Personality relates to commonly held attitudes and perceived behavioral orientations, and it is these factors that mediate specific buyer response.

Being able to describe a target receiver in terms of gross personality characteristics, which are in turn known to be good discriminators of a particular attitude or disposition, provide a much clearer picture of whom one is dealing with for purposes of developing advertising and marketing strategies directed toward them, and the mediating effect those characteristics will have on advertising response. This connection with attitudinal disposition is important from a strategic viewpoint, for it is generally a cognitive or affective response that the marketer or advertiser seeks to exploit, change, or modify through advertising.

However, it must be recognized that intervening factors may effect behavior contrary to that predicted by a given attitudinal disposition. As an example, imagine the man who hates lawn work, but finds himself with an unruly hedge on his hands. He may reluctantly purchase a hedge trimmer even though his personality profile matches that of a nonowner of lawn and garden tools. This fact of ownership does not make him a good prospect for additional lawn and garden tools, or likely to respond positively to lawn and garden tool advertising. The intervening factors of an overgrown hedge and complaining neighbors could perhaps have affected his prior behavior. Figure 2.7 illustrates the possible action of intervening factors.

In the work reported by Percy (1976b), one of the product categories studied was power tools, a light durable of primary interest to men in which ownership was known to be widely distributed over a number of different products, with individual subjects likely to own none, one, a few, or many items. Each item is available in a broad range of price, quality, and sophistication. Examining the personality profiles between nonowners and involved owners (so-called multiple product ownership coupled with ownership of more sophisticated items) revealed opposite profiles (correlating -.595). These profiles are shown in Figure 2.8.

Interpreting these profiles, one could say that those who own no items in this category may be described as unsure of themselves and their abilities, seeking stability and continuity in their environment, and apprehensive of ill-defined or risk-involving situations. They try to avoid situations calling for choice and decision making, and are dubious about the results of expending effort or becoming involved with their labor. On the other hand, the involved owners are determined to do well, and are usually successful. They have a quiet confidence in their own abilities and worth, welcoming the challenges to be found in disorder and complexity. Sincere and dependable, they are adaptable, resourceful, and comprehend problems and situations rapidly and incisively.

There was clearly a relationship found, and a significant one, between the two extremes of category behavior and receiver personality profiles. However, when one attempts only to correlate these profiles with behavior, other receivers are found exhibiting similar personality profiles who are not similar to one another in terms of the "predicted" behavior. But, when correlations were made at an attitude level, a correlation of .613 was found between those positively disposed toward buyer response and the involved owners; and a correlation of .851 between those negatively disposed and the nonowners. Although personality as a receiver characteristic may not be a unique predictor of actual buyer behavior, it does significantly discriminate the underlying behavior and attitude factors that tend to lead to specific product behavior.

From an advertising standpoint, this means that personality traits, when

FIGURE 2.7

Personality-Attitude-Behavior Link

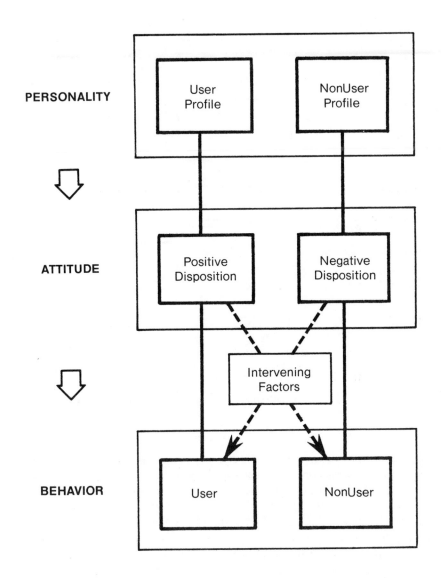

PERSONALITY

User Profile

NonUser Profile

ATTITUDE

Positive Disposition

Negative Disposition

Intervening Factors

BEHAVIOR

User

NonUser

FIGURE 2.8

Personality Profiles of Nonowners versus Owners

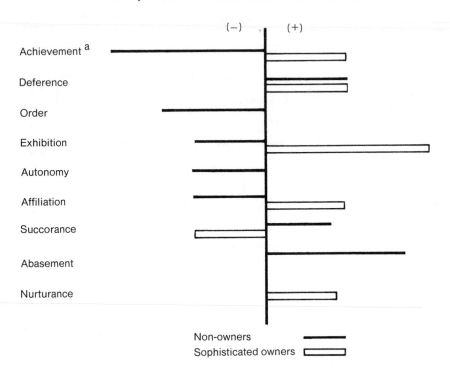

^aScales derived from a modification of Gough & Heilbrun Adjective Check List.

considered as profiles (or even "clusters" or bundles of traits), will predict the likelihood of a receiver being persuaded by advertising for one's product or brand. To the extent that a receiver's personality is known and found to be different from nontarget receivers, this information will mediate a more positive response to advertising, at least to the extent that those receivers' attitudes presage a disposition toward positive behavior. As a result, when personality characteristics of receivers are available to the advertising or marketing manager (for example, through a syndicated media or research service), it may be used for more than the usual practice of guiding message "tone." It may be used to help identify those receivers more likely to respond positively to the advertising.

An Application

With Part I of this chapter as background, the reader should now be in a position to effectively evaluate and isolate potential groups of receivers most likely to positively respond to advertising. The details of how the advertiser determines what to say and how, and where to present this message, is contained in later chapters. However, to help reinforce the reader's practical understanding of receiver selection through attitudinal segmentation and how that leads to specific advertising strategy, an in-depth look at an actual case study follows.

A major condiment manufacturer, facing an uncertain share of market with the introduction of two nes competitive products, sought guidance for developing a marketing and advertising program designed to most effectively blunt the impact of the new entries, as well as enhance the company's position with respect to the existing market leaders. An advertising-oriented, attitudinally based market segmentation was undertaken, in order to provide the company with a better understanding of how condiments such as theirs fit into a home-maker's meal-time routines, what the important condiment-related attitudes of homemakers were, and, finally, to isolate and fully describe groups of attitudinally similar homemakers from which "prime receivers" could be selected for the purpose of maximizing buyer response.

Following the general methodology outlined above, including an initial phase of qualitative group sessions and in-depth interviews, a second phase of highly quantitative pilot studies, and a final phase nationally projectable study among 1,000 homemakers, a number of key attitudinal dimensions mediating product use were uncovered. Basically, usage was found to depend upon developmental taste acquisition, immediate situational factors in usage, and consideration of both add-on (that is, table use) as well as add-in (that is, ingredient use) variety in usage. An ideal product was seen as one that "enhances" the taste of other foods rather than adding a taste of its own, and one that is "all purpose."

A series of factor analyses were applied throughout the study in an effort to isolate those attitudes most likely to discriminate among homemakers. An initial sample responded using a five-point Likert agreement scale to a series of some 80 different attitude statements suggested by the qualitative study. These measures were factor analyzed first in the R-mode (that is, variables reduced or grouped over subjects) to arrive at a more parsimonious grouping of the statements, then in the Q-mode (that is, subjects grouped over variables) for purposes of identifying which of the statements from each of the R-factors should be retained and administered in the nationally projectable phase of the study. The results of the national study were then factor analyzed in the R-mode to uncover the latent attitudinal structure of the condiment market and in the Q-mode to reveal those segments of the market holding generally homogeneous attitudes relevant to the condiment market.

The important dimensions of attitude revealed by the R-mode factor analysis were (1) could get along without any; (2) ideal for children; (3) brings out taste; (4) good for all types of food; (5) add-on but not add-in; (6) brand is not important; and (7) children must acquire taste. The Q-mode factor analysis of homemakers revealed six attitudinally based market segments of potential receivers (see Table 2.1). Each of these was extensively profiled using the more traditional product oriented segmentation variables, including category behavior, personality, and demographics. Three segments exhibiting strong positive attitudes toward condiment use, as well as compatibility with the advertiser's product, were selected as the "prime receivers." Reviewing those attitudinal dimensions that tend to describe the segments, segments one and two were clear choices, along with segment five, despite its poorer attitude toward ingredient usage. In total, these three prime segments accounted for some 58 percent of all homemakers.

It was then possible to draw a composite picture of the target receiver most likely to exhibit belief compatibility with using the advertiser's product from the profiles of the prime segments. Utilizing the prime segments general attitude as a foundation, and the more product-oriented variables as descriptors, it was found that the potential customer the advertiser should direct his primary marketing and advertising strategy toward was generally comfortable with the notion of using condiments, and using them for a variety of purposes. Much less likely than other homemakers to feel one could get along without condiments, the potential customer feels they are ideal for a variety of foods and for a variety of purposes. Condiments enhance or bring out the natural flavor of food. The strong belief in the suitability of condiments for children was perhaps a function of the greater probability that the homemaker's family used them when the homemaker was a child. Behaviorally, the homemaker tended to be more likely to use condiments than others, and to the family they are a desired part of the evening meal. The personality characteristics strongly suggested the type who is responsive to the needs of family and amenable to change, while the demographic characteristics revealed a somewhat younger woman (that is, under 50) and much more likely to have small children at home.

In addition to this detailed understanding of the target receivers selected, certain critical product beliefs were also uncovered: enhancement, variety of use, and spicy. With the possible exception of spicy each was highly related to the basic underlying attitudinal factors. The problem then became one of matching the congruent usage and product beliefs, relating them to the target receivers, and then creating marketing and advertising strategies that would tend to raise usage and product belief salience in connection with the advertised brand.

From behavior data, it was found that if a condiment such as the one in question was actually used at yesterday's main meal, that meal was generally considered to have been much more enjoyable for both the homemaker and the family to eat. This finding suggests a latent correlation between an enjoyable

TABLE 2.2

General Attitude Description of Market Segments

Factor Dimensions	Attitude Segments					
	Q_1	Q_2	Q_3	Q_4	Q_5	Q_6
Could get along without any				AS		AS
Ideal for children	AS	A	D		A	
Brings out taste	AS	A	D		A	
Good for all types of food		AS	D		AS	
Add-on but not add-in	DS				A	
Brand is not important				A		
Children must acquire taste						A

Note: AS = Agree Strongly; A = Agree; D = Disagree; DS = Disagree Strongly.

meal and serving the product (at least such a scenario would be believable). In addition, when the product was used, the day itself was perceived to be busier than usual. The meal, however, required no more time or effort than usual to prepare, suggesting that in serving the product the homemaker is not attempting to cover up the taste of a quickly prepared meal (which would of course be inconsistent with the beliefs that condiments only enhance food, which specifically excludes the possibility of adding a condiment to impart a taste of its own). Knowing the receivers selected strongly agree with the "brings out taste" and "good for all types of food" attitude factors, coupled with their general behavior data, would suggest a strategy element for message development one might think of as "enjoyable meals."

Although most homemakers do not consider the use of condiments very important for themselves, a large portion of the selected receivers felt it was important to their families, particularly children. This finding, in fact, ran somewhat counter to a category nostrum that considered the product specifically male oriented, with little appropriateness for children. Because the attitudinal findings suggest these receivers feel the product is ideal for children, understanding the almost universal desire among homemakers to please their families, this finding became actionable through a strategy element one might think of as "family experience." The generally larger number of children and the personality characteristics of the receivers selected (their responsiveness to family needs and willingness to change) would also tend to reinforce the enjoyable meal idea within a context of family experience.

In summary, using an advertising orientation for segmenting the condiment market on the basis of attitude provided documentation of an attitudinal bias in favor of usage for children along with an expressed need, a strong suggestion that an opportunity exists for a likely responsiveness to family needs in conjunction with enjoyable meals, plus an integration of product beliefs and general attitudes indicating an enhancement of flavor and variety of use orientation to advertising strategy. This led to advertising featuring a family orientation within a variety of meal-time situations, a radical departure from the traditional narrow usage and male orientation position. This redirected advertising, directed toward receivers selected from an advertising oriented market segmentation, along with marketing efforts reflecting this new knowledge of the target receivers, successfully blunted the impact of the two new product entries, which despite early and significant share gains, ceased to be a factor in the market. In addition, the overall market position of the advertiser's brand was enhanced.

Part II
Receiver Interaction
with Message

In addition to the specific individual-difference characteristics associated with receiver selection, it is important to understand how a receiver is likely to react to particular message situations. This section deals with different affects upon a receiver as a result of his interaction with the message itself.

EFFECT OF INITIAL ATTITUDE ON PERSUASIBILITY

The persuasive impact of a communication message is affected by the extent to which the receiver is initially opposed to the position being advocated by the persuasive communication. This constitutes the receiver's cognitive "state" at the time of presentation of an advertising message. While only temporary, this state is nonetheless causal, with particular impact on advertising response.

In this section we shall discuss the effect of discrepancy between the receiver's initial opposition and the position urged in the communication message, and what this can mean in determining how far to urge the receiver to change in order to maximize one's probability of positive change. If only a slight change is advocated—for example, when one is introducing a new brand name to a product category and wishes to bring this to consumers' attention—then very little movement from the receiver's initial position would be required for the persuasive communication to succeed. The receiver would need only to become aware of the new brand's introduction. On the other hand, if something more ambitious is required—say, persuading a group of currently satisfied product users that another product, quite different from the one they now use, would offer them even more satisfaction—the receivers may reject the entire message as unbelievable. The receivers would not have been convinced that current product satisfaction could be improved upon. Two general areas will be considered: notions of discrepancy and selective avoidance. In addition, the affect of prior attitude on immunization to subsequent persuasive efforts will be reviewed.

Discrepancy and Persuasibility

Sherif and his associates (Sherif and Hovland 1961; Sherif, Sherif, and Nebergall 1965) have developed an assimilation-contrast or social judgment theory dealing with an ordered series of positions along any dimension. People

FIGURE 2.9

Assimilation-Contrast Theory

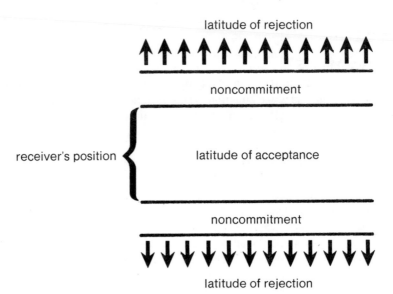

have a range of acceptable attitudes known as their latitude of acceptance; this acceptance band is surrounded on both sides by a borderline area of indecisiveness constituting their latitude of noncommitment, and an area outside their attitude of noncommitment constituting their latitude of rejection (see Figure 2.9). Generally speaking, the more discrepant a given communication from a receiver's position, the less likely it is to fall within his latitude of acceptance. If the persuasive message does fall within a receiver's latitude of acceptance, there tends to occur an assimilation error such that the receiver perceives the persuasive communication as closer to his own position than it actually is and he tends also to adjust his own position closer to it. If the persuasive message is clearly one to which the receiver objects, and it falls into the latitude of rejection, then a contrast effect occurs, in which the receiver perceives the persuasive communication as being farther away from the receiver's position than it actually is; there may also be a tendency to move the receiver's position still further away, creating a so-called boomerang effect. With respect to acceptance or rejection of a given persuasive communication, the receiver's perception of the position advocated in the message becomes a crucial factor. It follows that acceptance should be inversely related to the discrepancy between a receiver's own position and that advocated in the persuasive communication (see Figure 2.10).

With this social judgment approach, a persuasive communication is as-sumed to put pressure on the receiver to change an attitude or behavior toward the object of the message. The greater the pressure, the greater the likelihood of change, provided the advocated position is not perceived to fall within the re-ceiver's latitude of rejection; at that point, change in position should decrease with the magnitude of the original discrepancy. For example, suppose one knows that the position of a group of target receivers on use of a particular type of product is quite favorable. This favorable position would be considered by Sherif and Hovland (1961) as the receiver's "anchor" or point of reference in the perception of any persuasive attempt dealing with that category of behavior. If one were to create advertising reinforcing this type of behavior and at the same time positioning a brand positively within that environment, it would be expected that the receiver would assimilate the position of the advertisement as falling within the receiver's latitude of acceptance (that is, the favorable posi-tioning of product behavior), and increase the probability of accepting that brand (evaluating it closer to the receiver's brand than it really is) for trial. If, on the other hand, one created advertising that relied on positioning a brand as clearly superior to comparable products in a situation in which most consumers were satisfied with the performance of these other brands, one would expect a receiver who uses one of these other brands to contrast the position of the ad-

FIGURE 2.10

Probability of Receiver Acceptance

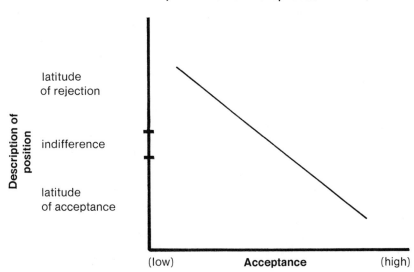

vertisement as discrepant from feelings of satisfaction with the receiver's current brand and thus falling into the latitude of rejection, where the brand advertised would be perceived as even more dissimilar from satisfactory brands.

In reviewing the effects of discrepancy on attitude change, McGuire (1973) finds that with a fairly wide range of discrepancy the obtained change is a positive function of the amount of change advocated, although the proportionate change tends to go down with discrepancy. This means that the more one advocates a change of attitude or behavior through a persuasive communication, the greater the change obtained, even though this obtained change becomes a progressively smaller percentage of the urged change. The amount of change is expected to be a curvilinear function of perceived discrepancy in which the point of inflection on the curve approaches the receiver's own position as the receiver's involvement with the issue increases (owing to the notion that the more ego-involved a receiver is with a communication message, the more the receiver's position serves as an anchor for evaluations).

Generally, Sherif and Hovland (1961) hold that, for any receiver, certain positions along an attitude dimension are acceptable, while others are not. The more a position advanced by a persuasive communication is perceived to be a receiver's own stand, the more likely it is to fall within the latitude of acceptance. Mediating message processing and advertising response, the receiver's involvement (among other factors) is expected to influence attention and comprehension by increasing assimilation and contrast effects (for example, displacing the advocated position of the communication) and to influence response by widening the latitude of rejection.

Selectivity and Persuasibility

It is frequently remarked in the communication literature that people are most likely to expose themselves to arguments with which they already agree and try to avoid information discrepant with their original opinions. This appears as a major explanatory factor in attempts to account for the all too frequent finding that mass media communication efforts do not easily persuade people to change their attitudes or behavior. Hence we have the generalization that communication campaigns through mass media (such as advertising) do little more than reach the already converted receiver, reinforcing held attitudes and behavior; others rarely attend to the communication and never have the opportunity to be persuaded. This concept of selective exposure will be dealt with from the standpoint of the receiver, and the extent to which the receiver does or does not select or avoid a communication. In part, this emphasis is explained by Katz (1968) as a shift of interest away from the study of mass media "campaigns" in favor of the study of the "uses" or "gratifications" that people derive from exposure to the media. This shift makes the concept of selectivity more important, in that one now explains selectivity in terms of the functional contribution of exposure to some social or psychological need on the part of the receiver, where selectivity for the purpose of attitude reinforcement may be only a particular case. But, as we shall see, while there may be this selective-avoidance tendency, there seems to be an equal or greater opposite tendency to seek out surprising or discrepant information (McGuire 1968c; Sears 1968; Sears and Freedman 1967; Freedman and Sears 1965).

Katz (1968) feels, despite Freedman and Sears' (1965) conclusion that neither experimental nor field studies provide convincing evidence of this notion of motivated selectivity, that there is no question that selectivity exists. The only question in his mind is whether people are disproportionately exposed to communications compatible with their attitudes or behavior because they are specifically motivated to seek such reinforcement, or merely find themselves exposed to such communications through more "de facto" circumstances. The former, which he calls supportive selectivity, is thought to be highly relevant, even though in some cases de facto exposure may be more important. For example, socioeconomic status may, in certain communication situations, be more casual than a supportive selectivity, such as advertisements for high priced luxury goods. Or, as Freedman and Sears (1965) point out, the findings that receivers favorable to the United Nations were disproportionately exposed to a UN information campaign may reflect nothing more than the well-known fact that better educated receivers are more likely to be in an audience for any communications in the field of public affairs and that better educated receivers are probably more internationally minded. Yet, Katz (1968) reviews a number of studies of the diffusion of information and other uses of mass media and feels satisfied that rather strong evidence exists in support of the motivated selectivity hypothesis, whether one chooses to regard it as selective exposure or selective retention.

In addition to de facto circumstances, such as socioeconomic status, two other alternative explanations for the discrepancies found in the study of selective exposure are offered: utility and interest as a basis of selectivity. Utility suggests a motivation on the part of the receiver to desire information when it answers a felt need or serves a practical purpose. Freedman and Sears (1965) feel that when nonsupportive information is useful, a receiver will prefer it to less useful information that is supportive. For example, the concept of utility might suggest that a receiver who is uninterested in do-it-yourself or handyman type activities, but none-the-less must perform some minor maintenance task, would be more likely in that particular circumstance to seek out information or advertisements for products likely to be useful in the successful completion of the task. These communications are clearly nonsupportive of the receiver's general hostility to this kind of activity. While the notion of selective exposure certainly does not apply in this case, one might speculate that upon the completion of the discrepant behavior, the receiver will, in all likelihood, cease attending to nonsupportive communications in the area of home maintenance.

In a number of studies (for example, as reviewed in Sears and Freedman 1967) mere interest in the topic of a communication message, whether supportive or nonsupportive, appears to be an important consideration in selectivity. Here the receiver's ego-involvement seems relevant, as do the notions of cognitive dissonance—for example, the fact that one is likely to attend to advertisements for the products one buys. Yet as Katz (1968) points out, the distinction between interest and utility or support-seeking is not always easy to make. Considering the idea that interest in a particular communication message is, or leads to, ego-involvement because of past history of exposure or what have you, illustrates this problem. If we think in terms of dissonance theory, the perceived reinforcement of one's attitudes or behavior through mass media communications that seem to reflect those attitudes or behavior, even when negative (cf. Feather's studies of smokers, 1963), might be considered a kind of supportive selectivity. This would presuppose that the receiver's ego-involvement had some built-in dissonance, and any search for reduction in this dissonance would be indistinguishable from the supportive motive in selectivity. Another consideration must be the relationship between a receiver and possible dimensions of interest. For example, it may be that interest in a particular product category is always positive for any receiver. The mere fact of interest would then reflect a singular position, and any communication for that product category would be attended by interested receivers only: interest and support would again be indistinguishable.

Although considerable research on the selective exposure hypothesis has been reviewed by a number of authors (cf. Sears and Freedman 1967; Katz 1968) with little confirmation for the predictive ability of the selective-avoidance hypothesis, few are willing to reject it outright. As McGuire (1968c) puts it: "Once again in psychology, a hypothesis that somehow seems to deserve to be true manages to keep surfacing despite submergence in a sea of empirical disconfirmation." Two reasons are generally offered in support of this lingering faith that the evidence for selective exposure is hiding out just behind the next experiment: methodological difficulties in current and past studies; and several intrinsic factors that tend to stack experiments against the selective-avoidance hypothesis, such as utility, familiarity, comprehensibility, and relevance. These factors could override defensive avoidance in some cases.

Opponents of the selective exposure hypothesis are just as quick to find alternative explanations for those occasional studies that seem to support the hypothesis. As McGuire (1968c) points out, most of these explanations of apparent selective exposure offered by its enemies posit a sociological, rather than psychological, basis for behavior. As a result, they claim it is not surprising to find that someone has more information in support of his own attitudes and behavior than against them, because the social system is structured to promote this seeming bias. It has been pointed out that ingratiating communicators tell the receiver what they think he wants to hear. This is certainly true with advertising communications. In fact, as we shall see in the chapter on message variables, a great deal of attention is paid to structuring a message to insure maximum buyer response. Advertisers seek out target audiences that would naturally be sympathetic to their message (such as current category or brand users) and search for the most efficient media to reach them. A reasonable question surely follows: do receivers selectively expose themselves to supportive advertising messages or do advertisers serve as communication gate keepers, directing only supportive messages to carefully screened receivers? There is certainly some doubt as to whether these circumstances would indicate any motivated tendency on the part of the receiver to seek out supportive and avoid discrepant communications.

While there are some theories that could be brought to bear, predicting results opposite those of selective-avoidance (for example, satiation theory, which would suggest that a receiver would at least temporarily try to avoid overly familiar information; or the notions discussed by Berlyne and by Maddi in *Theories of Cognitive Consistency* [1968], tending to make predictions opposite those of consistency theory). Perhaps the most interesting rebuttal to the selective exposure hypothesis is offered by McGuire (1973). He wonders how the human race could have survived on this earth, for a period that even the most conservative estimates place at a minimum of 6,000 years, if people operated on this redundancy principle, strenuously avoiding anything new or to correct any of their mistakes. Although there may, in fact, be a selective-avoidance tendency operating to some extent in some cases, it is equally probable that an equal or even greater opposite tendency to seek out surprising and discrepant information exists. More on this problem will be discussed in chapter 4, "Message Strategy."

IMMUNIZATION TO PERSUASION

Although the major thrust of most persuasive communication is to maximize advertising response through the effective presentation of believable arguments, it is also possible to increase one's probability of an attitudinal response by insuring against subsequent counterarguments from competitive persuasive communication. However, one must not think that to effect such immunization to subsequent persuasive attempts is only the reverse of persuasion. In order for one's communication effort to have an immunizing effect requires much more than a mere reversal of those characteristics that make a communication message more persuasive. Rather, one must consider positive pretreatments that will render the receiver less prone to change his attitude when subsequently exposed to competitive persuasive messages, by providing him a specific message that makes him more resistant to other persuasive influences, regardless of their strength.

   An important component in many types of approaches to this problem of producing resistance to persuasion is a forewarning, through some mechanism, of the likelihood a receiver will be confronted with a future counter-communication. Research in the area of anticipated belief change has postulated both a "demand" interpretation of forewarning affects on immunization (cf. Papageorgis 1967) that suggests that receivers infer from forewarning that the source wishes them to adopt the advocated position, as well as a "self-esteem" interpretation (cf. McGuire and Millman 1965) which argues that, when a receiver anticipates persuasion by an impending communication, the receiver is likely to become apprehensive that conforming to the position advocated may indicate a susceptibility to persuasion, and a corresponding loss of self-esteem if the receiver were to comply. Either interpretation makes it quite difficult to measure the actual results of forewarning for immunization in a research environment, because of the high degree of possible subject-experimenter interaction.

   Nevertheless, studies such as that reported by McGuire and Papageorgis (1962) indicate that one of the affects of forewarning the receiver of a position to be advocated in a subsequent communication is to stimulate a receiver in preparing defenses against the anticipated message, thereby increasing the probability of counter-arguing. However, one also runs the risk of possibly increasing the likelihood of agreement with the counter-position to be advocated prior to its presentation. In an advertising sense, messages that suggest "others may say they are good, but you know we are the best" forewarn the receiver that there will be a confrontation with conflicting claims sometime in the future. On the one hand, the advertiser may strengthen existing beliefs in anticipation of competitive attempts at counter-persuasion; yet, on the other hand, the advertiser may encourage initial counter-arguing to the message, thereby increasing the probability of the receiver accepting the persuasive arguments of subsequent competitive communication.

   One variation reviewed in the literature of forewarning a receiver in hopes of producing resistance to subsequent competitive persuasive communication is an attempt to generally increase the receiver's critical capacity. It is speculated that, if a receiver is trained to recognize the persuasive intent of a communication, or more generally trained in analyzing and refuting persuasive arguments, one would enhance the receiver's resistance to influence. However, as McGuire (1969a) points out, numerous studies on this question have tended to find, at best, only a slight immunizing affect. Only when the pretraining (forewarning) involves prior refutation of arguments and source derogation for specific issues does a noticeable immunizing affect occur. This could have important implications for advertising. For example, these results would seem to indicate that any attempt to generate a generalized resistance to advertising per se would prove unsuccessful. And, from a pragmatic standpoint, it would seem to suggest that immunization through forewarning-type techniques should have its greatest impact against brand-specific or item-specific references, rather than broad or general categories of competition. In other words, if one is interested in minimizing the persuasive impact of competitive advertising, particularly if it is significantly greater than one's own, one should be quite specific in these efforts, mentioning the competition by name rather than referring to it generally.

McGuire (1969a) offers several reasons why generalized resistance to persuasion by training in critical techniques have thus far proven unsuccessful. First, it could be that one of the critical assumptions underlying these attempts, that if a receiver recognizes a persuasive intent in a communication it would lessen its impact, has been naive. We will discuss circumstances in both the chapters on "Source Factors" and "Message Strategy" in which impact of a persuasive communication can actually be increased when the persuasive intent is known (particularly with refutational appeals). Also, it could be that training in analyzing and evaluating arguments may enhance the effective reception of the persuasive message more than it lowers the level of persuasion, resulting in an overall increase in buyer response. Finally, the "discounting cue" hypothesis (discussed in more detail in Chapter 6) suggests that anything tending to heighten a receiver's discounting of a message argument would induce only short-term immunizing affects. After a period of time, the impact of the discounted argument would exhibit a delayed-action effect as the message content is disassociated from the original critical evaluation of its attempt to persuade.

Although attempts at inducing a general immunization against persuasive communications have not been completely successful, other immunizing techniques directed at making the receiver more resistant to persuasion on specific subjects or to particular sources, while leaving the receiver's more general resistance unaffected have proved somewhat useful. A review of these more successful techniques may be found in McGuire (1964, 1969) and Tannenbaum (1967). We shall consider four of these approaches in this section.

Motivational Change Approach

Altering a receiver's general motivational orientation can have an important impact on resistance to subsequent persuasive communication. As we have already discussed, certain individual-difference characteristics of a receiver related to persuasibility can be manipulated. It is possible, for example, to raise a receiver's self-esteem by providing a successful experience (Mansuer 1954; Samelson 1957). In an advertising context, it would perhaps be possible to provide the receiver with such an experience through a demonstration that the receiver is likely to identify with, either from experience or through identification with the source-presenter. To the degree that the receiver has already used and found the advertised product or service acceptable, the receiver's own experiences would contribute positively to such an approach. This kind of presentation could perhaps be made even more meaningful by juxtaposing the simulated success experience with the failure of competitive alternatives, for Mansuer and Bloch (1957) have shown that the resistance-inducing effect of a success experience is augmented for a receiver if the receiver simultaneously sees the failure of a source found in subsequent persuasive communication. One must be careful, however, in considering this approach, if one anticipates complex persuasive messages from competitive sources. It was pointed out in the section on personality traits that, although self-esteem is positively related to message reception, it tends to be negatively related to attitudinal responses. As a result, efforts to raise the receiver's self-esteem through a successful experience or some other means would be less likely to prove successful against a complex communication because of the difficulty in reception. On the other hand, with simple messages (as is the case with most advertising communication), everyone should comprehend the message, permitting the negative influence on response for alternatives to operate through resistance to subsequent competitive persuasive communication.

A second individual-difference characteristic mediating motivation and amenable to possible immunization effect is anxiety. However, it, too, is influenced by the now familiar dual effect on advertising response: heightened anxiety is negatively related to the message reception and positively related to persuasion. As a result, Millman (1965) has shown that immunizing attempts through fear-arousing communication do tend to enhance resistance to subsequent persuasive communication for receivers exhibiting high levels of chronic anxiety, while lowering resistance among receivers exhibiting low levels of chronic anxiety. Although these experiments dealt only with general anxiety levels, for which the induced fear need have no relationship to the attitude value in question, similar immunization possibilities occur in attaching anxiety to specific issues. For example, if a specific subject is made to be anxiety producing for a receiver, in the receiver's evaluation of subsequent messages on that subject one should expect a lower probability of persuasion and hence an increased immunization to such communication.

Commitment Approach

To the extent that an individual tries to keep his internal beliefs, his verbal expression, and his actual behavior consistent with one another, immunization to future persuasive communication should be possible through some form of prior commitment. While actual behavior should prove the most binding form of prior commitment from a consistency theory point of view, followed by some form of public endorsement of a position, Bennett (1955) has found that even an internal review of the receiver's beliefs in the receiver's own mind can function as an effective means of inducing resistance to subsequent persuasive communication. This suggests that advertising that seeks a commitment or decision from the receiver should produce an effect immunizing the receiver from competitive advertising. The receiver, once committed to an advertiser's argument, will be less susceptible to counter-arguments in other advertising. This effect could quite possibly overcome the impact of a greater frequency in message presentation among competitive alternatives, assuming they, too, are not specifically addressing cognitive commitment in their messages. McGuire (1972) has noted that there is some evidence to suggest that the more active a receiver's rehearsal of beliefs and the less pressure put upon the receiver to elicit this rehearsal, the stronger will be the committing effect and thus the greater the resistance to counter-communications. This argues for a subtle rather than a hard-sell approach in the creative message of advertising seeking immunization through commitment. Obvious examples of this approach in advertising include those messages that seek active closure on the part of a receiver to a message conclusion, as well as those with jingles or "tongue-twisters" that benignly encourage rehearsal.

Even though it would, no doubt, be more effective if the receiver could be persuaded to publicly express his beliefs prior to his exposure to competitive persuasive communications, it is not a realistic advertising goal, despite McGuire's (1969a) observation that a number of studies have shown public commitment to be more effective than private decisions in conferring resistance to subsequent influence attempts. But, even more committing than a public expression of one's beliefs should be actual behavior on the part of the receiver reflecting the beliefs. This could become extremely important to advertising in the introduction of new products or new uses for existing products. The advertiser who is able to most effectively generate buyer response, be it behavioral change in the sense of brand switching or the purchase of a new product, or an advertising response such as an attitudinal change reflecting a new understanding of an existing brand or product, creates a commitment in the form of a prior response, which should help induce resistance to advertising for competitive alternatives. As intuitively appealing as this may seem, one is cautioned that such behavioral commitment confers resistance to subsequent influence only under certain conditions (cf. McGuire 1961, 1964). A study by Kresler and Sakumura (1966) has indicated that resistance to subsequent attack is most readily apparent when the behavior involves only a small reward rather than a large reward. Since most consumer advertising involves very little risk and a correspondingly small "reward" in the product, for most advertising this notion should hold. However, for such high-priced consumer durables as major appliances or automobiles, the product itself holds a large "reward" and hence advertising for such products should be less dependent on prior brand or product behavior (cognitive states important to a receiver's reception of a message).

One final example of external commitment mentioned by McGuire (1969a) involves preannouncing to the receiver that other people believe the receiver has a certain initial belief on the subject of the communication. It has been found that receivers who have been provided with such a preannouncement tend to be more resistant to subsequent persuasive communication attacking that belief. For advertising, this suggests a variation of the refutational strategy, for which one begins by stating that most people similar to the receiver (that is, those the receiver is most likely to wish to identify with) believe that the receiver agrees with the advertiser's arguments, then supplies support for the belief, and closure such as: "That's why you and all these others hold these beliefs."

Anchoring Approach

The anchoring approach to immunization involves linking the beliefs presented in a persuasive communication to other aspects of a receiver's cognitive domain. As such, it is generally related to the commitment approach, since both assume a consistency need on the part of the receiver. But, whereas the commitment approach involves the receiver acting on the basis of his beliefs, the anchoring approach involves making the belief resistant to subsequent counter-argument by correcting it with existing beliefs. Immunization to subsequent counter-belief persuasive communication follows because it would then require not only a change in the given belief, but also a change in all corresponding cognitive links before effective counter-persuasion could occur.

Several studies have been reported that link beliefs to accepted values, showing that it is conducive to behavior or attitudes the receiver finds favorable. The subsequent resistance to persuasion occurs in this case because prior to a persuasive attack the perception of either the positive saliences the receiver attaches to the belief or the instrumentality of the belief to those saliences has been raised. Carlson (1956) conducted a test in which he sought to determine whether in fact attitudes or beliefs could be changed by altering a receiver's perception of the significance of the belief object as a means for attaining a valued goal. Changes in attitude were found to be significantly related to changes in perceived instrumental relationships, and to changes in an index based upon both satisfaction and instrumentality ratings. This suggests that resistance to persuasion on a given belief can indeed be enhanced by raising the receiver's perception of the belief's instrumentality to an already positively valenced goal. Nelson (1968) tested the anchoring approach by linking the belief to be immunized to specific values or goals held by the receiver. On the basis of a need-instrumentality theory of attitude it was predicted that a pretreatment which enhanced the perceived instrumental relationship between the belief under consideration and highly valenced goals would make the belief more resistant to persuasion. Specifically, the study was designed to determine whether amount, activity, and difficulty of the anchorings of the beliefs to the receiver's values affected the belief's subsequent resistance to persuasion. It was found that active participation in establishing the instrumental link did confer a significant amount of resistance to persuasion; however, the number of values to which the belief was shown to be instrumental was not crucial, nor was the difficulty of their establishment. Further support for the anchoring method of inducing resistance to persuasion is provided by Holt (1970).

It should be clear to the reader, at this point, that much of the reasoning behind the anchoring approach to immunization, particularly its clear association with consistency theory principles, is the same as that which argues for attitudinal segmentation of markets for purposes of effective advertising strategy development (Percy 1976a). Not only should the linking of accepted values or other beliefs and behavior patterns enhance response for one's own persuasive communication, but to the degree that such beliefs are linked to the advertiser's message, they also induce resistance to subsequent competitive advertising via anchoring. In fact, following McGuire's (1969a) "Socratic effect," one can see how the presentation of relatively consonant beliefs on related subjects tends to set off cognitive activity or reorganization, which will bring all the related beliefs into greater logical consistency within the receiver's mind. Once completed, the strength of the message belief anchored to the existing beliefs becomes more resistant to counter-communication.

One final consideration for anchoring is suggested by reference-group theory. To the degree that a highly valued source is associated with the message belief, this link should help anchor the belief positively in the receiver's mind. Or, as McGuire (1969) points out, preexisting links can be made to have greater impact by raising the salience of the source within the message (this, of course, assumes a prior knowledge of highly valenced sources). Subsequent persuasive communication that goes against this perceived source-belief norm would more than likely be resisted by the receiver. For example, if a high-valence source is linked with a particular product in a receiver's mind, competitive advertising that claims another brand is more appropriate (for whatever reason) would be unpersuasive because of the strength of the belief identification with the reference group.

Innoculation Approach

This approach to immunization suggests that resistance to persuasion can be increased by prior exposure to small amounts of a future attacking argument, strong enough to stimulate a defense such as counter-arguing, but not so strong as to be persuasive. Its name derives from the obvious analogy to medical innoculations—a patient is immunized against a disease by the introduction of a small amount of that same disease into the patient's system. Originally suggested by Janis (1958), it has been heavily explored by McGuire (1964) in the area of cultural truisms related to health. He assumed that the characteristic mode of belief defense is avoidance of exposure to opposition argument. It was found that a preexposure to a weakened form of an attacking argument created a greater resistance to subsequent heavy persuasive counter-communication than merely providing the receiver with a prior message in support of his own beliefs. In general, it was found that a certain period of time was necessary for the "innoculation" to become truly effective, and that such preexposure innoculation tended to also develop resistance to additional arguments against the belief, arguments not originally presented in the innoculation material.

The mechanism at work here seems to suggest that, if a receiver is made aware that a strongly held belief is open to argument, the receiver will seek to bolster cognitive defenses against any subsequent attempt to attack that belief. Wyer (1974) speculates that this may imply that a simple mention of arguments against a proposition may be sufficient to make a receiver aware of the vulnerability of held beliefs, causing the receiver to cognitively reorganize all relevant beliefs, regardless of which ones are actually refuted in the original innoculation communication. Also, the more vulnerable the receiver feels, the more likely the receiver will be to take the necessary cognitive steps required to effectively counter-argue when held beliefs are attacked through subsequent persuasive communication, and hence the more resistant to such persuasion the receiver may become. The work by McGuire (1964) cited above, as well as a study by Papageorgis and McGuire (1961) seem to support these conclusions. Specifically, the simple awareness of arguments against a proposition will be sufficient for a receiver to prepare counter-arguments for any subsequent attack upon that proposition, and the greater the number of arguments the receiver is aware of, the better prepared the receiver will be.

A convenient message appeal for effecting an innoculation approach to immunization in advertising is a refutational defense. This is, in fact, the message appeal used by McGuire and his colleagues in testing the effects of the innoculation hypotheses. One interesting finding arising from this line of thinking is that refutational strategies seem to derive their immunizing efficiency from mentioning the attacking arguments rather than from the reassuring refutation of them. And, while McGuire cautions that, because his work dealt only with cultural truisms and as such is really only generalizable to the immunization of cultural truisms, two studies reported by Chase and Kelly (1976), using an issue that was not a cultural truism also revealed the effectiveness of low intensity pretreatment messages in conferring maximum resistance to persuasion. Additionally, a large body of empirical evidence does exist supporting innoculation theory.

ACTIVE PARTICIPATION IN THE
COMMUNICATION PROCESS

A final receiver variable to be considered is the extent to which a receiver actively participates in the communication process. Thinking first of the particular state of an individual receiver upon receipt of a communication message, predictions from the areas of learning and psychotherapy would indicate that persuasibility should be greater to the extent that the communication message requires the receiver's active participation in the process. However, communication research often tends to lead to quite opposite conclusions. In our discussion of source objectivity in the next chapter, it is pointed out that a persuasive communication has at least as much persuasive impact when an explicit conclusion is drawn for the receiver as when it is implicit, and must be drawn by the receiver. Learning and psychotherapy predictions would hold that the implicit conclusion that called upon the receiver to participate actively by formulating its conclusion would be more persuasive than the explicit conclusion that was already drawn for him. McGuire (1969a) suggests that this nonconfirmation of the prediction by analogy from the supposed psychotherapy and learning findings should not come as a great surprise. For example, a receiver viewing a television commercial is typically a "captive audience" whose main motivation with respect to the persuasive communication is to get through with it (and this condition would be even more likely in a commercial testing environment). Generally, the receiver would have little interest in or acquaintance with the subject of the advertisement and even less motivation to utilize effectively any active participation opportunities presented. While this may be less true for a finely honed target audience known to be active in the product-market being advertised, for the majority of receivers it remains a cogent analysis. Additionally, regardless of the degree of receiver interest in the subject of the persuasive communication, a receiver typically will not have a supply of relevant arguments to use within the receiver's cognitive repertory even if motivated to argue.

McGuire's (1964) work on immunization and attitude change (which has just been considered in some detail in the previous section) describes the inability of receivers to utilize effectively the improvisation opportunities afforded them in attitude change situations. Findings from this work suggest that a receiver is generally unprepared and unmotivated to find the needed information with which to actively participate in a persuasive communication, and, as a result, is more affected by the passive reading of an explicit message. He does point out that there is some evidence that the opportunity for active participation does tend to catch up with passive reading in effectiveness under certain motivated conditions. However, it never surpasses the passive-reading condition in persuasive effectiveness.

Insufficient Justification

A rather complex aspect of the relationship between active participation and the communication process involves the effect of counter-attitudinal advocacy with insufficient justification. One might feel that almost any persuasive communication, particularly advertising, would involve insufficient justification for any receiver holding an attitude or behaving in a manner contrary to that being advanced by the communication message. But, what is at issue here is the amount of internalized belief change that results when a receiver is forced to advocate overtly a position highly discrepant from his internal belief, when the persuasive message carries varying degrees of real or perceived sanction. From a theoretical viewpoint, there is a controversy involved between dissonance-theory predictions on this insufficient justification issue and incentive-theory predictions.

Dissonance theory is examined extensively in our discussion of source factors in the next chapter. Its presence here bears on several predicted receiver reactions under various sanctions for compliance to counter-attitudinal persuasive communication with insufficient justification. For example, if a receiver is persuaded by a communication effort to engage in some form of counter-attitudinal advocacy (such as buying a certain advertised product the receiver is not particularly interested in, because outside pressure demands it), there results a discrepancy between internal beliefs and actual behavior that creates cognitive strain. Dissonance theory would demand some resolution of this conflict. If the receiver can justify discrepant behavior (such as buying and using a particular product to facilitate family harmony, or in hopes of advancing the receiver's position within some social or business group, then a certain cognitive balance is retained. If such external justification is weak or lacking, and the behavior persists, one should expect a change in the receiver's internal beliefs in the direction of more stable cognitions. In either process, a certain unpleasantness is felt in confronting the discrepant choice, owing to a disconfirmation of expectation—a name given to a line of research initiated by Aronson and Carlsmith (1962). Once a receiver makes a choice in the full knowledge of information that suggests the decision was irrational (as would occur in the purchase of a product the receiver was not fond of using, even though the receiver rationalized the purchase for other considerations), it violates the receiver's self-expectation of rational behavior. The problem is, of course, intensified to the extent that the receiver perceives an insufficient justification for the behavior.

This dissonance theory prediction that when a receiver is required to openly express attitudes or behave in a manner highly discrepant from internal belief, the amount of resultant internal belief change in the direction of the discrepant position will increase as the amount of positive incentive for the actual compliance decreases, frequently stands in apparent contradiction to predictions made on the basis of incentive theory. Incentive theory would suggest that the greater the perceived reward or reinforcement for actively participating in a counter-attitudinal or behavioral advocacy (such as the scenarios discussed above, or perhaps even message rehearsal for a product not currently used), the greater will be the likelihood of movement toward the advocated position (see Figure 2.11). In other words, if the receiver really finds sufficient justification for counter-attitudinal behavior, the receiver will be more likely to repeat such behavior, in order to sustain the rewards associated with that attitude or behavior,

FIGURE 2.11

Incentive-Dissonance Controversy

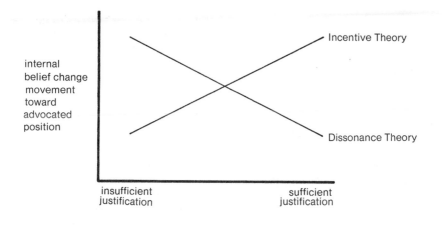

internal
belief change
movement
toward
advocated
position

Incentive Theory

Dissonance Theory

insufficient
justification

sufficient
justification

and, as a result, be more likely to be persuaded of the correctness of the advocated position.

While there would seem to be a discrepancy in the dissonance theory versus incentive theory predictions on this insufficient justification issue, Aronson (1968) reviews a number of studies that minimize their differences. McGuire (1969a), too, feels that the controversy is more apparent than real. He points out that dissonance-theory predictions deal most specifically with the effect of receiver commitment to engage in counter-attitudinal behavior prior to the actual carrying out of the commitment, while incentive-theory prediction deals primarily with what happens when the receiver actually carries out the counter-attitudinal behavior. In other words, in terms of a persuasive communication such as advertising, in which one is advocating the use of a product the receiver would not ordinarily purchase, dissonance theory should deal with those responses associated with an affective predisposition to engage in the advertised behavior, whereas incentive theory should "skip" the affective changes and focus more directly on providing reasons for purchase (an intention objective). The amount of internalized belief change in either case would be related to degree the receiver finds insufficient justification to engage in the counter-attitudinal behavior.

In summary, it is doubtful that a dissonance theorist would take issue with the fact that receivers of persuasive communication frequently behave in a counter-attitudinal way in order to obtain rewards, and that the activities associated with those rewards tend to be repeated, thus leading to greater self-indoctrination of the advocated message. Nor would an incentive theorist be compelled to deny the prediction of dissonance theory that the commitment to carry out a counter-attitudinal behavior tends to cause cognitive strain, and that the results of this cognitive strain will be the assimilation of the internal belief in the direction of the commitment to the advocated message, at least to the extent that there is insufficient justification for behaving (McGuire 1969a). It is only when the receiver actually carries out this commitment that the incentive prediction is made.

Transactional Model of Communication

We have seen that a receiver, far from being passive in a communication situation, may actively seek out information for such diverse purposes as refining or consolidating his existing attitudes, preserving or strengthening his self-image, or ingratiating himself with other individuals or groups. On the other hand, even though he may not actively seek out information, he may react to persuasive communication in similar ways, even to the extent of using communication messages to deal with cognitive problems. The specific reaction is mediated by his individual characteristics. Moreover, in addition to this activity as an individual within complex sets of often seemingly contradictory effects, a receiver reacts to persuasive communications as a member of social groups (Freidson 1953) that condition his response to a given communication's message. The more salient his membership in one or more of these groups, the more complex are the interactions of individual characteristics and group norms in determining a receiver's reaction to any particular communication. In general, one would expect the groups to which a receiver belongs to act as a reference in reinterpreting, dampening, or amplifying the original communication message to conform with the beliefs held by each group. In certain extreme cases, in which a particular persuasive communication attracted strongly held group beliefs, a "boomerang" effect could result, so that the message is discredited because it is at variance with group beliefs, and the receiver's originally held beliefs are further reinforced.

Because of these persuasive communication reactions within a group situation, Bauer (1964, 1973) has suggested that, if people communicate as members of groups and receive and react as members of groups, then any one communication cannot be seen as having an impact on a single individual receiver, but must be seen as the start of a chain of events or as input into a more complex system. One early formulation of this chain is offered by Katz (1957). He addresses the notion of a two-step process in communication, in which "opinion leaders" use the information they get from mass media to influence others. The receivers in this case (or at least a subset of them) become, in turn, sources of communication. This, of course, positions the receiver in an active role. Much has been made of this possibility among advertisers, as they attempt to communicate with these so-called "opinion leaders" in an effort to broaden the effectiveness of their persuasive message.

If one accepts the basic idea of a two-step process in communication, it is not difficult to imagine that, if feedback occurs and the source of the communication (for example, the advertiser) responds to it so as to correct any errors that may have resulted from the original communication, then it is only reasonable to assume that the initiator of a communication would attempt to figure out in advance what the target receiver would like and how the receiver is likely to react to the messages communicated. This is precisely what goes on, in many cases, as an advertising campaign is put together. Research or other available information is digested, in order to position the creative execution of the persuasive communication in a manner that will have maximum impact on the receiver's response to the communication. In other words, as Bauer (1973) puts it, the receiver would have influenced what is said before the receiver ever heard or read what the communicator had to say. If this logic is accepted, then it is just as proper to say that the receiver influences the communicator as it is to say the communicator influences the receiver.

This notion of a transactional model of communication as a mutual two-way influence is built around the idea that one of the functions of mass media is to activate the receiver to become a communicator also. And, as we have seen, both individual characteristics and group memberships will affect the way in which the receiver reacts to any particular persuasive communication. As a result, the course of this transactional model will be a function of the structure and state of the social system, of which the first receiver of a persuasive message is a member. The importance of these receivers to subsequent events in the model should be evident; for, as Bauer (1973) feels, whatever the nature of the initial persuasive communication, its impact will be only in part, and perhaps in small part, a function of its own content and form. For, while it is possible to predict the probable reactions to various forms of persuasive communication messages, it is the characteristics of the receiver, including membership in social groups, that mediate an advertising response. And, within the framework of the transactional model, it is the reception of the communication by the receiver that effects eventual feedback and subsequent second-step communication.

Although a great deal of discussion is frequently given to the proposition that the communication process is a transactional one in which the communicator and receiver play equally active roles, little by way of formal impact is evidenced in the literature. The flow of influence is treated predominantly as a linear one from the communicator to the receiver, with any effect being some change in the receiver's attitude or behavior toward the subject of the communication. The receiver, for the most part, is seen as exercising a mediating role, concerned with the intent of the persuasive communication. This is, in fact, the primary position taken in this text. It is not necessary to consider an acceptance of the transactional model of the communication process as refuting the mediating role of the receiver in response to advertising. It is more that this mediating role is central to how a communication's message persuades, even though a receiver may react, in part, also because of membership in a social group and as an active participant in a two-step process of communication. At whatever point in a two-step or more complex receiver-communication system, the key to understanding is the receiver and how the receiver mediates a particular response objective. While this transactional model sees the receiver as a second-stage communicator (and a certain body of evidence supports this—cf. Bauer 1973), this view is easily embraced within the notion of the mediating role of the receiver; for the person must certainly be a receiver before becoming a second-stage communicator.

REVIEWING VARIABLE 1: RECEIVER SELECTION

The overall objective of this chapter has been to provide an understanding of how to maximize the strategic impact of advertising by successfully identifying and understanding the target receivers for a message. Specifically, one should be able to:

1. Discuss the need for segmentation in identifying target receivers
2. Contrast the differences between traditional market segmentation and market segmentation with a communication orientation
3. Compare how a receiver's initial attitude and an advertising message will effect response to the advertising
4. Identify important individual difference characteristics that can affect selection of a receiver, and understand how such characteristics will mediate a particular receiver's response to advertising
5. Develop strategies that will tend to increase the probability of positive retained receiver intention
6. Illustrate how receiver involvement with advertising can facilitate advertising response

KEY CONCEPTS

Target Receivers	Immunization
Market Segmentation	Commitment
Product Orientation	Counter-arguing
Communication Orientation	Forewarning

Initial Attitude
Latitude of Acceptance
Selectivity
Individual-Difference
  Characteristics
Personality as a Trait versus State

Anchoring
Active Participation
Dissonance
Transactional Model
  of Communication

3

SOURCE FACTORS

The source of a message, while real in many respects, must be studied in terms of how it is perceived by the intended receiver. A source may be someone we know, a newspaper or magazine we read, a television or radio announcer we hear; almost anyone or anything could be perceived in a source role by someone. The same message could, in fact, be attributed to a number of different sources, depending upon an individual receiver's perceptions. As an example, consider a typical television commercial. It would be possible for source attributions to be made for the medium itself, the advertiser, the brand, or any of the message or execution variables present (for example, testimonials by well-known personalities, supportive information ascribed to reputable institutions, relevant general "authority" figures such as doctors or engineers). Some or all would be present in any communication (even if not in precisely that fashion), suggesting a source level effect that must be accounted for in an understanding of advertising and communication.

The detailed discussion of source variables that follows may be applied to any source level, and the reader should bear in mind that perceived source factors of a particular message at one level may not always be in harmony with the perceived source factors at another level. We shall want to examine this notion in more detail after we acquaint ourselves with various source characteristics.

Part I
Source Characteristics

Traditionally, the most generally studied source characteristics may be grouped together under three subclasses on the basis of a target receiver's motivation for accepting the message being offered. These characteristics of the perceived source that add to the persuasive impact of a communication message attributed to it may be considered as three component valences: credibility, attractiveness, and power. While others have suggested additional distinctions, such as Bauer's (1965) prestige, likability, and dynamism of the communicator dimensions or Triandis's (1971) familiarity and hostility, we adhere to this tricomponential analysis because it has the strongest traditional support and the greatest degree of applicability to advertising. The theorist who is most often credited with working out the general question of the tricomponential analysis of source characteristics in the fullest detail is Kelman (1958, 1961). In the first component, a source gains in persuasive valence to the extent that a target receiver is motivated to be "correct" on a given issue, and perceives the source to be credible (for example, when the source is perceived as being objective or expert on the subject of the communication message). A second component occurs when an individual receiver wishes to identify in some real or emotionally satisfying manner with a source (for example, when the source is perceived to be similar to the receiver, as in "slice-of-life" advertising; or when the source is perceived as likable in some way). The third, while less involved with mass media effects, bears directly on both personal selling and word-of-mouth communication. Here, a receiver may respond to a message because the receiver is anxious about the source's ability to reward or punish; and, the source is perceived to have such power that it can actually control the receiver's reward and punishment, has concern about compliance, and can ascertain whether the receiver has indeed complied. Kelman's analysis of how these characteristics affect attitude change is thought of in terms of internalization, identification, and compliance. Internalization is generally dependent on the credibility of the source, identification is dependent on its attractiveness, and compliance on its power.

AN OVERVIEW OF KELMAN'S ANALYSIS

Strictly speaking, the Kelman (1961) typology is concerned with types of social influence, and restricted to personal communication. Nevertheless, as McGuire (1969a, 1973) and others have pointed out (Howard and Sheth 1969;

Triandis 1971), his conceptualization of the interaction through motivation of source effects on receivers is extremely helpful in understanding how source characteristics function in advertising and communication. This is particularly true from the point of view of advertising response.

Internalization

Internalization may be thought of as occurring when a receiver accepts the influence of a source because the induced behavior is congruent with the receiver's value system (beliefs). As a mode of change in buyer response, the receiver adopts a change in behavior (or attitude leading to behavior) because of perceiving it as inherently conducive to the maximization of the receiver's beliefs. The receiver is motivated to have some objectively correct solution to a problem or verifiably "right" position on an issue. While the obvious characteristics of a source (such as, for example, the clothes, accent, rate of speech, loudness of voice, physical attractiveness, and demographic characteristics) do play an important part in internalization, the key source characteristic is credibility; that is, the extent to which the source is perceived in relation to the communication content as knowing the right answer and as motivated to communicate it. In short, this is the source's perceived ability and motive for personal gain, or what Hovland, Janis, and Kelley (1953) term "expertness" and "trustworthiness."

To the extent that the source (at whatever level) is perceived as having high credibility, the arguments are learned and recalled, and the conclusions are integrated into the belief and value system of the target receiver. Typically, though, the receiver will not totally accept the source's conclusions, but rather will modify them to some degree so they will fit the receiver's own particular problems and values. As a result, the receiver will tend to manifest attitude and behavior changes consistent with the conclusions advanced by the source in the message. The new behavior is now independent of the source (no longer depending on reinforcement by the source), and dependent upon extent to which underlying values are made relevant in new situations—hence the term "internalization."

Identification

Identification may be thought of as occurring when the receiver's response is derived from the perceived behavior of the source because this behavior is associated with a satisfying self-defining relationship to the source. As a mode of change in affecting response to communication, it is the receiver's motivation to establish a gratifying role relationship with the source, either in an actual reciprocal role (for example, in personal selling or word-of-mouth communication) or within some perceived self-concept. To the extent that such a relationship with the source is established, the receiver defines the receiver's role in terms of the role of the source. The receiver attempts to be like or to actually be the source. A source likely to be perceived in this manner would be one whose role or outward characteristics—characteristics the receiver often lacks—are sought by the individual receiver. The essential source characteristic involved for this process is attractiveness, as determined by the receiver's similarity to, familiarity with, or liking for the source.

To the extent that the receiver finds the source attractive, the receiver will tend to adopt a position similar to that advocated by the source and coincident with the role relationship, as perceived by the receiver, between the receiver and the source. To produce a change through a response to advertising, the source need not supply any evidence to substantiate position (for example, testimonials by well-known sports or show business personalities in advertising), but need only make the role relationship salient. In other words, the receiver need only wish to identify in some fashion with the source in order to respond to the message and behave accordingly. The receiver will then proceed to elaborate the newly adopted position in a way that will reinforce his identification with the source. While the receiver does not alter the response pattern because of finding the source's argument compelling, the receiver will, in fact, believe in the new attitude and behavior adopted. Additionally, one should point out that source attractiveness could be negatively valenced, such that the receiver has a negative identification with the source and thus uses the source's position as a guide to what not to believe or how not to behave. In this way, the receiver will be reacting in a similar mode to that just described, only for opposite reasons.

When changes in the receiver's response pattern are occasioned by the identification process, they do not, as in the internalization case, become functionally autonomous of future changes in the source's position. Such changes remain tied to the source and are dependent on social support. The maintenance of the new attitude or behavior depends on the source's continued advocacy of it, the receiver's continued role relationship with the source, as well as the salience of this role relationship. They are not integrated within the receiver's value system as was the case with internalization, but rather tend to remain isolated from the rest of the receiver's values.

Compliance

Compliance may be thought of as occurring when the receiver is willing to accept the influence of the source in hopes of obtaining some sort of favorable reaction. This involves the receiver's public acquiescences to the position advanced by the source in the communication, without any necessary private commitment to it. The receiver is complying with what the receiver thinks the source wishes, because the source is seeking a desired response from the receiver;

TABLE 3.1

Source Characteristics and Behavioral Response

Source Characteristic	Behavioral Response Change Mode	Attitude-Change Effect
Credibility	Internalization	functionally autonomous of future changes in source's position
Attractiveness	Identification	tied to source and dependent on social support
Power	Compliance	expressed only when receiver is either in presence of the source or his perceived agent

the receiver feels that adopting this behavior will be instrumental in the production of a satisfying social effect. In essence, the receiver reacts the way the receiver perceives that the source expects, regardless of what the receiver's personal attitude may be. The source characteristic essential to this mode of response is power—specifically, the source's power over the receiver's means to attain a desired goal.

The source has the influence to produce this compliance mode of change in responding to advertising to the extent that the source has the power to apply positive and negative sanctions to the receiver (either directly or indirectly), is desirous of the receiver's compliance, and is able to determine or observe whether compliance occurs. While this has more immediate application to situations involving personal or one-to-one communication, one should not overlook mass media implications. For example, there are people who compulsively try to say and do the expected thing in all situations in an effort to please everyone; and there are people who infer from a source a particular set of needs in an attempt to curry favorable responses from some group. To the extent that the source of an advertisement or other communication is perceived to be an agent or surrogate of a desired social contact, compliance may be brought about. The receiver will react to the message by exploring the limits of compliance within the desired group, and manifest induced attitude or behavior change to the extent that the source retains sanctioning power and an ability to monitor the compliance through such surrogate pressure. And, as such, attitudes and behavior adopted through compliance will only be expressed when the receiver is either in the presence of the source or the perceived agent of the source.

These relationships between the source characteristics and Kelman's expression of the psychological modes leading to change in the receiver's response probability are summarized in Table 3.1. It should be stressed, in addition, that the three relationships are not mutually exclusive. Although they have been discussed individually, they do not generally occur in such a precise way in real-life situations. The distinctions are drawn primarily to emphasize some of the processes involved in source perception.

CREDIBILITY AS A SOURCE CHARACTERISTIC

Crane (1972) has called credibility the most important source characteristic in marketing communication. Howard and Sheth (1969) also feel it is perhaps the most important attribute of the source. As we have seen, a credible source gets a receiver to incorporate or internalize into the belief structure the views expressed in the message. One might speculate that a problem for advertising communication may be that receivers of advertising messages perceive a lack of credibility in the message based solely on one source level: that is, the fact that the source is an advertiser, and as such would have its own motives, which are generally perceived to be in opposition to the receiver's beliefs. A receiver may use or even need advertising (or other commercial sources, such as salespeople and displays) as a source of information, while remaining immutable in complaining about the lack of source credibility. On the other hand, Arndt (1967) has shown that credibility in personal word-of-mouth communication is extremely important, because the receiver perceives the message coming from friends or even neutral sources as unlikely to be biased against the receiver's own value system or welfare. It is, therefore, extremely important to understand how each source level is perceived by various target receivers.

Credibility has been defined traditionally in terms of the source's attributes, which are perceived by the receiver as relevant to the topic being communicated. It follows that believability of the communication reflects the extent to which the message (via the source) is perceived by the receiver as being correct, and more particularly on the receiver's perception of the source as knowing what is correct and being motivated to communicate what he knows. Or, as McGuire (1969a, 1973) characterizes it, the perceived expertise and objectivity of the source (corresponding to our earlier expressions of "expertness" and "trustworthiness" attributed to Hovland, Janis, and Kelley 1953). Both of these perceptions will now be considered in some detail.

Perceived Expertise

There is a considerable literature (reviewed in chapter 2 of Hovland, Janis, and Kelley [1953]) showing that the amount of attitude change produced by a given communication message can be varied by ascribing the message to sources that differ for socially desirable dimensions, such as knowledge, education, intelligence, social status, professional attainment, and age (McGuire 1969a). And, as one might suppose, it has generally been found that the more a source is perceived as expert, the greater the persuasive impact of the message on the receiver. Even irrelevant characteristics of the source's status have been found to have an effect on persuasive impact, owing to source credibility. In an experiment conducted to test the relative importance of objectively relevant and objectively irrelevant aspects of a source's credibility on changes in receiver opinion, Aronson and Golden (1962) found that both the relevant and the irrelevant characteristics of the source had a significant influence on the effectiveness of the communication. A speech extolling the virtues of arithmetic was recited to sixth-grade students by one of four different sources: (a) high relevant and high irrelevant credibility (a white engineer); (b) high relevant and low irrelevant credibility (a black engineer); (c) low relevant and high irrelevant credibility (a white dishwasher); (d) low relevant and low irrelevant credibility (a black dishwasher). The expected result was a strong tendency for engineers to be more effective than dishwashers. But, there was also a strong tendency for those subjects who were prejudiced against Negroes to be underinfluenced by the Negro source and for those subjects who were not prejudiced to be overinfluenced by the Negro source. These results suggest again the importance of understanding the receiver's perception of each source level in the development of advertising communication, for even the irrelevant source levels may affect overall source credibility.

McGuire (1973) draws attention to a qualification of the common-sense positive relation between expertise and persuasive impact. There might be such a thing as too much perceived expertise. He mentions a study by Stukàt (1958) in which it was found that children tend to be influenced more by children somewhat older than themselves than by their age peers, while being less influenced by those considerably older. Additional support is offered by the so-called "pratfall" experiments (cf. Aronson, Willerman, and Floyd 1966; Helmreich, Aronson, and LeFan 1970), which suggest that a highly prestigious person actually becomes more attractive if there is evidence of some human failing which would be cause for rejection of a less prestigious individual. So it would seem that a source perceived to be slightly superior to the receiver would be more credible than a source who was not superior at all or who was a great deal more superior to the receiver. The more expert source benefits from being perceived more knowledgeable than the receiver, but suffers from being perceived as much different from the receiver. This nonmonotonic relationship between the source's expertise and the persuasive impact is illustrated in Figure 3.1, in which

FIGURE 3.1

Nonmonotonic Relationship between Source Expertness and Persuasive Impact

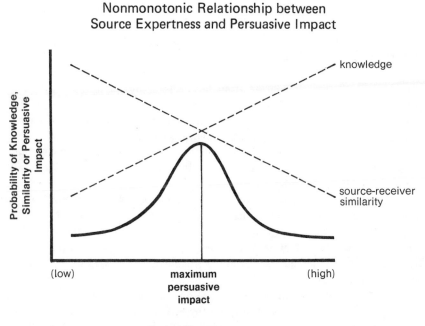

each are related through the mediation of the underlying factors such as knowledge of the source and similarity to the receiver. In this case, maximum persuasive impact occurs at some intermediate level of source expertise.

Perceived Objectivity

Not only must a source be perceived as knowledgeable to be considered credible, it must also be perceived as objective enough to be motivated to provide an unbiased account. It would be expected certainly that the less objective a source is perceived to be by the receiver (that is, the more the receiver suspects that the source is really only trying to persuade), the less change in response one should expect; and there is an abundance of empirical literature dealing with this commonsense notion in one form or another (for a review, see McGuire [1969a]). The rub is that, although there is a great deal of research available relevant to this question, the evidence in support of the "obvious" hypotheses that a source loses persuasive effectiveness when there is a perceived bias or persuasive intent by the receiver is almost nonexistent. In fact, out of this research has frequently come support for quite the contrary notion: that the receiver's awareness of source bias and intent to persuade may actually increase the amount of attitude or behavioral change.

There is evidence that a soft-sell advertisement or other communication that goes to some lengths to mask its intent to persuade and thus give an appearance of objectivity in fact may decrease change in attitude or behavior through failure to communicate the source's point. Rather, if the source draws the conclusion explictly in the message instead of permitting or expecting the receiver to arrive at a logical conclusion from the support presented, more immediate change is induced. McGuire (1969b) presents a number of circumstances in which blatant attempts to persuade are more effective in producing change in attitude or behavior than the more "commonsense" notion of minimizing persuasive intent. The extent to which the strategy and execution of the communication bears on these questions of persuasibility and source credibility will be discussed in chapter 4, "Message Strategy."

On the specific question of the objectivity or "trustworthiness" of the source, there is some indication that this may be a function of time. By manipulating the "trustworthiness" component of source credibility, Hovland and Weiss (1951) observed what they termed a "sleeper effect." Compared with a measure of attitude taken immediately after a communication message, they found a decrease, after four weeks, in the extent to which receivers agreed with a position advocated by trustworthy sources, but an increase in agreement when the message was presented by an untrustworthy source. They concluded that there had been equal message content learning under the two conditions of "trustworthiness," but less yielding to the arguments of the untrustworthy source. After four weeks, a "dissociation of source and content" occurred, so indicating resistance to the acceptance of the arguments of the untrustworthy source was reduced, which, actually led to greater acceptance of the message by the untrustworthy source than by the trustworthy source. This "sleeper effect" is illustrated in Figure 3.2.

The implications of the sleeper effect for advertising communication are intriguing. It suggests that when a strongly persuasive argument is called for (for example, when one is attempting to refute a generally held highly negative salience) by a clearly biased source (such as an argument by potato growers that potatoes are not fattening), one would be better off acknowledging the source rather than attempting to conceal it. This would assume that over a period of time the message would gain credence as it was dissociated from the source.

Yet, in another study of the sleeper effect, Kelman and Hovland (1953) found that reinstatement of the source obviates the improved level of persuasion otherwise noted for a clearly biased source. They presented identical communications ascribed to three different sources: (a) one well informed and fair, (b) one neutral, and (c) one poorly informed and biased. In terms of credibility, the two extremes utilize both expertise and objectivity. After three weeks, one-half of the subjects were again reminded of the source of the original communication,

FIGURE 3.2

Sleeper Effect

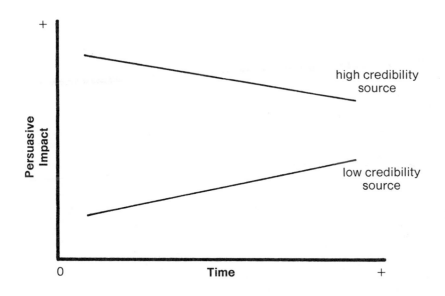

while the other half was not. Attitude change reflected the sleeper effect when the source was not reinstated, but when it was reinstated, the reduction in attitude change for the biased source paralleled that of the positive source. In other words, their results seem to indicate that attitude change follows a "forgetting curve" without reinstatement of the source; when the source is reinstated, it has the effect of improving the memory of the receiver. Returning to our example, how confident now could we be that a sleeper effect would hold true when most advertising is exposed potentially a number of times. Wouldn't this have the effect of reinstating the biased source in the mind of the receiver? The problem now becomes one of message strategy and execution, as well as the expected effect of the media schedule (see chapters 4, 5, and 6). More than likely, if a truly high negative salience is being addressed, one would be interested in long-term rather than short-term effect. This would tend to discount early problems of source reinstatement in favor of eventual reduction in the negative salience and introduction of positive saliences to reinforce behavioral change.

At present, the work in the area of source credibility may be summarized by saying that the perceived expertise aspect of credibility adds to persuasive impact more than the objectivity aspect does (McGuire 1969a). And, by expertise we mean such things as the perceived competence, status, and intelligence of the attributed source; by objectivity we mean the source's perceived disinterested-ness, trustworthiness, and lack of persuasive intent.

ATTRACTIVENESS AS A SOURCE CHARACTERISTIC

In our discussion of source credibility, we were concerned with the moti-vation of a receiver to be correct in judgment or behavior with reference to a persuasive communication. To assure correctness, the receiver relies on the re-ceiver's perception of the source's expertise and objectivity. Now, in considering the attractiveness of a source, we are concerned with a receiver's motivation to attain a level of self-satisfaction through adoption of the position advocated by the source (see the earlier discussion of Kelman [1961] in this chapter).

Identification with the source in a communication is a common ploy in ad-vertising, particularly when one level of the source (the person communicating the message) is a well-known personality, such as a sports or show business star. One can easily manifest strong evaluative judgments toward a product or brand found attractive because it is identified with an attractive source. Despite this commonsense notion, Crane (1972) feels that, while source attractiveness may have some influence in selling, it has little when advertising is used for buyer-seller communications. This is decidedly a minority opinion.

Just as we found components to source credibility, there are components to source attractiveness: similarity, familiarity, and liking. There is a great deal of evidence that the greater the perceived similarity between a source and re-ceiver, the greater the persuasive effectiveness of the source in influencing ad-vertising response. There also seems to be evidence that sources who are liked are perceived to be more similar to the receiver than they actually are, and that those who are disliked tend to be perceived as more dissimilar. In other words, these three components are interrelated, perhaps even in a causal way. Triandis (1971) describes their relationship as circular. Similarity may lead to familiarity and from there to liking; or liking may lead to familiarity and from familiarity to liking. This analysis is also given by Newcomb (1961). Once this circular pro-cess starts, it is likely to increase (or decrease) all three variables as they mutually reinforce one another. Sources who are perceived by the receiver as highly similar to the receiver become familiar and are liked; as a result, the source tends to be more effective in changing attitude or behavior.

Perceived Similarity

As we mentioned above, there is a great deal of evidence suggesting that a receiver is influenced by a persuasive message to the extent that it is perceived as coming from a source similar to the receiver—and, by extension, we might consider a case where the source is perceived to be similar to how the receiver would like to think of himself. The assumption here is that the receiver probably feels that if the receiver and the source share certain diverse characteristics, they are more likely to share consumer goals or needs. The position advocated by such a source would then be understood by the receiver as representing a position that people like the receiver (or people that the receiver would like to be associated with) ought to hold, and the tendency to respond would be altered accordingly. An extension of this notion seems to be embodied in Burke's (1962) "strategy of identification" in which the source begins the persuasive effort by showing the receiver that they both have similar needs. This is, of course, a familiar tactic in personal selling, and one not unfamiliar to advertising, particularly in the "slice-of-life" approach, in which an empathy is sought between the receiver and the source communicator. Here a problem situation is usually presented—one that the receiver should readily recognize—thus showing a common bond of interest between the source communicator and receiver. With this similarity established, the probability of persuasion by the source communicator increases, aided by additional source levels, such as the medium and advertiser.

Recalling our discussion of source expertise, it was pointed out that source-receiver similarity works in conflict with source expertise in maximizing persuasibility (see Figure 3.1 above), because most people are not expert on the subject of most communications (although with many advertised consumer goods receivers may consider themselves expert), for the source to be similar to the receiver, the source's expertise must suffer. This, perhaps, places a limitation on the obvious relationship discussed by Burke (1962). While this probably is true of communications in which the receiver is actively seeking a credible source for information, recognizing a lack of knowledge, this is not the usual advertising situation. As a result, source similarity can take on a more personal or social significance.

McGuire (1969a) reviews a number of studies addressing the question of similarity between source and receiver. In addition, he raises several interesting points, such as the possible importance of the issue bearing on the source-receiver relationship and the question of whether demographic or ideological similarity has a greater effect on liking of the source. Both are important concerns in the understanding of advertising communication. In the first instance, if the importance of the message does affect the relationship, this would tend to support the idea that attitude similarity tends to function as a reinforcer rather than a cue for liking. If the message subject has no effect on the relationship, then similarity would seem to be operating as a cue. This difference bears on the second question. While McGuire (1969a) states that, from a theoretical point of view, the question of whether demographic or ideological similarity has the greater effect on liking of the source is unanswerable at the present time, from a practical viewpoint it is a real concern. His argument is that, even if, say, the demographic dimension accounted for more of the variance in a particular experiment, one wouldn't know if this was because similarity on the demographic dimension is indeed more powerful in determining liking, or because the particular points chosen on the demographic dimension happened to be farther apart than those picked on the ideological dimension. In the case of a casting problem for an advertisement, one would still attempt to maximize source-receiver similarity demographically and attitudinally, assuming these data were available (see the section on attitudinal segmentation in chapter 2, Identifying Target Receivers with Market Segmentation), without concern for the theoretical problem of ideological versus demographic similarity. The problem remains, however, when personal selling or word-of-mouth communication is involved.

An important theory, relevant to the degree of perceived similarity between the source and receiver is the Sherif and Hovland (1961) assimilation-contrast theory. They suggest that a critical range of similarity called the "latitude of acceptance" bounds an individual's attitude in a given context, and, if the source's expressed attitude falls within this range, the receiver perceptually distorts it as being even closer than it actually is; the receiver has a change in attitude in the direction of the source. On the other hand, if the source's position lies outside this range of similarity and beyond an indifference zone in an area called "latitude of rejection," the opposite will occur. The receiver, in this case, will distort the source's position, so that it is perceived to lie even farther from the receiver's position than it actually does, and the receiver will proceed to a change in atittude away from that of the source. (This assimilation-contrast theory was discussed in chapter 2 and is summarized in Table 3.2.) McGuire (1969a) points out, too, a similarity between the assimilation-contrast theory

TABLE 3.2

Summary of Assimilation-Contrast Theory

Source Position	Receiver Perception	Communications Response
latitude of acceptance	more similar to receiver's position than really is	likely reception
latitude of non-commitment	unclear	possible reception
latitude of rejection	more dissimilar to receiver's position than really is	unlikely reception

and Festinger's social comparison theory, which predicts that when evaluation of the appropriateness of one's behavior is impractical (for example, in a novel situation), one will judge one's own behavior in terms of those perceived as similar rather than those considered dissimilar. This theory would predict, for example that an individual would seek out others within critical similarity range so as to satisfy the self-evaluation need. An extension of this theory might be made to explain certain notions of selective attention to advertising communication at particular source levels: for example, when attention is given or not to an advertisement becuase of a perceived similarity (and thus attraction) to the source communicator.

Perceived Familiarity

Because of its close correlation to liking, only a brief discussion of the familiarity component of source attractiveness is necessary. To begin, contrary to the old adage that familiarity breeds contempt, the bulk of the research into the matter has shown that, as the interaction between individuals increases, so, too, does their affection for one another. While this has obvious implications for personal selling, and for the sources of word-of-mouth communication, it doesn't appear to be particularly appropriate to advertising communication. The source and receiver relationship in advertising is rarely one offering any degree of actual interpersonal contact (although a receiver might perceive such a relationship). Yet, a great deal of additional evidence exists that suggests that familiarity per se will enhance liking (McGuire 1969a). Given a wide range of different stimuli, the more frequently they were presented, the greater they were liked and the more positively they were evaluated. Although this seems to be contradicted by work in satiation theory, McGuire (1969a) believes this may also suggest that, for the entire range, liking would be an inverted U-shaped function of familiarity (see Figure 3.3). The implication for advertising communication would involve, among other things, wear-out (which is discussed in some detail in chapter 6, "Scheduling Strategy"). How many impressions are necessary to insure a positive reaction to the source? If McGuire's formulation is correct, liking is a nonmonotonic function of familiarity, so there would be a limit to the number of times one would wish to expose a particular source level. This is a particularly good example of the idea of source levels. Familiarity with the source communicator may be affected by over-exposure in other communications (perhaps creating a credibility problem as well); the product category as a source may be extremely active; the advertiser as a source may be overly exposed, with a wide range of products. Any one level of source attribution may be too familiar, thus dampening potential liking for the specific message subject. Again, a good knowledge and understanding of independent variables in the communication model will alert the advertiser to possible trouble.

FIGURE 3.3

Stimulus Satiation

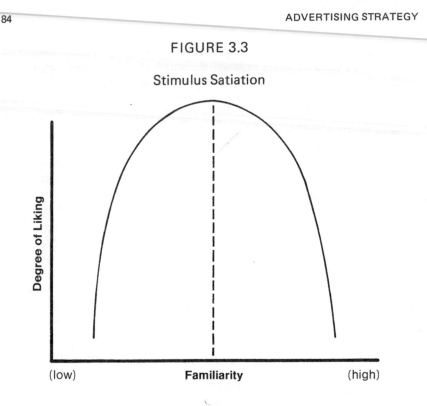

Perceived Liking

Much as we discussed in the section on perceived familiarity, one finds that people tend to agree most with those whom they like. This, in fact, is one of the underlying principles of balance theories (Abelson et al. 1968), which will be discussed later in the section on theories of attitude and the source. Liking of the source will enhance the source's persuasive impact on the receiver, such that if the receiver likes a source who expresses a liking for something, then the receiver will also tend to like that same thing. This is, of course, the identification principle discussed earlier in the section on Kelman (1961), and the basis for the use in advertising communication's sources perceived as attractive by potential receivers. In addition to theory, a number of empirical studies are referred to by McGuire (1969a) to support this commonsense reading.

Yet there are some interesting contradictions suggested by dissonance theory (also discussed later in another section). In some studies just the opposite finding seems to hold: the source's persuasive impact increases as the receiver's dislike for the source increases. According to the predictions of dissonance theory, if a receiver agrees to listen to a disliked source, the receiver is in less of a position to justify his listening on grounds that he finds the source attractive, and must consequently justify listening to the message for its own value, and thus be more influenced by it. In a study reported by Zimbardo, Weisenberg, Firestone, and Levy (1965), the source at all times was positioned as credible (both expert and objective), but in a "positive source" condition was additionally polite, informal, considerate, and pleasant. In a "negative source" condition the source was additionally snobbish, demanding, tactless, bossy, cold, and formal. Each condition was designed to simulate either a liked or disliked source. Attitudes toward eating a highly disliked food (fried grasshoppers) were measured before and immediately after an inducement to eat the food by the source communicator, adopting either the friendly, positive role, or an unfriendly negative role. The findings revealed that those who complied with the request from the disliked source and actually ate the fried grasshoppers increased their liking for them significantly more than those who were exposed to the liked source. Noncompliance with the urging of the source was associated with boomeranging effects in which grasshoppers became even more disliked.

In making any inferential leaps from these results to potential advertising implications, one is reminded first that the source was a personal communicator, and second of Zimbardo et al.'s (1965) conclusion that in their study the perceptual association was between the source communicator and the receiver's own behavior, while in most cases the perceptual associations are between the source and the message. Hence, they suggest that their resulting perceptual associations are stronger and the attitude change made of sterner stuff. Attitudinal advertising responses, as we describe them, are accelerated under heavy, "hardsell" conditions, much as in a high-pressure personal selling situation. In such personal selling situations (such as door-to-door selling) dissonance theory would predict that, once the receiver's resistance is broken and a purchase is actually made, the original attitude toward the purchase will improve. It is doubtful that a disliked source in mass media advertising would be as successful in generating such compliance. However, one could conceive of a situation in which, over a short time span, a "sleeper effect," similar to that described in the section on source credibility, could repress the disliked source, improving the likelihood of a change in attitude or behavior. If the attitude or behavior were publicly acknowledged (for example, in discussions with friends or in the actual purchase and use of the product), subsequent reinstatement of the disliked source through additional advertising exposure could cause a further strengthening of the changed response. Although this is theoretically possible within the framework of our discussion, it would be a highly perilous scenario to assume in practice.

While this reversal of the commonsense liking-persuasiveness relation offers little constructive theory for the advertising practitioner, another such reversal shows more promise: the "praise from a stranger" phenomenon. Again, McGuire (1969a) reviews several studies on this point. For example, it has often been found that social reinforcement influences children's behavior more if it comes from a stranger than if it comes from a familiar person or a parent (Gewirtz and

Baer 1958). Extensions to advertising communication would suggest that completely familiar or liked sources are not requisite for effective persuasion.

A final thought on the perceived liking component of the source attractiveness characteristic concerns group theory. Here again, we find a rather straightforward assumption that membership in some group or category, similarity to the other members, liking for the group and its members, and being liked by them, all contribute to the persuasive impact of the group in changing or moving attitude and behavior closer to group norms. If real or imagined group memberships coveted by the receiver are perceived in some level of the source from an advertising communication, the persuasive power of the message should be increased for that receiver. This is, of course, the principle behind a great deal of advertising: an effort to convince the receiver that the behavior encouraged by the communication is an essential qualification for membership in a particular life-style (such as, for example, young moderns, sophisticates, active-outdoor) or other identifiable image group. The reason such advertising is not completely successful, even when profiles of the target receivers are well understood, is that an individual is a member of, and shapes behavior on the perceived expectations of a number of groups and categories; such as, for example a single individual can simultaneously be athletically inclined, a parent, work in a bank, and belong to a gourmet club. The question of the liking between the receiver and a group as the perceived source will inevitably give rise to conflicts of loyalties and salience of characteristics.

POWER AS A SOURCE CHARACTERISTIC

As a result of the authority perceived in the source by the receiver, the receiver may respond to what the source wants because this is seen as a way of achieving some desired response from the source (or a representative of the source). McGuire's (1969a) analysis of the perceived power of the source breaks down the psychodynamics into three components: first, the receiver appraises the extent to which the source can administer positive or negative sanctions (perceived control); second, the receiver estimates how much the source cares about whether or not the receiver conforms (perceived concern); and finally, the receiver judges how likely it is that the source will be able to observe whether or not the source's position is accepted (perceived scrutiny). While it is easy to see applications of these power components on the level of personal selling or word-of-mouth communication, it is more difficult to imagine examples in which it is an advertising communication that relates the buyer and seller (Howard and Sheth 1969; Crane 1972). An exception noted by Howard and Sheth (1969) could occur if the receiver has a high perceived risk (Bauer 1960; Cox 1967) because of lack of competence to evaluate alternatives or ignorance. The receiver would then be likely to comply because of finding the source in a powerful position. As a derivative, they suggest that, in a seller's economy (such as in most of the developing countries), power is likely to be an important source attribute vested in the selling company. We might add that in some service advertising or health care communication, the perceived power of the source could operate in a similar fashion.

Perceived Control

In the first of the three contingencies mentioned by McGuire (1969a), a number of studies are cited whose results tend to support the commonsense notion that the bigger the stick the greater the compliance—in other words, the more control perceived by the receiver, the higher the likelihood of a positive response to the communication. Cohen, Berger, and Zelditch (1972), in analyzing the results of work on the effects of power on the relations among group members, infer a line of reasoning that suggests a link of occupational status, prestige, and perceived power to influence. This would seem to indicate that there could be possible social psychological needs associated with a receiver's perception of the source's power to control; these are in addition to whatever source credibility or attractiveness characteristics follow from a source's occupational status or perceived prestige. Hence, more control would be likely in an advertising communication, if the message were attributed to a highly valenced source: for example, through endorsements by medical or other high status groups such as a presidential council or agency.

Perceived Concern

The second contingency of source power involves a concern by the source for the receiver's compliance. This, of the three, is probably the most easily generalized to cases of advertising communication (although one must continue to bear in mind that all three contingencies are necessary for a full accounting of power as a source characteristic). McGuire (1969a) reviews several studies showing an appreciable relation between the source's concern over the receiver's compliance and the source's persuasive impact. Once again we find this a rather commonsense notion. It is certainly reasonable to expect, for example, that if a receiver perceives a genuine concern on the part of the source (say the American Heart Association) for the receiver's well being, the receiver would be somewhat more likely to respond to the message. This feeling, of course, should be much more readily communicated through personal selling or word-of-mouth communication. One is cautioned, however, that this generalization of the source's power to induce attitudinal or behavioral change conforming to one's own increasing with the source's concern about the compliance of the receiver, is applicable only when the source is concerned that the receiver be imitative of the source's behavior. The old saying "do as I say, not as I do" will not induce compliance under these conditions.

Perceived Scrutiny

This final contingency of perceived scrutiny, the source's capacity to scrutinize the receiver's conformity, is again almost entirely concerned with personal selling or word-of-mouth communication. To be applicable to advertising communication, a group to which the receiver belongs or seeks membership must be perceived as the implied, if not actual, source of the message. Otherwise, there would be no means for the source to discern whether or not the receiver has in fact, complied with the message. Another assumption of this aspect of the source is the prediction that, when the receiver is complying with a source perceived as powerful in order to manipulate the bestowal of positive sanctions by the source (for example, acceptance into group membership), the receiver will be more influenced in public response, which the source or its representatives can detect, than in more private attitudes. In other words, while outward behavior may conform under scrutiny, there is no assurance of a resulting attitude change. Yet, such a condition of tension is unlikely to persist over a period of time. Holding private attitudes that conflict with overt behavior would, under most conditions, be too demanding. A reading of consistency of dissonance theory would suggest that in time the public behavior would tend to be introjected as a private attitude. So, while an internal change in attitude is not required under the source power scenario, there is every reason to believe that, if the behavior persists, attitude too will conform.

THE VISCAP MODEL OF SOURCE EFFECTIVENESS

Thus far, we have discussed three main source characteristics: credibility, attractiveness, and power. Add to this a source's visibility, or the perceptual characteristics of the source, and one is now in a position to judge a source's potential overall impact on advertising responses. These four dimensions are summarized by the VisCAP model of source effectiveness shown in Table 3.3.

As we know from the discussions in this chapter, there is more than brand or product image involved in advertising source effects. Frequently, a company seeks someone to act as a spokesman or endorser for their product. Suppose you were the advertising manager of a telephone company, and you were asked to approve the use of Emmett Kelly, Jr. in his hobo-like portrayal of "Weary Willie" as a source figure in your residential long distance advertising (a source which was actually used by a mid-western telephone company). In order to judge his

TABLE 3.3

The VisCAP Source Effectiveness Model

Source Attribute	Psychological Mechanism	Response Measure
Visibility	Attribution of who is responsible for or who is endorsing the ad message	Perception–initial comprehension
Credibility a) Expertise b) Objectivity	Internalization of the message as true and sincere	Comprehension–cognitive believability and acceptance
Attractiveness a) Likability b) Similarity	Identification with source, which transfers partially to the product	Evaluation–affective reaction
Power* to reward or punish receiver	Compliance with the message because of source's status	Yielding–behavior intention

*Less relevant in (indirect) media persuasion although power has some advertising applications. More common in interpersonal persuasion, e.g., personal selling.

potential impact as a source on buyer response, one must evaluate the source on four main dimensions: visibility, plus the three major characteristics of source effectiveness—credibility, attractiveness, and power. For convenience, the manager might utilize the VisCAP model of source effectiveness as a guide in his evaluation.

Considering first *visibility* or the perceptual characteristics of the source, the use of Emmett Kelly could certainly become a highly visible component in the advertising. However, one can not be sure everyone would know he was actually Emmett Kelly portraying a clown rather than merely "a hobo." Neither the clown role, nor hobo role, nor Mr. Kelly himself constitutes an appropriate source for long distance telephone advertising. Regardless of which of these roles is perceived by the receiver, each has limitations in terms of the two critical source characteristics of credibility and attractiveness.

The *credibility* of a source, as we have seen, refers to its expertise and objectivity. Expertise is the source's perceived knowledgeability concerning the item of endorsement. As a hobo or a clown, there is certainly little to suggest experience in long distance calling; and Mr. Kelly as himself is hardly known as an experienced telephone user or long distance caller. There is a serious expertise problem. But what of the second subcomponent of credibility, objectivity? This refers to the source's perceived sincerity or trustworthiness in communicating what the source knows. Neither hoboes nor clowns are seen as the most objective of characters, and why should Mr. Kelly be seen as knowing anything about long distance calling to pass on to the receiver, regardless of how objective he might be.

A source's attractiveness also has two subcomponents: likability and its similarity to the target receivers. Mr. Kelly in his "Weary Willie" role does seem to be a fairly likable character. However, he certainly bears little similarity to the target receivers. It would be difficult for a receiver to identify with him because he would not be seen as typical of either a long distance user or of people in general.

Power refers to the source's perceived ability to instill compliance on the part of the receiver—in this case, to reward or punish their long distance calling behavior. As we have discussed, power is not usually a salient source dimension in advertising (except for certain fear appeals), and it is not really relevant here in evaluating "Weary Willie." It is, however, possible that the telephone company itself (as an alternative source) has some implied power over the receiver's behavior, and the manager should not overlook this aspect of source impact in his advertising.

In a more general sense, too, the "poor" and "cheap" source connotations of "Weary Willie" are not the right associations for the long distance caller. Light users in particular, but, in fact, all users, see long distance calling as an expensive business. It is not cheap, and it is not for poor people (such as hoboes). A more correct connotation in this regard would require a source spokesman perceived as a smart saver, in a more sophisticated vein, trying to reduce the expense of long distance calling through more prudent use of direct-dialing and low-rate periods.

Overall, in evaluating source effectiveness in terms of the VisCAP model, one can see that Emmett Kelly, Jr., in his "Weary Willie" role, is not an appropriate spokesman for residential long distance advertising. There are very definite source effectiveness problems that would be expected to negatively affect an advertising response: most notably role appropriateness (visibility), perceived lack of telephone usage experience (credibility), and lack of identification with the target receivers (attractiveness).

Combined Influences of Source Characteristics

As we have hinted in the preceding sections, there is not always a perfectly compatible set of source characteristics present in every source communicator. It was pointed out that highly credible sources are often likely to be viewed as quite dissimilar from ordinary receivers, and as such be less attractive. And what, for example, could be predicted regarding the persuasive impact of a highly attractive, low-power source versus an unattractive, high-power source; or in terms of advertising communication, a persuasive message for similar products delivered in one case by a well-known personality, highly attractive to the receiver but unrelated to the product category (for example, a sports figure promoting a stomach remedy), versus a perceived knowledgeable source unfamiliar to the receiver (for example, studies by medical laboratories). Obviously, it is quite essential to understand what the functional bases of the particular attitudes involved are, and how these will relate to the receiver's response to advertising. If the attitudes of the receiver critical to a particular product category reflect a need for information more than sociability, one would expect a source perceived as an expert to be more persuasive than one perceived attractive. Conversely, for ego-defensive attitudes, the attractive source may be more persuasive than the expert.

Just how a source is judged when it exhibits contradictory source characteristics has been well studied. In one study reported by Mehrabian and Wiener (1967) three degrees of attitude (positive, negative, and neutral) were communicated by a source using three different tones of voice, testing all nine possible combinations. It was found that the major influence on the way the message was perceived by the receiver was the tone of voice, not the subject of the communication. If a positive message was delivered in a hostile manner, the receiver perceived the message as hostile. This would seem to suggest that source attractiveness has a strong influence on message perception.

In studies of source similarity versus source credibility, an interesting observation has been made by McGuire (1969a). It seems that most laboratory studies of intercharacteristic conflict where peers are pitted against authorities as sources of persuasive messages, one finds receivers more influenced by the extent to which the source is one's superior in expertise rather than one's peer. Yet, quite a different picture emerges from field studies of the relative persuasive impact of peers and experts. One almost always finds that in natural social settings the peer as a source has significantly more persuasive impact than the expert. In a study by Katz and Lazarsfeld (1955) of who influences housewives in marketing, fashion, movie-going, and public affairs (all areas well advertised) they found that in all four areas the influences were predominantly sources with the same demographic profile as the receivers. Where influence did cross demographic category, it generally tended to flow down; for example, the source of higher social class tended to influence those of lower social class more than the other way around. In fact, despite the persuasiveness of mass communication and advertising, it is difficult to demonstrate in sociological experiments any impact at all by the expert source or authority figure. Word-of-mouth communication seems all important.

The apparent anomaly, however, is explained by McGuire (1969a). He feels that the reason field studies generally find greater impact of peers over authorities is perhaps due to a difference between the field and laboratory situations in how exposure mediates persuasion. In actual social settings, sociologists have repeatedly found that people have little contact outside their peer group, and, as a result, are much more exposed to peer than to expert influence. Laboratory experiments, on the other hand, are typically designed to equate exposure to both the expert and the peer source. The implication of this difference is that when the expert does get his message attended to, he has more impact than the peer, but, in the natural community, the expert source is much less often heard and attended to than are one's peers. While other explanations and theories are offered by Weiss (1969), this appears to be a sufficient and satisfying rationale. Its implication for advertising communication lies in the importance of maximizing efforts to gain attention as an initiator of message processing and subsequent advertising response.

Part II
Source Impact

In addition to understanding the specific characteristics of a source and how they affect an advertising response, it is important to grasp the influence of a source upon message strategy and communication in more abstract ways. This section reviews how source perception affects an attitude response, and illustrates the impact of source image in developing advertising strategy.

THEORIES OF ATTITUDE AND THE SOURCE

There is much in the literature of attitude theory that has broad implications in many of the source relationships we have been discussing, and now that we are familiar with the components of the source, some considerations of it would seem to be in order. No attempt here will be made to treat theories completely; the interested reader is referred to the volume by Insko (1967) for a useful collection of theories on attitude change, and to the references cited below for detail. Rather, we will present an overview of how certain conceptualizations of attitude and attitude change within theories of cognitive consistency (the general conceptualization most relevant to the source variable) relate to our understanding of the source as an independent variable in communication. The basic notion of the consistency theory approach to attitude and attitude change is that an individual will adjust attitudes and behavior in such a way as to maximize the degree of internal harmony within the belief system and between attitudes and actual behavior. We have already mentioned one such theory in connection with our discussion of the liking component of source attractiveness: a reference to balance theory actually derived from Heider's (1946) "p-o-x formulation" which states that person, p, tries to keep sentiments regarding another person, o, in line with their mutual liking for an object, x. Below we shall consider three specific consistency theory formulations: congruity theory, dissonance theory, and expectancy-value.

Congruity Theory

As described by Tannenbaum (1968), congruity theory focuses on a receiver's attitude toward the source and toward the assertion of the message. Communications are judged not only in terms of their message content, but in terms of the source as well. He hypothesizes that not only can the degree of attitude change toward the concept or object of a communication be affected by existing attitudes about the source, but also that attitude toward the source could change as a result of similar pressures in the same situation. As a result of the attitudes the receiver brings along into the communication situation to begin with, attitudes toward both the concept and source of a message can be modified. Thus, it is possible in an advertising situation to overcome source derogation at one level, given an understanding of the preexposure attitudes of the receiver.

In specific studies of source credibility within the congruity theory model, two approaches have been taken (Feldman 1966)—molar and atomic. Molar studies attempt to explain attitude toward source credibility in terms of the characteristics of the communicator; the atomic studies attempt to do so in terms of general processes found in attitudinal behavior. Of the two, Feldman (1966) leans strongly in favor of the atomic approach because of its greater relevance to the process of attitude organization and change, the combining properties of psychological matter. If one is less concerned with the processes involved, however, and more interested in the source characteristics of a particular case, the molar approach is quite adequate. For example, if one were testing several advertising communications with various source characteristics, and measured attitude preexposure and postexposure, the source characteristics of the advertisement with the greatest positive attitude change would be inferred to have the greatest persuasive ability—a perfectly correct conclusion for a practical problem, even if it contributed little to understanding why those source characteristics registered the greatest persuasive impact.

Prior to being exposed to a communication message, the congruity model recognizes that a receiver can maintain any type of attitude toward any number of potential sources and concepts, as long as they have not been linked to one another by the receiver. If the communication situation is one in which an identifiable source makes an assertion for or against a particular object or concept, the consistency question arises when that particular source and that particular concept become associated through the message as the source takes a position. If the receiver's preexposure attitude toward both the source and the concept is favorable and the direction of the assertion is positive, there is essentially no incongruity, and, according to the theory, there will be little or no pressure for a change in attitude or behavior. However, should the initially favorable source make a negative assertion about an equally favorable concept, incongruity would obtain and pressure for change in attitude or behavior toward either the source or the concept, or both, will occur, always in the direction of making a newly congruous situation.

The implications this has for advertising communication are many. For example, consider the case in which a receiver initially holds positive attitudes toward two brands in a product category, and uses both interchangeably. He then sees an advertisement for one brand which compares itself to the receiver's other favorite brand, strongly criticizing the second brand. An incongruous situation has been created. The receiver must now either (a) change the attitude and behavior toward the second brand, using only the first (the object of the advertisement); (b) change the attitude and behavior toward the brand being advertised, deciding from now on to use only the second brand; or (c) in addition to no longer buying the advertised brand, the receiver could also have a change in attitude toward the source, and decide to no longer buy or use any products made by it. There are obvious perils in creating states of incongruity.

Dissonance Theory

Festinger's theory of cognitive dissonance (1957) has resulted in a great deal of research, and as McGuire (1966) has pointed out, probably more hostility than any one other approach to attitude change. The core notion of the theory is really quite simple: dissonance is a "negative" drive state occuring when two cognitions (such as ideas, beliefs, opinions) that are psychologically inconsistent are held simultaneously by the same individual. Put another way, dissonance produced by some overt behavior that does not follow from one's relevant attitudes is inversely proportional to the amount of justification supporting performance of the discrepant behavior. If one wishes to reduce dissonance created, for example, by a highly credible source communicator advancing a position that is discrepant from the receiver's, the receiver can either (1) change the attitude to make it coincide with the communicator's or (2) derogate the communicator (Aronson 1968). But, as we have just seen, from the advertising communication standpoint this could create problems of incongruity.

Zimbardo et al. (1965) in the study mentioned in the discussion of liking in the section on source attractiveness in this chapter, also found that, under certain conditions, a source having low credibility would produce greater change than one having high credibility as a result of irrelevant aspects associated with the source. Suppose the receiver has a definite attitude and a source communicator attempts to induce a behavioral change, rather than merely a modification of attitude. If pressure is put on the receiver (for example, through perceived power of the source) to comply with behavior discrepant with the receiver's attitudes and values, then obviously the intensity of the felt pressure to comply will be a determining factor in how the receiver will comply and the attitude structure will remain unchanged. If the perceived pressure is indeed great, the receiver will comply with a behavioral change, but with no guarantee of an attitudinal change. If this behavioral change can be completely justified in terms of the perceived power of the source, then, as we have seen, there is really no need to change one's attitude also. But, as the probability of compliance within a given population approaches one-half, it becomes increasingly likely that attributed characteristics of the source that are essentially irrelevant to the actual behavior encouraged will be used as justification.

If, on the other hand, a receiver complies to the inducement of a negatively perceived source, such as someone disliked, clearly the receiver cannot rationalize this discrepant behavior by invoking the personal characteristics of the communicator as justification. In that case, Zimbardo (1960) suggests that the receiver would be likely to change the attitudes, bringing them in line with behavior. This would be a case of cognitive dissonance resolved through the change in attitude. And, as we remarked in an earlier discussion, the likelihood of someone retaining any attitude dissonant to a public or acknowledged behavior is slight, unless, as Zimbardo et al. (1965) seem to feel, the receiver would have access to certain irrelevant aspects of the source as justification for the behavior. This would not, however, be something one should wish to count on in the development of an advertising communication.

One final comment on source credibility and dissonance is in order. If the receiver in a communication situation begins with the feeling that a source communicator is credible, the more arguments put forth in the message, the more persuasive the source might well become, provided nothing intervenes to change the receiver's judgment of the source's credibility. If the receiver should sense in the source a need for reinforcement, then it may be that the more insistent the source in making the point, the more it will appear to the receiver that the source "doth protest too much," and the less likely it will be that the receiver actually perceives the source's statements as expressions of "actual" attitudes (Bauer 1965). In terms of advertising communication, this would seem to argue in favor of a certain amount of restraint in the presentation of claims for an advertised product or claim. Too many, or too forceful a presentation by the source, may actually reduce credibility by creating a dissonance reaction in which the receiver can no longer believe anything could be so good. Resolution of the dissonance would result in the lower evaluation of the source and message.

Expectancy-Value Theory

In the current attitude literature, much is being made of the so-called expectancy-value model which defines attitude as a sum total of beliefs and evaluations. Fishbein & Ajzen (1975) have suggested a presentation of the persuasive communication process in terms of beliefs. In their approach, a persuasive communication is directed at one or more proximal beliefs, and, via a series of intervening processes, changes in these proximal beliefs may produce change in the dependent variable (belief, attitude, intention, or behavior). The crucial question concerns the factors that are responsible for change in the proximal beliefs; and therein lies the reason for introducing Fishbein's approach in this chapter. According to his approach, changes in proximal beliefs are determined primarily by the acceptance of source beliefs. It is these source beliefs that are of interest to us here.

In any persuasive communication, there are a number of statements made by or attributed to the source. Fishbein & Ajzen (1975) would identify each of these statements as corresponding to one or more beliefs—each is an informational item that represents a source belief or source probability. Corresponding to each source belief would be a receiver's proximal belief or subjective probability that the object was the attribute specified in the message. For example, in an advertising communication, this could correspond to several claims being made on behalf of the product or service advertised (source beliefs) and the degree to which the receiver believes each (proximal belief or probability). Suppose an advertiser wished to raise the subjective probability that the advertiser's brand was superior to a competitor's (the dependent variable in Fishbein & Ajzen's formulation). The advertiser may attempt to change the belief that the brand "tastes better" by including this claim in the communication message. Then, in order to increase the likelihood of obtaining the desired change in this target belief (that is, persuading people that the brand in fact does taste better), the advertiser may provide supportive evidence. Additional source beliefs such as "made with real butter" or "finest ingredients" could serve as supportive belief for the target belief.

In sum, they suggest that a persuasive communication comprises, for the most part, a set of belief statements. Each statement corresponds to a proximal belief held by the receiver (in other words, the receiver's a priori belief). Some of these proximal beliefs may serve as dependent beliefs, others as target beliefs, and still others as beliefs that are assumed to support the target beliefs. Associated with each belief statement in the message is a probability representing the strength of the source belief and a probability representing the strength of the receiver's initial belief; the strength of the source belief will, it is hoped, bring about a positive change in the strength of the receiver's belief (the proximal probability). Although the positioning of the source in this alternative model in terms of beliefs and belief probabilities offers an interesting reconceptualization of the way a communication persuades, it really suggests little to change the perception of source characteristics. In fact, the evaluation of the source in terms of the characteristics presented earlier could be viewed as mediators of source belief or source probability.

SOURCE IMAGE

The reader should now be in a position to evaluate various source components in advertising, and assess their probable impact on advertising response. An additional aspect of source is now considered: the perceived "image" of a brand among target receivers. Consider the perceived image of a set of fast-food

FIGURE 3.4

Nonmetric Multidimensional Unfolding of Restaurants by Usage Scenarios Via Mdscal 5M

restaurants. Looking at Figure 3.4, we have the results of a multidimensional unfolding of seven different fast-food restaurants measured over six situational usage scenarios. Target receivers ranked each of the restaurants in order of their likelihood of visiting in each usage situation. These results were then "unfolded" to provide a joint-space configuration of the perceived similarity of the restaurants in terms of the possible usage situations, as well as the situational uniqueness of the usage situations in light of the alternative fast-food restaurant options. This sort of information is quite useful in evaluating brand source effects in their advertising.

Because this is a spatial representation of the receiver's general cognitive understanding of the fast-food market, one is concerned with the various interpoint distances among the stimuli. The closer together any two fast-food restaurants, the more alike they are perceived to be by the target receivers (in terms of their likelihood of visiting in these situations); the closer together any two situations, the more likely it is that the receivers rank all of the restaurants in the same order for those situations; and, finally, the closer a restaurant to a usage situation, the greater the likelihood the receivers would visit that particular fast-food restaurant under those circumstances.

In this solution we see that McDonalds clearly dominates the selected usage scenarios. When taking the family out for dinner, however, Steak & Shake, Bonanza Steak House, and Kentucky Fried Chicken are more likely choices (being the closest restaurants in the space to that scenario). If, on the other hand, one were looking for a change of pace (presumably from McDonalds), Steak & Shake, H. Salt Seafood Galley, and Bonanza Steak House would be likely choices.

If one were a brand manager for Bonanza Steak House, it would be critical to know that target receivers saw it as a good place to take the family for dinner, or as a change of pace. In the first instance, the competition would be Steak & Shake and Kentucky Fried Chicken; in the second, Steak & Shake and H. Salt Seafood Galley. To the extent that the marketing goals are compatible with this user image, advertising strengthening these associations will enjoy brand source compatibility and a greater probability of response. If the goal is to position Bonanza Steak House as the place to go for lunch or an inexpensive meal, source credibility would suffer without some accounting for the strong position of McDonalds. To accomplish this, a strategy that seeks to position Bonanza Steak House as an inexpensive or lunch-time alternative to "the same old hamburger" would be able to capitalize on the credible change of pace image, while tacitly acknowledging the strongly held McDonalds inexpensive and lunch perception.

REVIEWING VARIABLE 2: SOURCE FACTORS

The overall objective of this chapter has been to provide an understanding of how various source factors may affect the receiver's response to advertising. Specifically, one should be able to:

1. Recognize various "levels" of potential source attribution
2. Distinguish between the various components of source credibility and how each mediates response to advertising
3. Understand the implications of the "sleeper effect" for advertising
4. Distinguish between the various components of source attractiveness and their effect on response to advertising
5. Distinguish between the various components of perceived power in a source and their effect on response to advertising
6. Interpret the combined influences of multiple source characteristics on the overall likelihood of a positive response to advertising
7. Relate general attitude theory to potential receiver response to a source factor in advertising

KEY CONCEPTS

Tricomponential Analysis of
  Source Characteristics
Internalization
Identification
Compliance
Source Credibility
Perceived Expertise
Perceived Objectivity
Sleeper Effect
Source Attractiveness
Perceived Source-Receiver
  Similarity

Assimilation-Contrast Theory
Perceived Source Familiarity
Perceived Liking
Contingencies of Power
Contradictory Source Character-
  istics
P-O-X
Congruity Theory
Dissonance Theory
Expectancy-Value Theory

4

MESSAGE STRATEGY

For many, persuasive communication is thought to involve nothing more than a message, or, in the special case of advertising, a creative execution. While we have already seen that there is actually much more involved in effective communication, more research has probably been done on message factors than on any other class of communication variable. There is no doubting either the impact of a message on persuasion or the complexity involved in creating an effective message that will maximize the desired advertising response. It is the responsibility of the execution of a message to seize the attention of the receiver and communicate in an understandable and believable manner what the communicator (for example, an advertiser) wishes to say. Crane (1972) suggests that two factors seem to constrain the ability of a persuasive message in meeting these goals: a need for the message to combine both the novel and the familiar so as to be both attractive and understood, as well as the need to use various sets of symbols to reach diverse audiences.

A good advertising message will reflect a motivating strategy based upon a thorough understanding of the environment in which an advertised product or brand is used, as well as the attitudes, behavior, and background characteristics of the target receivers (those consumers most likely to be persuaded). In effectively executing a strategy known to be motivating, the message will provide the receiver with a believable communication that is compatible with the receiver's attitudes and behavior, one that the receiver is able to evaluate favorably, placing the advertised brand or product within a set of desirable choice alternatives. The difficulty comes in being able to effectively implement such a strategy.

In this chapter we shall consider the complex problem of message execution, always assuming a well-developed, motivating strategy. Our discussion will center on three major classes of message characteristics: (1) message appeal, (2) message structure, and (3) specific message content.

Part I
Message Appeal

One question that arises in considering the types of persuasive appeals available in message construction is whether one should appeal to the receiver's moral principles, emotions, or intellect, which are, as McGuire (1969a, 1973) reminds us, the distinctions Aristotle makes in the *Rhetoric* between ethos, pathos, and logos (or ethics, passions, and logical argument as alternative processes for changing attitude. This typology is useful for an initial classification of the alternative options available for message appeal.

By ethos, Aristotle meant persuasion based upon an appeal that concentrates on the source rather than the message. In our discussion of source variables in chapter 3, emphasis was placed on the effects on advertising response by such things as source credibility, which, in a way, reflect the use of ethos appeals. Rosenthal (1966) has distinguished ethos appeals from pathos and logos on just that point, suggesting that ethos appeals attempt persuasion by forcing the receiver's attention on the source, while the others are more impersonal, focusing on message content. In advertising, there are many examples of persuasive messages appealing to a highly personable source element, such as an esteemed or credible spokesperson.

Persuasive messages using an appeal characterized by Aristotle's notion of pathos would involve creating an appropriate feeling in the receiver by appealing to feelings, values, or emotions, by associating strong affective cues with the product or brand. Examples from advertising again come easily to mind. Almost any appeal that does not rely heavily on source identification or require the receiver to make a decision based upon logical argumentation would fall into this category—cosmetic advertising aimed at one's feelings of well being, advertising emphasizing quality for durable goods, automobile advertising that stimulates emotional reactions. All these are examples of pathos appeals.

The so-called "functional theorists" feel that an individual's attitudes are held in order to protect or bolster self concept, and to support the individual's view of the world. This notion (cf. Katz and Stotland 1959) leads to a formulation of attitude quite similar to the more familiar expectancy-value models. They would construe attitude to be a composite of how one's perceptions of an attitude object's characteristics facilitate the attainment of various goals and how these goals are evaluated; this is a reasonable approximation of Fishbein's attitude model (1967). In a study of this self-insight approach to attitude change, Stotland, Katz, and Patchen (1959) predicted that the individuals most susceptible to attitude change in relation to a socially undesirable behavior (here, racial prejudice) would be moderately ego-defensive. Those highly ego-defensive would fail to associate undesirable behavior with their own behavior, when a pathos-type appeal is used, and those less ego-defensive would already understand the basis for their behavior without caring that it was socially undesirable. Again, we have an example of how two different characteristics of the communication process (source and message) interact in mediating response to advertising.

Other examples of pathos-based appeals are suggested by Carlson (1956), who found that attitudes can be changed more effectively by communication aimed at perceived instrumentality to goals already held by a receiver rather than by attempting to change the attractiveness of the goals to which the attitude object is already perceived as being instrumental. This, of course, is reflected in the desirability of creating advertising designed to be compatible with existing attitudes, values, or feelings. In the long run, Katz (1960) has found that attitudes can be changed by addressing, in the communication's message, the motivations that are reinforced by the attitude. If beliefs (as opposed to "attitude" in an expectancy-value sense) can be modified through advertising, the corresponding attitudes that are a function of those beliefs (again, in an expectancy-value sense) would also be expected to change in a similar direction; hence the importance of a thorough understanding of the belief sets associated with the use of a particular brand or product category. Extensions of this type of appeal could involve specific stylistic considerations such as novelty or humor (discussed in more detail below). It would follow that the more relaxed or amused a receiver, the better the disposition, and perforce the probability of persuasion.

The third general classification of persuasive appeal tends to be the most difficult to execute effectively. Logos appeals require the receiver to deduce the desired conclusion from a message based upon certain general principles presented or implied within the message that the receiver accepts as true; or they may require the receiver to induce the desired conclusion as a result of believable evidence in the arguments presented. In other words, the receiver is encouraged to draw the receiver's conclusion from perceived logical argument based upon promised cognitive and affective benefits following the behavior advocated in the persuasive message. However, one cannot always count on a receiver to abide by the formal laws of logic in drawing conclusions. (This point will be covered in some detail in later sections dealing with message content and syntax.)

The fact that a receiver may draw illogical conclusions from a particular communication message need not be necessarily considered a bad thing. It is not uncommon for a receiver to commit logical fallacies in reading, listening, or viewing advertising, believing an advertisement or commercial has said something when it hasn't. Since it is the receiver who has added new information through an invalid implication from the message, the fallacy must be attributed to the receiver, not the message. After all, if the receiver hadn't added the invalid point to the message, no fallacy would exist. This phenomenon was explored in an experiment by Preston (1967), in which 90 college students were asked to examine advertisements from an issue of *Life* magazine. The subjects were asked whether a set of five statements were accurate or inaccurate restatements of the content of each advertisement. One of the five statements for each advertisement was illogically derived, yet almost two-thirds of the subjects agreed that it was a correct statement. The original premise was that such a response on the part of the subject-receivers is due to illogical thinking, but additional ad hoc evidence suggested that some of this apparent "illogical" behavior may have occurred because people approach advertising with a set to perceive the advertising as saying what the advertiser would have been most likely to say—in other words, that advertising is expected to be self-serving. To the extent that this is true, logos appeals could be so constructed as to maximize positive inference through both logic and illogic.

An important issue to be considered in the question of logos versus pathos appeals, as McGuire (1969a) points out, is the relative effectiveness of logical versus emotional appeals. While earlier studies generally held that there is no difference (cf. Knower 1935; Matthews 1947), or that emotional appeals have more impact than logical appeals (Eldersveld 1956; Hartmann 1936), it now appears that, in terms of psychological judgment, they are not at opposite ends of a single continuum, but tend to be almost orthogonal dimensions (cf. Knepprath and Clevenger 1965). McGuire (1969a) explains this distinction by considering as logical those appeals that argue for the truth of a given belief by presenting evidence in favor of the likelihood of the antecedents from which a belief follows being true, and considering as emotional those appeals arguing for a particular belief by stressing the desirability of results that would follow from a given belief. From an advertising viewpoint, one might consider advertising stressing the attributes of a product as more logical in appeal, and advertising stressing the "reward" of product use as more emotional. It is interesting that, from a media standpoint, logical appeals lend themselves more to print than broadcast media, while emotional appeals are generally more effective in broadcast rather than print media.

POSITIVE VERSUS NEGATIVE APPEALS

Turning to a more basic characterization of message appeal, when an advertiser or other source presents a persuasive message urging a receiver to adopt some new attitude or behavior, he has the option of using either a positive or negative appeal. Quite naturally, a positive appeal stresses the benefit to be gained from yielding to the persuasive message and modifying one's attitude or behavior accordingly, while a negative appeal will focus on the undesirable consequences of not yielding. This choice is always available in creating an advertising message, regardless of the subject, even though some products or brands obviously lend themselves more to one kind of appeal than another. For example, in advertising deodorant soap, one could use the positive appeal of stressing the benefits of a clean and fresh-smelling body, or, on the other hand, the negative appeal of stressing the social consequences of body odor. In advertising breakfast cereal, however, one must stretch the imagination to come up with a negative appeal that points out the horrible consequences of not buying a particular brand.

The use of positive versus negative appeals in mediating attitude or behavior change through response to advertising is analogous to the use of reward versus punishment in learning situations. In such cases, reward may be thought of as increasing the probability of the desired response in two ways: (1) the situation in which a reward is given becomes attractive for the learner and the learner would tend to seek out such situations; and (2) when the learner finds such a situation, the learner will tend to be more likely to repeat the previously rewarded response. Punishment generally works in quite the opposite manner. Situations in which the learner has experienced punishment become unattractive, and the learner tends to avoid them; but if in such a situation, the learner is unlikely to respond in the punished fashion. When one uses a positive appeal in a message to persuade the receiver to adopt the desired attitude or behavior (for example, buying a particular brand), the probability of thinking about the subject (that is, evaluation) and making the desired response is increased. If, instead, a negative appeal is used in seeking a particular attitude or behavior change, both a beneficial and detrimental effect are likely. The receiver will be more likely to respond to a negative appeal by taking the desired preventive action, providing the receiver is aware of the situation presented in the communication, but unfortunately a negative appeal will also tend to increase the likelihood that the receiver will repress the situation completely, because of the anxiety the message stimulates. Consequently, it would not be unusual for a strongly positioned appeal to actively reduce the probability of persuasion. This point is considered in more detail in the following discussion of fear appeals.

Fear Appeals

The use of fear appeals in persuasive communication has been extensively researched and reported in the literature, dating from an early study by Janis and Feshbach (1953), through more recent studies specifically concerned with the use of fear in advertising messages (Ray and Wilkie 1970; Sternthal and Craig 1973). Because fear is an obvious negative appeal, one would expect the chance for both the beneficial and detrimental effects discussed in the last section. In fact, from our discussion of anxiety and receiver variables in the last two chapters, one recalls that fear has both a cue and drive state that correspond directly to this dual effect. On the one hand, fear or anxiety in its drive aspect will tend to increase likelihood of persuasibility and compliance with the communication message, while on the other hand, in its cue aspect it tends to elicit avoidance of the source or message. This leads to a consideration of the relationship between fear appeals and subsequent attitude or behavior change as nonrectilinear and even nonmonotonic, taking the shape of an inverted U-shape curve requiring specification in terms of second-order and even higher-order interaction effects (see Figure 4.1). At low levels of fear the receiver will not be particularly interested in the message, thus minimizing the probability of message reception. As the level of fear increases, so too will the likelihood of reception, and along with reception, a probable increase in response. Once the level of fear becomes relatively high, however, message reception will decrease as the receiver tends to repress the message because of the perceived consequence. This explanation corresponds closely to McGuire's (1968b) two-factor analysis, which finds the same nonmonotonic relationship such that some intermediate level of anxiety arousal is more conducive to persuasion than very low or very high anxiety arousal. He further predicts that the level of anxiety arousal that is most efficacious goes down as message complexity increases and as the receiver's chronic anxiety level goes up. McGuire (1973) reports partial support for this contention by Millman (1965), although Lehmann (1970) and Leventhal (1970) suggest that there is still higher order interaction with a receiver's self-esteem.

Janis (1969), like McGuire, predicts an inverted U-shaped relationship between fear or anxiety arousal and attitude change. But, he argues that by intro-

FIGURE 4.1

Relationship between Reception and Fear Appeals

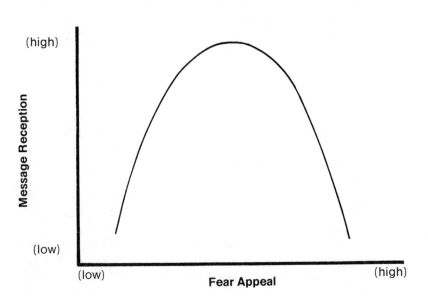

ducing intervening mechanisms that will reduce the defenses of the receiver, one will be able to produce more attitude change. Janis and Mann (1965) arranged a role-playing experiment in which subjects were asked to play the role of medical patients beginning to suffer from the harmful consequences of using tobacco. All of the subjects were young women who had expressed no interest in cutting down on their smoking. The experimenter assumed the role of a physician, complete with white coat and various props, such as X-ray pictures of the lungs. Each subject in the experimental group was encouraged to express her spontaneous reactions as a patient. Five different scenarios were acted out, including one in which the role-playing patient waits while the experimenter-physician arranges for her hospitalization in the surgical ward (a scene that was exceptionally effective in arousing the subject's emotions). Results of this study showed definite changes in behavioral intention among those participating, and actual behavioral change in the number of cigarettes smoked. Mann and Janis (1968), in a follow-up study 18 months later, found that those subjects in the experimental group continued to smoke fewer cigarettes than those in a control who had only listened to a tape of the role playing by the experimental subjects. These results certainly indicate the potential positive benefit of involving a receiver with the message of a persuasive communication.

In another study, Mann (1967) compared a general fear-arousal procedure, such as the one just discussed; a cognitive experiment in which the subjects assumed the role of a debater arguing against smoking; and a shame-arousing exercise in which the subjects assumed the role of helpless smoking addicts. The fear-arousal approach proved to be significantly more effective in changing attitude. A number of other studies involving interaction between the level of fear arousal and subsequent attitude or behavior change report similar results. Leventhal and Watts (1966) have found that high fear arousal is better than moderate levels in getting subjects to reduce their amount of smoking, but that low arousal is better for inducing them to seek chest X-ray checkups for the possibility of lung cancer. Leventhal, Watts, and Pagano (1967) found that messages with high fear arousal concerning the health danger attached to cigarette smoking produced higher intention of quitting smoking (yielding) than did low fear arousal, but, in terms of actual behavior change resulting, there was no significant difference between the high and low arousal messages. Insko, Arkoff, and Insko (1965), in testing the effects of high and low fear appeals in messages about the health hazards of smoking, found that high fear arousal was more effective than a low fear appeal in immediately convincing nonsmokers that they should not take up the habit. After one week, a "sleeper-like" effect became evident. Although the effect from the high fear appeal message was still greater, the effectiveness of the high fear appeal condition had decreased, while that of a low fear appeal message increased slightly.

The effects of high versus low fear appeal in a persuasive message as measured over a period of time has been studied by Evans et al. (1970). They tested five different message conditions in a program designed to improve the tooth-brushing habits of junior high school students. After presentation of either a high or low fear arousal message, or a positive social approval message, an identical set of four specific procedural recommendations about proper tooth care followed. In the fourth message condition, only the four specific procedural recommendations were presented; and in the fifth message condition, a more embellished version of the same recommendations was presented. A number of different attitudinal and behavioral measures were taken immediately following exposure, five days later, and again after six months.

As one might expect, the high fear appeal increased reported anxiety more than the low fear appeal message; both produced greater levels of anxiety than the other three conditions, but the magnitude of these effects decreased over a period of time. Surprisingly, the fear appeals resulted in the least amount of retained information (retention) from the five message conditions, while the social approval messages generated the most. However, over a period of time, the differences in the level of retained information among the five message conditions decreased to nonsignificant levels. In terms of immediate behavioral intention (yielding), once again the fear appeals were significantly more effective than the nonfear message appeals, but, as the effects of each message decreased over a period of time, only the high fear appeal produced strong persistence effect, remaining significantly higher than all other conditions after six weeks. Considering reported toothbrushing behavior over a period of time, the high fear appeal message was most effective, followed, interestingly enough, by the embellished four recommendation message. Yet when actual behavior is recorded (as reported elsewhere by Evans et al. [1970]), one finds that it differs dramatically from the subject's reported behavior. Utilizing disclosing wafers after five days and six weeks, it was found that the embellished recommendations and the positive social support appeals were most effective in changing actual toothbrushing behavior; and these were the two least effective messages on reported behavior. The high fear appeal that occasioned the greatest change in reported behavior managed only third best in actual behavior change.

While this short review only begins to cover the reported research on the effects of fear-arousing message appeals on attitude and behavior change, it is certainly sufficient to demonstrate that many, if not all, of the effects of fear-arousing communication, and contingencies of these effects upon individual difference variables, are potentially interpretable in terms of the effects the variables have upon response to advertising. It is conceivable that in some instances the fear-arousing appeal of a communication message may not affect either the probability of reception or attitude change, but rather may affect the tendency to agree publicly with the desired message ends (regardless of whether or not the message is effectively refuted). To be sure, strong appeals are more likely than mild appeals to give receivers the impression that the position being advocated is important to the source. This is a point perhaps even more applicable to advertising than to other types of communication. Differences between the effects of appeals on reported attitudes and the effects of these appeals on actual behavior (as noted above and reviewed by Leventhal [1970]) suggest that this could certainly be the case. High fear-arousing appeals positively affect advertising response and reported behavior change, although it may be less likely retained, and as a result less likely to effect the desired actual change.

Pleasantness Appeals

Pleasantness as the appeal of a communication's message provides a positive contrast to the negative appeal of fear. A pleasant message appeal could be reflected in the general mood of the communication or in some specific element of style, such as humor. Although there is some evidence that a pleasant message appeal may facilitate immediate attitude change (Rosnow 1965), the question of the overall effectiveness of pleasant message appeals, and of humor in particular, remains somewhat controversial. Early work by Lull (1940) found that the addition of humor to a speech on an otherwise serious topic did nothing to facilitate persuasion or interest. Later, Gruner (1965) found that satirical speeches were simply not persuasive, leading McGuire (1969a) to comment on the findings as another example of how adequate reception of the message can be a considerable hurdle in the way of persuasive impact—the point being that satirical speeches have a low probability of reception. DeLozier (1976), on the other hand, remarks that in general, humor appears to be very effective in gaining attention to an advertising message, and, in addition, seems to aid in recall and comprehension—a contradiction to Gruner and McGuire. Yet, in other work, Gruner (1967, 1970) himself has found some evidence that source credibility can be enhanced by the use of humor, particularly when dealing with topics of low interest. This could have important implications for advertising, for, as Robertson (1976), among others, has pointed out, most consumer product purchase decisions are of low involvement. Karlins and Abelson (1970), however, doubt the effectiveness of humor in facilitating persuasion, while Osterhouse and Brock (1970) have found that humor in a communication's message appears to reduce counter-arguing and increase attitude change, along with a corresponding persistence to such change. Sternthal and Craig (1973), though, failed to find any superiority in the use of humor.

Although the question of using humor as our approach to pleasantness in message appeal may be somewhat unsettled, pleasantness itself enjoys a more certain position. In their execution, pleasant communications (and particularly advertising) tend to be more "soft-sell," and are characterized by the subtleness of their conclusions. This low-key nature of pleasant appeals generally requires implicit or subtle claims that must be comprehended by the receiver. Krugman (1962) has speculated that such subtleties would result in less message wear-out than a more explicit message, given the usually high number of exposures occurring with most consumer package goods advertising. Work by Silk and Vavra (1974) appears to offer additional support to this notion. Finally, experiments that have compared messages of a more pleasant appeal and subtle conclusion with those that are more "hard-sell" and explicit in their conclusion have consistently found greater immediate attitude change resulting from the explicit conclusion message (cf. Hovland and Mandell 1952).

Implicit Versus Explicit Conclusions

While it is true that implicit conclusions in persuasive communication tend to accompany more positive or pleasant message appeals, they are by no means excluded from messages with negative appeals. Because of this, the question of whether it is more effective to draw a conclusion explicitly within a message or leave it for the receiver to draw the conclusion becomes an interesting question in its own light. McGuire (1969a) suggests that research into this question probably stems from the belief that nondirective psychotherapy is more effective than directive. Freud believed that when a patient was left to draw a conclusion, the patient was much more likely to accept its validity than when a therapist draws it for the patient. However, it has been shown that in persuasive communication it is more effective to explicitly draw the desired conclusion within the message (Hovland and Mandel 1952; McGuire 1964). When dealing with a persuasive communication in a real life situation rather than a patient undergoing psychotherapy, the receiver is much less likely to be motivated to draw the advertiser's conclusion. In terms of advertising response, one is dealing with the reception stages. As McGuire (1969a) puts it: "In communication, it appears it is not sufficient to lead a horse to water; one must also push his head underneath to get him to drink." If a message with an implicit conclusion manages to move beyond the reception stages, the fact that the receiver has drawn the conclusion should enhance the likelihood of responding, since the receiver would come to regard the conclusion as the receiver's own, rather than one imposed by the advertiser or other source. But, as we have so often found, the rub comes in being able to maximize both reception and response.

In any effort to accomplish this task, it would be helpful to consider the nature of an implicit conclusion versus an explicit conclusion message. It would seem reasonable to suppose that each would interact differently with temporal and individual-difference variables. We have already noted that immediate attitude change is more likely when the conclusion is explicit. Perhaps what is needed to balance this immediate persuasion is more time. If the frequency of exposure was high for an implicit conclusion message, the probability of reception should increase, and, with reception, the likelihood of a greater response.

REFUTATIONAL APPEALS

A fundamental question in the development of a persuasive message is whether or not it is better to ignore possible opposing arguments or to include, but refute, them.* One could, for example, create a message that presents only supportive points in favor of the advocated position (for example, the product or brand in advertising communication) without mentioning any drawbacks to the argument or recognizing any conflicting claims. A refutational appeal, on the other hand, would present both sides of a position, but argue against the position that is contrary to the source argument. This type of appeal is characterized by the type of advertising in which two or more competing products are presented, but the advertised product is shown in a more favorable light. Another situation that frequently leads to a refutational strategy in the message is one in which a single negative cognitive salience is juxtaposed with one or more equally strong positive saliences. When this occurs, it is necessary to refute the negative salience in order to gain acceptance of the positive saliences as persuasible. If the negative salience is ignored, it will tend to override the positive saliences presented in the persuasive message at the evaluative stage of the buyer-response hierarchy, because negative characteristics subjectively outweigh positive ones in determining attitude or behavior change. Only when the possible counter-arguments to a message, or particular negative beliefs, are either weak or nonsalient should one consider ignoring them in message execution.

Some of the earliest work on the efficacy of refutational appeals came out of research during World War II by Hovland and his associates (cf. Hovland, Lumsdaine, and Sheffield 1949), which showed that neither ignoring opposition arguments nor explicitly refuting them has greater efficacy under all conditions. In general, ignoring the opposition was found to be more desirable if the receivers were initially favorable toward one's conclusion, but that mentioning and then refuting the opposition is somewhat more desirable if the receivers were initially opposed to one's position. Also, refuting the opposition argument was found to be more effective with receivers of higher intelligence, and when the receivers could be reasonably expected to already know the opposition arguments. Work by others (mentioned by McGuire 1969a) has likewise indicated that both refuting and ignoring opposition arguments are about equally effective overall in producing direct attitude change, although earlier studies by McGuire (1963) found that explicitly refuting opposition arguments, rather than ignoring them and presenting only one's own arguments, does produce more direct attitude change. In contrast to these findings, Janis and Feierabend (1957) have sug-

---

*Frequently referred to as a one-sided (ignoring the opposition) versus two-sided (refuting the opposition) communication.

gested that the mere presentation of opposition arguments, even to refute them, could put the receiver in a situation of conflict, especially if the opposition arguments are dealt with before the arguments supportive of the desired position. Mentioning the opposition arguments might cause the receiver to switch sides, giving rise to possible problems with defensive avoidance when the supportive arguments are presented later.

In an extension of the direct effects of refutational appeals, studies have focused on the extent to which refuting the opposition arguments rather than ignoring them confers resistance to subsequent counter-communications (McGuire 1964). While this subject was treated extensively in the sections of chapter 2 that discuss the concept of immunization to persuasion, a review of the effects of refutational appeals on persuasibility over a period of time will be considered here. McGuire (1964) has presented evidence to support the prediction that immediately after either a refutational or supportive message, the message built upon the supportive appeal will prove to be more persuasive. However, if a competitive opposition message follows the original message, the message based upon a refutational appeal will sustain greater retention. In another experiment, McGuire (1962) tested the effects of time between original and competitive messages on three original message conditions: (1) a refutational-same appeal, in which a refutational appeal refutes the source arguments that are subsequently used in the competitive opposition message; (2) a refutational-different appeal, in which the messages refute opposition arguments different from those subsequently used in the opposition message; and (3) a supportive appeal, in which the original message ignores all opposition arguments. The opposition arguments were presented either immediately after the original message or two to seven days later. The refutational-same appeal persisted for the first few days, then decayed; the refutational-different appeal showed some increase with time during the first few days, then decayed to about the same level as the refutational-same message; while the supportive appeal began at a lower level than either refutational appeal (as found above), and simply decayed over a period of time. These findings would seem to suggest that in highly competitive advertising environments, a strong presumption for refutational appeal elements in persuasive communication should be made.

In any attempt to replicate McGuire's results using advertisements about the effectiveness of safety air bags in automobiles, Szybillo and Heslin (1973) found a similar order of persistence of effectiveness when the opposition message was presented immediately following the original message, but little difference in the level of decay after three days. The supportive appeal showed no appreciable decay, while the refutational appeals decayed down to the level of the supportive appeal. However, the credibility of the source of the opposition argument (either a government agency or an automobile manufacturer—high versus low) was also varied in their experiment, and they did find a somewhat lower rate of attention from the higher initial levels achieved by the refutational appeals in the low-source-credibility condition. Gillig and Greenwald (1974) also dealt with this question of refutational appeals and source credibility over a period of time, and they, too, found that messages relying on refutational appeals proved more effective over a period of time in a low-source-credibility condition. The implication of these findings for advertising communication is merely to reinforce the conclusion that refutational appeals are more conducive to retention in the buyer response hierarchy, given the comparatively low source credibility of most advertising.

Counter-arguing

To the extent that the persuasive impact of a communication is affected by counter-arguing, one should expect a greater probability of response when the arguments used in the message are less subject to receiver refutation or counter-arguing. Likewise, to the extent that one's own persuasive communication effectively stimulates counter-arguing against possible counter-positions, the probability of yielding to the advocated position should increase as compelling competitive arguments are refuted. In a test of this general notion, McGuire and Papageorgis (1962) compared the effectiveness of refutational messages, as well as supportive messages, in minimizing the effects of a persuasive communication. If counter-arguing is indeed an important mediator of persuasive effectiveness, the message most likely to stimulate counter-arguing should also prove to be the most effective in maintaining adherents to the original position. In other words, a persuasive message should be effective in proportion to the arguments provided, which help the receiver refute subsequent messages which argue a different position. Since supportive messages contain only message-points that deal positively with the position advanced by the source of the communication and do not deal directly with any arguments that might be used against it, the information provided should minimally affect the receiver's ability to refute them. On the other hand, since a refutational appeal brings up possible counter-arguments and refutes them (as described in the previous section on refutational appeals), the information provided in such a message should effectively increase the probability of successful counter-arguing in the face of subsequent efforts to dissuade.

The McGuire and Papageorgis results support these predictions. Those receivers who were presented supportive messages exhibited no significant differences in topic beliefs from a control group who received no prior supportive or refutational message, after they had been exposed to an attacking message. Those receivers who were presented the refutational message prior to being exposed to an attacking message, on the other hand, showed significantly stronger postattack beliefs. In this study, the arguments were sometimes presented by the experimenter and read by the subjects, and at other times they were written by the subjects themselves. Surprisingly, postattack beliefs were stronger when the original refutational message was already prepared and only read by the subjects, rather than when the arguments were written by the subjects on their own. This suggests that effective counter-arguing is more likely when the arguments are made explicit by an outside source, rather than merely being left to the receiver to arrive at himself. In terms of advertising, of course, it is quite easy to explicitly present the necessary message-points for counter-arguing within a refutational framework. To the degree that counter-arguing is a desired effect in one's advertising strategy—for example, when a clear market leader appears to have co-opted a particular attribute, or when a new use for an existing product runs counter to existing beliefs—the appropriateness of a refutational appeal in the message would appear to be well founded.

While this may all seem straightforward enough, it sometimes happens that the very message-points provided by the refutational strategy to encourage counter-arguing may be negatively correlated with stimulation provided by these message-points to actually effect counter-arguing. McGuire (1961) attempted to separate these two effects by asking subjects to either read or write message-points designed to counter arguments that were to be presented in a subsequent communication. Some of the subjects refuted message-points that were the same as those in the second message; some used arguments that were different from those used in the second message. He found that when the refutational strategy of the first message dealt with message-points that were the same as those contained in the persuasive message of the second communication (which, in effect, was attacking the first), it was effective to the degree that the specific message-points employed provided a means of refuting the subsequent arguments. On the other hand, when the message-points of the initial communication pertained to arguments different from those in the subsequent attack, they proved to be effective only to the extent that they made the receiver aware of the vulnerability to attack, and as a result, to stimulate the receiver in considering and practicing counter-arguing prior to exposure to the second message. (This entire question was dealt with in more detail in the section "Immunization to Persuasion," in chapter 2.)

Wyer (1974) speculates that if this is so, it perhaps follows that when a receiver attends to and comprehends a weak message containing arguments not found in subsequent message attacks, the receiver should become more aware of vulnerability and hence more resistant to those attacks than a receiver who reads a strong message against subsequent arguments. Although this implication is interesting, there is little to recommend it to advertising planning, for it would be difficult to anticipate competitive advertising accurately enough to gauge (a) when a refutational strategy is appropriate, and (b) the strength and content of future competitive claims in order to provide only a weak basis for counter-arguing in one's own advertising.

While investigating the effects of various types of message-points on increasing the probability of resistance to subsequent counter-communication, McGuire (1964) discovered that, although receivers no doubt have a large set of socially-accepted beliefs they accept as unquestionably true, there may, in fact, be little or no actual grounds for many of those beliefs. He presented specific persuasive messages designed to refute many of these social truisims (for example, "Everyone should brush his teeth after every meal if possible") and found a significant decrease in the receiver's belief that they were true. One possible explanation advanced by McGuire is that, since the receivers had never before questioned the validity of those general beliefs, they were unequipped to effectively counter-argue the message-points presented in the attacking communication. He speculates that the receivers' ability to effectively counter-argue would be increased as they were exposed to arguments that reinforced their original beliefs. The parallels to advertising seem equally clear. When beliefs are known to be strongly held by receivers, one should concentrate on messages compatible with one's strategy designed to reinforce those beliefs; when beliefs are weak or must be altered, a refutational appeal designed to stimulate counter-arguing would seem to be in order.

DISTRACTION

Another way in which the appeal of a persuasive message may influence advertising response is through the use of irrelevant positive reinforcement or irrelevant punishment. McGuire (1969a) mentions a number of studies that have addressed this question, and concludes that, in general, irrelevant positive reinforcement strengthens and irrelevant punishments weaken elicited opinions, to the extent that the reinforcement or punishment is administered without delay. In advertising communication, a parallel may be drawn to the use of sweepstakes, premiums, or even coupons. All are irrelevant reinforcements to the actual purchase of the advertised product or brand to the extent that they do not reflect direct product benefit. Given McGuire's conclusion, it would seem that only those irrelevant reinforcements that occur immediately with trial (such as a price-off coupon or dual promotions offering other immediately available products) would be successful in positively effecting behavior change. Longer term reinforcements, such as "bounce-back" coupons, which must be mailed to the manufacturer, or sweepstakes and premiums that must be sent for, should be less efficacious.

Examples of external manipulation of attitude through distraction are also helpful in understanding the effects of message appeal. While it is true that it is usually not within the power of an advertiser using mass media to control external distractions during message reception, the advertiser should be aware of the probability of distraction through partial attention, and, by extension, the degree to which a particular communication execution contains elements that might encourage distraction from the main point of the message. A successful demonstration of the effect of external distraction on persuasibility is presented by Janis, Kaye, and Kirschner (1965). The objective of their research was to determine the effect of eating while reading on the persuasiveness of a message. One group of subjects in the "food condition" was presented four persuasive messages to read, along with an ample supply of peanuts and soft drinks. The control group was given only the four persuasive messages, without anything to eat or drink. Their results indicated that those subjects in the "food condition" were persuaded more than the subjects who read the same persuasive materials under the "no-food condition." This would seem to suggest that at least some irrelevant distractions may have positive effects on advertising response.

DeLozier (1976) reports another study of distraction effects that bears more directly on possible advertising implication. Male college students were asked to listen to taped messages that presented views dissimilar to their own. As they listened to the tape, slides of pleasant scenery such as clouds and mountains were shown simultaneously to one group, while slides of nude females were shown to a second group. The results showed that subjects who viewed the nude females were more likely to be persuaded by the message they heard than subjects viewing picturesque secnery. These findings strongly suggest the likelihood of increased persuasibility due to certain distraction effects (a point made by Karlins and Abelson [1970]), but also point out the importance of selecting an appropriate distraction for message execution. Too much of a distraction could easily prove inefficacious if the receiver becomes so involved with the distraction that no attention is paid to the content of the message as it is presented.

Other factors influencing the effects of distraction on communication effectiveness include (1) communication characteristics, (2) individual differences, and (3) counter-arguing. Considering the effects of communication characteristics in message distractions, Regan and Cheng (1973) presented subjects messages that were either quite simple but not very convincing or difficult to understand, but convincing if understood. The messages were heard under two distraction conditions—music played at either high or low volume. They found that distraction (especially the music played at a high volume) increased the influence of the simple message but decreased the impact of the complex one. The effects of individual differences and distraction has been studied by Festinger and Maccoby (1964). A tape-recorded message attacking the fraternity system was played for both fraternity members (presumably in favor of fraternities) and nonmembers (presumably neutral or opposed to fraternities), along with a visual stimulus that was either highly distracting (a humorous silent film satirizing the Jackson Pollack drip-style of art) or minimally distracting (a film of the speaker). Distraction tended to increase the influence of the message to fraternity members, but the level of influence upon nonmembers was the same for both levels of distraction. Yet, in another study reported by Haaland and Venkatesan (1968), distraction decreased the influence of the communication. This suggests that both the magnitude and the direction of distraction effects will depend upon the particular levels of distraction selected. Finally, the effects of distraction on a receiver's likelihood to counter-argue (or resist) a message was studied by Oster-house and Brock (1970). The amount of counter-arguing to a presented message was measured as the number of such arguments occuring in a written elicitation following presentation of the message. Once again, it was found that, as dis-traction increased, the number of counter-arguments decreased, while yielding to the advocated position became greater. Overall, it appears that distraction, when not severe, tends to facilitate advertising response.

REPETITION OF INFORMATION

The amount of information included in a persuasive message and the de-gree of repetition can have important effects on advertising response. Research on the question of repetition and persuasive impact has been extensive and varied, ranging from a study by Peterson and Thurstone (1933) which showed that several commercial films, when shown individually, produced no detectable effect on persuasion, but did when the films were shown together, through a study of the effectiveness of repetition in newspaper advertising by Stewart (1964). Overall, however, one is struck by the absence of any consistently true significant effect on attitude change. McGuire (1973) points out that, while an increase in the impact of a message is usually apparent for one or two repetitions, this quickly reaches an asymptote beyond which further repetition has little effect. While most of the research that led to this conclusion was based upon repetitions of the overall message, the principle would seem to apply to repeti-tition of points within messages. The reader is also reminded that these effects do not necessarily translate directly to the concept of repeated exposure in media, since one is usually dealing with a changing audience, and presentation is the required first step for message processing (see discussion on reach and fre-quency in chapter 5, "Media Selection"). In this case, although the effect of repetition on a given receiver may quickly reach an asymptote, repetition (or frequency) within a media schedule is designed to build exposure to the message among successive samples of receivers.

Repetition of the same message-points within a single communication a number of times has been shown to be useful for increasing retention (Cook and Wadsworth 1972; Weber 1972). This would seem to suggest that copy in adver-tising communication would be more effective if fewer message points were used, and those that were used were repeated often. In fact, experience with the communications effectiveness of various executions by the authors tend to sup-port this conclusion. Advertisements that stress eight to ten major product attri-butes communicate only a few of those points to any one receiver (although overall each message point is communicated to at least some receiver) while executions stressing three to four attributes consistently communicate all of those message-points to the majority of receivers.

Considering only the amount of information in a given communication, from a memory standpoint it would seem logical to assume that the fewer message-points the better, particularly if they are repeated often. One could reason that with less to learn or comprehend in a persuasive communication, the likelihood of retention and subsequent attitude or behavior change should increase. While this notion has nice intuitive appeal, Cook and Insko (1968) found that a communication with six message points was superior to a communication of comparable length dealing with only two message points in both effecting attitude change and in maintaining that change over a period of time. They reasoned that an attitude is more likely to be internalized as a greater number of values, or more important values, are linked to the new attitude. This internalization of attitude should explain the resistance over a period of time to decay, but not the initial learning. Perhaps, the number of message-points, given the length of the communication (some 2,000 words), were not sufficiently different to effect short-term memory and subsequent storage. As is fairly well known, short-term memory appears capable of handling something like six to eight functional units; it may be that once this constraint is violated the likelihood of retention decreases.

One final note on the amount of information contained in a persuasive communication addresses the overall length of the messages. Calder, Insko, and Yandell (1974) have found that longer messages tend to have a more enduring effect on attitudes than shorter messages. The implication for advertising communication, particularly broadcast, could be significant. One could be led to the conclusion that 60-second commercials would greatly enhance the probability of advertising response, compared to 30-second (or even shorter) commercial messages. With the increased noise in television advertising, and the trend to shorter and shorter commercials, this is one area that would seem to suggest careful study.

Part II
Message Structure

Any single communication message is usually composed of a number of message-points, and, as a result, one must perforce be concerned with the order in which they are presented within the total persuasive communication effort. We have already discussed such things as repetition of multiple message points, drawing a conclusion or leaving closure to be provided by the receiver, and the possibility of using a refutational appeal. In all of these cases a question of ordering sequence arises. If a number of message-points are to be included, which should be presented first? If one draws a conclusion explicitly, should it be presented at the beginning (a primacy effect) or at the end of the message (a recency effect), and, if one employs a refutational appeal, should the opposition's argument be refuted before or after one's own arguments?

A great deal of research has addressed this question of the order of presentation in a message. Hovland (1957), in reviewing several specific experiments in this area, arrived at a number of general conclusions. When contradictory information is presented in a single communication, by a single source, there appears to be a pronounced tendency for those message-points presented first to dominate the overall impact of the message. Messages that provide information relevant to the satisfaction of needs, after those needs have been stimulated, bring about a higher level of response than a message order that presents the supportive information first and then follows it with need-arousal. Communicating message-points first that are highly desirable to the receiver, followed by those less desirable (though not necessarily negative), tends to produce more attitude change than the reverse order; and, similarly, when nonsalient arguments or message points are included with strong persuasive arguments, if an authoritative source is used, the strong arguments should precede the weaker or negative message points. He also reports that, overall, the order of presentation in communicating message-points tends to be a more significant factor in influencing attitude among receivers with a relatively weak desire for understanding or comprehension, than for those receivers with a "high cognitive need."

Currently, there is probably more research available on the general issue of primacy-recency effects (for example, that reviewed by McGuire [1966]), than any other message order question. In this section, we will present first a general discussion of primacy-recency effects, and then the effect of order on specific message appeals.

PRIMACY-RECENCY EFFECTS

In discussing the question of primacy-recency effects, McGuire (1969a) offers three theoretical explanations for its results: learning theory, perceptual theory, and intention-to-persuade. Although he considers each of these conceptual frameworks in light of two message sources, each arguing for different sides on a given issue, the reasoning applies equally to the order of presentation within a single message. He begins by suggesting that research on primacy-recency effects has two historical roots: (1) research on judgments about personality, especially in the problem of halo effect and the importance of first impressions; and (2) investigations of whether it is more advantageous to have the first or last say in debate. Early work in the area of impression formation confirmed the intuitive feel that first impressions are important. Since then, studies have shown that primacy effects are by no means universal, and that both primacy and recency effects are based on rather complex underlying processes.

Looking at primacy-recency effects from a learning theory perspective, Miller and Campbell (1959) have shown that attitude change resulting from either a primacy or recency effect in ordering may be explained in terms of an underlying learning process. Initial learning is enhanced by primacy because of proactive inhibition, which could interfere with the learning of subsequent communication in accordance with the so-called negative-transfer paradigm. Retention, however, should be maximized by recency, since it is closer to actual attitude or behavior change within the buyer response hierarchy, and a negatively accelerated Ebbinghouse-type forgetting curve would be expected for both the initial and second message. Following this logic would also suggest that primacy tendencies should be more manifest when the second side follows immediately after the first (as would be the case in a single message presenting two sides, or when two opposing advertising commercials are seen, one immediately following the other), while recency tendencies should be more acute as the time between message presentation increases, or when yielding or attitude change is measured immediately following the second message.

If a perceptual theory of order effects is considered, one would be led to conclude that primacy effects are more efficacious. The reasoning here would follow from the perceptual-theory hypothesis that early exposure to a situation tends to provide a specific (and favorable) frame of reference against which subsequent situations are attended and understood. As Sherif's (1935) early work in this area found, belief sets appear to be formed quickly during one's early exposure. If should then follow that any primacy effect associated with new information should indeed be strong, but become less pronounced as the message content becomes more familiar. Both the learning theory and perceptual theory explanation predict better communication efficiency through primacy effects, but learning theory bases its prediction on a lower likelihood of learning the later message, while perceptual theory bases its prediction on a general likelihood of distortion in the second message.

The final theoretical explanation of primacy-recency effects offered by McGuire (1969a) is the intent-to-persuade argument advanced by Hovland (for example, in Hovland, Janis, and Kelley 1953). He has suggested that a receiver's awareness of an intent-to-persuade on the part of the source will be less likely to occur when the receiver is first exposed to a persuasive message than after hearing a second argument, especially when the receiver is being presented a message dealing with essentially trivial or unimportant matters in a situation that is not initially perceived as being argumentative (a situation analogous to advertising communication, in which interest is generally low and media not usually considered a source of controversial messages). Only after the receiver begins to hear the second and contrary position is the receiver likely to realize the receiver has just listened to or read an essentially biased message. Unfortunately for the second source, even though the receiver may now be suspicious of the first message, the receiver is definite about the second and any damaging impact would fall largely upon it, since receivers do not tend to react to knowledge of persuasive intent retroactively.

FACTORS INFLUENCING ORDER EFFECT

A number of studies have been reported that deal with the contribution of various factors to primacy-recency effects, and whether information presented first in a persuasive message is more effective than information presented later in positively influencing advertising response. While these different effects usually covary in any actual communication situation, it is perhaps helpful to consider them independently in order to better understand the mediating role of each on response to advertising. Table 4.1 summarizes the typical reactions occasioned by each of five factors on the order of message point presentation in communication: receiver attention, consistency of meaning, message point contrast, message point weighting, and forgetting.

Receiver Attention

With any given communication, a receiver may not pay equal attention to all of the message-points. As is the case with most advertising communication, receivers have a low level of interest in the message topic, and, as such, may be hypothesized to attend only to the first part of a message (such as the headline in print advertising) without attending to what follows. If this were the case, a primacy effect would be predicted; that is, a more positive response to the mes-

TABLE 4.1

Factors Influencing Order Effect

Order Factor	Response		
	Reaction Stimulus		Effect
Receiver attention	a. low level of interest		primacy
	b. strong belief set		recency
Consistency of meaning	initial points provide context for evaluating subsequent message points		primacy
Message point contrast	initial points provide level of comparison		recency
Message point weighting	inconsistency among message points are noticed		primacy
Forgetting	back-to-back advertising		primacy

sage would be expected if the most important message point was presented first. However, in those cases in which a strong belief set is present, the most important point should probably be presented after any refutation or less favorable message points are introduced—in other words, a recency effect. As Wyer (1974) points out, this recency effect should dominate regardless of the receiver's initial attitude, so long as his attitude is not neutral. In order to maximize the probability of gaining receiver attention (a necessary preamble to any advertising response), it would seem the most important or favorable message points should be presented first in all cases, except those in which it is likely the receiver will suspect initial beliefs are being challenged.

Message Point Contrast

When the various message points contained in persuasive communication are open to several possible interpretations, each with a different evaluative implication, those points presented first could provide a context for the evaluation of those that follow. If this were indeed the case, it would argue for a primacy effect where the most favorable or important message point would be presented first in hopes of influencing the evaluation of the less favorable or less important points that follow. This hypothesis has been suggested by Chalmers (1969), and supported by Wyer and Schwartz (1969) who found that when information presented in a message tends to be inconsistent, a primacy effect is more pronounced.

Consistency of Meaning

A similar situation, albeit leading to a different conclusion, occurs when the first message point in a series of points is used as a reference in judging the subsequent information. In a case in which a message point is indefinite or inconsistent in meaning with the message as a whole, it has been noted that a primacy effect obtains because an evaluative mood is established. A recency effect is expected where there is a consensus as to meaning. To the extent that early points in a message provide a level of comparison, other message-points will be judged as less favorable when preceded by acknowledged favorable points than when they are preceded by message points generally felt to be unfavorable. This would suggest that when a message must contain a number of message-points, with various levels of desirability (none of which are necessarily undesirable), it would be better to leave the strongest points for last, in order to benefit from positive comparisions with the earlier message points.

Message Point Weighting

When a number of message points are presented in a single communication, certain inconsistencies may be perceived by the receiver. When such inconsistencies are noticed by the receiver, the receiver may tend to give certain message points less weight than others in the overall evaluation of the message. To the extent that order of presentation is effected by such weighting, one would expect a primacy effect. This assumes that a typical receiver will expect the source to present the most effective or important points first in a communication, and hence ascribe greater weight to them. If certain points occurring later in the communication appear inconsistent with the earlier message points, the receiver is likely to discount them, or even disregard them completely.

Forgetting

A final and obvious factor effecting order of presentation in a communication message is length, and the likelihood of the receiver forgetting. While this may be less of a concern with advertising communications (owing to their generally short length), when one is considering media placement for a message some consideration of persistence effect is noted. In a study by Miller and Campbell (1959), two messages were presented to subjects, one immediately after the other (analogous in advertising to back-to-back commercials or contiguous print advertisements), but no response was elicited until one week later. After the week, a strong primacy effect was evident. While no really satisfactory explanation was advanced for this finding, it does seem to suggest that message points presented at the end of a communication will tend to be forgotten more than those presented at the beginning.

ORDER EFFECTS ON SPECIFIC APPEALS

In most communications, each message contains a number of points or arguments in favor of the advocated position that differ in strength. A question arises in constructing the order of presentation as to whether one should start with the strongest argument or leave the most important point(s) to last—what one would call an anticlimax versus a climax appeal order. Unfortunately, as McGuire (1969a) points out, while a number of studies have addressed this point, the results are quite ambiguous. Considering the effect of order on advertising response objectives, it is not surprising that no one order of presentation in this regard stands out as the most efficacious. Because attention is generally highest at the beginning of a communication, if the strongest arguments are placed first, the likelihood of them being attended to should increase; and the earlier one attracts attention, the longer a receiver is motivated to attend to the message (McGuire 1957). Comprehension of the message, too, should be enhanced by an early presentation of the strongest message points. Work in the area of serial-positioning effects in learning indicate that material is best learned when placed at the beginning of a message (a primacy effect); the next best position is at the end of the message (a recency effect); the worst position for learning is in the middle. In other words, for message comprehension, one should present the strongest arguments as early as possible in the communication, avoiding what Bettinghaus (1973) has described as a pyramidal order, in which the most important message point is found in the middle. To maximize an attitudinal response, however, McGuire (1969a) feels a climax order is more effective. Once again, we are confronted with a situation in which in order to maximize persuasion one tends to minimize reception.

DeLozier (1976) goes beyond these main effects, and finds some useful generalizations from interaction effects. Specifically, he feels that when a receiver has a low level of interest in the material being presented, an anticlimax order tends to be most effective; but when a receiver's interest is high, a climax order creating a recency effect becomes more efficacious. Following Hovland, Janis, and Kelley (1953), he concludes that when receiver interest is low, greater attention potential is required, and hence an anticlimax order occasioning primacy effects. When interest is high, however, attention is less of a consideration, and a climax order becomes more effective, because the expectation created by the earlier, weaker arguments are exceeded, once the stronger arguments are presented. To the extent that these conclusions are justified, it would seem to indicate that most advertising communication, due to its generally low level of product and brand interest, should be executed with the strongest arguments or message points first. This would then be likely to maximize the potential for message reception, although, as we have seen, it would not be as likely to maximize persuasibility.

A similar dilemma occurs when considering the question of whether a conclusion (assuming it is to be explicitly drawn for the receiver) is most effectively placed early in the message or left until last. Each ordering has some advantages and disadvantages. An advantage of placing the conclusion first, much as newspaper journalists are encouraged to do in reporting a news story, is that it increases the comprehension of the message. On the other hand, when the conclusion is presented first, there is a chance of losing the attention of those receivers mutually opposed to the argument, the group one is usually most interested in reaching to effect a positive response. Also, by presenting the conclusion first, a significant source bias is introduced, which tends to increase the likelihood of the source being perceived as intending to persuade, with a subsequent decrease in the probability of the receiver attending to the message. Since it is frequently more important to maintain attention than to attempt maximizing persuasibility, one could conclude that generally it would be more effective to place the conclusion first. Mediating this conclusion, however, must be an appreciation for the obvious implication of the interactive effects at work: such variables as initial receiver hostility and its effect on source credibility, the complexity of the message, and individual receiver differences (such as intelligence, familiarity with message material), all occasion interaction effects with the ordering of a conclusion. As a consequence of these interaction effects, it becomes even more important to ensure a thorough understanding of one's target receivers if one wishes to effect maximum advertising response from the placement of a message's conclusion.

Beyond this general problem of where the conclusion of a message should be placed for optimum effectiveness is the more specific problem of ordering the individual message points. When a number of message-points are to be included in a persuasive message, inevitably some are more important or desirable (to the receiver) than others. A question then arises as to the optimal ordering for the message points within a message in order to maximize the desired advertising response. On the basis of learning theory principles, McGuire (1957) has shown that there is greater total agreement for all of the message points presented if the most desirable ones are given first. He argues that if the early content of a message rewards the receiver with an agreeable position, the receiver is more likely to pay attention to the remainder of the message; while if an undesirable point is made initially, the receiver will tend to avoid paying attention to the message, thus never really attending to the more favorable or acceptable message points that arise later. In fact, McGuire (1957) did find that presenting the more agreeable message points first produced significantly more attitude change as well as increased learning of their content. A frequent situation in advertising communications which would occasion attention to this ordering question is the inclusion of a high price or particularly difficult purchase or use requirement (such as traveling a long distance to a vacation resort) in a message that is otherwise agreeable. McGuire's results would seem to indicate that such possibly disagreeable points should be left until the end of the message.

McGuire (1969a) mentions that a number of studies support this "agreeable first" strategy, finding that the receiver tends to ascribe a positive valence to the source of a message when the receiver notes the more agreeable message points first, and that this association carries over through the more disagreeable message points presented later. But following Crespi (1942), one could conclude that if a disagreeable point were presented last in a persuasive message, it could tend to be perceived as even more disagreeable than otherwise, having followed the agreeable message points. It would appear that one must weigh the advantages of increased attention (and with it comprehension) against the possibility that the disagreeable message points will be intensified. It is obviously important to ensure that any heightened salience of disagreeable message points will not minimize the advantage gained through increased reception.

Analogous to whether one should present agreeable or disagreeable message points first in a communication is whether, assuming a refutational strategy, it is better to refute the opposition argument before or after presenting your own position. To the degree that a receiver is unaware of the opposing argument, Janis and Feirabend (1957) predict that it is better to present one's own position before refuting the opposition's. With more aware receivers, Anderson (1959) predicts that it is more effective to present the opposition argument first. This could have the effect of positioning the source in a more favorable light, by making the source appear more knowledgeable or even more trustworthy, although you are forewarning the receiver you will be trying to persuade.

GRAMMATICAL CONTEXT

One final comment on order effects is appropriate. Since most communication efforts (particularly advertising communication) are built upon sentences, the importance attached to the message might be suggested by its grammatical structure, as well as by the position of the sentences within the message. Consider a typical comparative claim, in which competitive products are described as "not as good as us, but good." It may be that receivers are more likely to infer that the competitive product is "good" than would be the case if the claim "good, but not as good as us" were made. The importance attributed to the words *following* "but" in that case would have received a greater weight than the words preceding "but," and, hence, a recency effect.

In an exploratory study of order effects within grammatical context, Wyer (1973) considered both consistent and inconsistent pairs of favorable and unfavorable adjectives. Along with varying the order of presentation for the adjective pairs, he also varied the grammatical context in which the adjectives appeared. Under a controlled condition, the adjectives were presented side by side, and subjects were asked to estimate the likableness of a person so described. In the test conditions, adjectives were presented either in the form "X is —— and ——" or "X is —— but ——," with instructions to estimate the likableness of X. Results indicate a recency effect for the control condition, uneffected by inconsistency between adjective pairs. When the adjectives were presented in the sentence format connected by "and," primacy effects increased when the adjective pairs were consistent, while recency effects increased when the adjective pairs were inconsistent. In the second test, in which adjective pairs were connected by "but," the opposite result was observed; recency effects increased when the adjective pairs were consistent, while primacy effects increased when the adjective pairs were inconsistent.

The effects of connecting adjectives by "and" are interesting to consider in light of the Wyer and Schwartz (1969) study of context effects mentioned earlier. Recall that they found primacy effects for individual message points only when the message point being considered was inconsistent in meaning with the overall context of the message. It may be that a similar effect occurs when "and" is used to connect two adjectives (or by extension, two message points). When two adjectives are inconsistent, the favorableness of the second may become displaced toward that of the first, resulting in an overall evaluation based upon the adjective pair shifting toward the favorableness of the first adjective presented, producing a primacy effect. On the other hand, when adjectives are consistent, the evaluation of the second may displace away from that of the first, resulting in an overall evaluation based upon the revised component judgment being relatively closer to the judgment of the second adjective, producing a recency effect.

Considering adjectives or message points connected by "but," although it may be intuitively logical to expect an increased emphasis on the second adjective or message point, Wyer's (1973) results would suggest that this is only the case when the adjectives involved are inconsistent, and the first adjective appears to be discounted. He speculates that if the message points are consistent, "but" seems to increase the relative importance of the first message point. Consider the two adjectives "efficient" and "ugly." It is quite possible that these two attributes could both be used in describing the same product in an advertisement, presented as "efficient but ugly." Following Wyer, we would expect this claim to be encoded by receivers as meaning "efficient" is a more critical characteristic than "ugly," while a descriptive claim of "ugly but efficient" could create the opposite impression.

Another possible explanation offered by Wyer (1974) is that the relative influence of adjectives connected by a conjunction depends in part upon whether the use of the conjunction in the message context is consistent with consumer usage. In everyday conversations, one usually finds "and" connecting semantically consistent pieces of information, while "but" is more often used to connect points with at least partially inconsistent implications. As Wyer (1973) found, recency effects are substantially greater when conjunctions are used in a usual as opposed to an unusual way. Atypical uses of conjunctions in communication may produce a tendency for the receiver to discount the second piece of information presented in a message. Further implication of grammatical context on advertising response is considered in some detail in the next section.

Part III
Message Content

The content of a persuasive message involves much more than the execution of a strategy in a creative way, for any strategy may be executed in an infinite number of ways; and depending on the manner of execution, a message will be more or less correctly interpreted by the receiver. In this part of the chapter, we will be dealing with the perception of message content, discussing first vocabulary, and then the structure of sentences within a message and how a receiver's reasoning process mediates individual comprehension of those sentences or combinations of sentences.

The relationship between the linguistic or grammatical structure of a sentence and the psychological effects occurring when the information contained in that sentence is processed by the receiver has only recently begun to interest psychologists, spawning the study of "psycholinguistics." While it is not our purpose to go into any great detail discussing various theories of psycholinguistics (the interested reader is referred to the works of Neisser [1967]; Fodor, Bever, and Garrett [1974]; and Glucksberg and Danks [1975]), we shall, nonetheless, borrow heavily from such theories in presenting the implication of sentence structure and reasoning processes on message comprehension and memory.

Finally, we will consider the visual content of advertising, present in all but radio commercials. Drawing upon recent research by psychologists, as well as a few advertising researchers, three visual components are explored: product symbols, pictures, and the dynamic system of symbols which is television.

While this chapter may at times seem tedious or difficult, the reader's patience should be rewarded with a new appreciation of the impact words, and how they are arranged as sentences, have upon understanding advertising and other communication messages.

LEXICAL STRUCTURE

It is almost too obvious to suggest that when one is writing advertising it is important to use words so that they will be understood. Yet, the meaning of words and how they should be used is by no means obvious. Some words have more than one meaning, others quite precise meanings, still others opposite meanings. Advertising will only be effective if it is attended to, decoded, and encoded properly. This can only be accomplished by message copy which indeed will be understood by the receiver in the manner intended by the advertiser.

Word Meaning

In this section we shall approach the problem of message meaning from the point of view of word-sense relations. A number of familiar word constructions, such as synonymous and antonymous, as well as a few more abstract relationships, such as hyponyms or relational opposites, go into making up something known as semantic components in word meaning. Semantic components are known by semanticists as a part or aspect of the sense of an expression: e.g. "male" is a semantic component of "man" (specifically a hyponym). For some semanticists (for example, Katz 1972), the notion of semantic components provide a good formal reason for thinking of word sense as in fact consisting of

TABLE 4.2

Semantic Components and Their Impact on Advertising Messages

Semantic Component	Definition	Importance to Advertising
Synonymy	sameness of meaning	are they interpreted as interchangeable or as communicating different shades of meaning
Homonymy or Polysemy	two different words with the same "shape"; or one word with different meanings	can cause confusion in comprehension and should be limited to their most common meaning
Antonymy	oppositeness of meaning	negatively modified adjectives are *less* desirable than an antonym of a different root word
Hyponymy	the notion of inclusion	word context must be easily understood
Relational Opposites	word pairs which exhibit the reversal of relationship between items	be certain of the implied opposite

semantic components (which may seem a bit circular). But considering them in advertising, however, one need only be aware of their usefulness in accounting for meaning relations among words within a receiver's vocabulary. The five major semantic components within lexical structure are listed in Table 4.2, and discussed in some detail below.

Synonymy

Synonymy is used to mean "sameness of meaning" between words. However, it could be maintained that actually there are no real synonyms, since no two words ever have exactly the same meaning. This points out the importance of realizing the "common" usage of a word (a theme emphasized throughout this book), and not using a synonym for purely stylistic reasons. Unfortunately, many advertising copywriters will use a synonym in place of a previously used word in a message purely for stylistic reasons.

There is some literature, however, that suggests that this practice might have a debilitating effect upon message comprehension. The only reason to use a synonym, according to many authors on the art of writing (cf. Perrin 1965) is when different shades of meaning are intended. The arbitrary use of a synonym to avoid repetition will only achieve an artificiality that can create confusion in message comprehension. In research studying the effect of semantic encoding of words in memory, a number of experimenters (for example, Anisfeld and Knapp 1968; Grossman and Eagle 1970; Kausler and Settle 1973) found that when people were asked to memorize a list of words, they often mistakenly recorded synonyms in place of the words originally learned. This suggests that even when synonyms are specifically used by a copywriter to indicate shades of meaning, his intent may be frustrated by a misinterpretation.

TABLE 4.3

Synonyms in Advertising

Headline	Synonyms
Europe begins with *me*	me-airline
We're shining/*bright* to/Amsterdam	bright-good service
The *well-bread*/Tartan sportcoat	well-bread-traditional
The *black sheep* of liquors	black sheep-"wicked"

Depending upon the receiver and the message context in which a synonym may be used, a receiver may interpret synonyms as interchangeable or as communicating different shades of meaning. One cannot be sure without testing to determine what shading of meaning is communicated, how a receiver will interpret a synonym. Unless one knows, it is best to avoid them when possible. Examples of synonyms from actual print advertising headlines are shown in Table 4.3.

Finally, in creating advertising, one must also guard against violating the evaluative or emotive (affect) meanings of words. While the basic meaning of words (cognitive meaning) may appear synonymous, there could be an obvious emotive reaction: such words as, for example, statesman versus politician; hide versus conceal; thrifty versus economical versus stingy.

Homonymy or Polysemy

Homonymy or polysemy is used to identify two different words with the same "shape" (homonymy) or one word with different meanings (polysemy). While sameness of meaning may be difficult to deal with, one would expect difference of meaning to be easy to handle. But even here there can be problems. First of all, one can't clearly distinguish whether two meanings are actually the same or different; nor can one determine exactly how many meanings a word might have unless some communication testing is done. Consider a word like "eat."

If one word form has several meanings, it is not always clear whether one would say that it is an example of polysemy (that is, one word with several meanings), or homonymy (several words with the same "shape"). Consider the word free, for example. Free, if considered as an example of polysemy could confuse the reader of an advertisement if the copywriter were to use the single word "FREE!" in a headline to mean "guiltless or innocent," rather than the more common meaning, "at no cost." As an example of homonymy, on the other hand, suppose the copywriter meant the headline "FREE!" to mean "to relieve or rid yourself of something that confines" (for example, in an advertisement for women's sportswear), rather than the more common "at no cost" meaning.

The point of this seemingly pedantic exercise is merely to underscore the potential that exists for confusing a receiver when advertising gets too "cute" with words that may be interpreted in several ways. And, in advertising, this problem is compounded, because people do not make the same distinctions in writing and speech. Some words are spelled the same but pronounced differently (homography) while others are spelled differently but pronounced the same (homophony). The potential for miscommunication in broadcast advertising should be obvious.

There is not much research reported in the literature indicating this need for making sure the intended meaning of a word is a familiar one and that the

TABLE 4.4

Homonyms in Advertising

Headline	Product
Easily comprehended:	
Quality never goes out of *style*	men's sportswear
The legendary *spirit*	liquor
Difficult to comprehend:	
The longer you stand/in line at a bank/[1]	bank service
The more interest/you *lose*	
Go out and *hug* a road/you like	automobile
We bring it back *alive*	stereo receiver
Our glass *reflects* the beauty/of saving energy	commercial window glass
A *concern*/for the future	corporate image
We have news in *store* for you	department store
For people/who like their water *dry*	vermouth

[1]*Note*: slash mark indicates separate line of copy in headline.

context of the sentence makes the meaning very clear (cf. Conrad 1974; Marcel and Steel 1973). Because semantic features are strongly encoded, work by Winograd and Geis (1974) has shown that when receivers see or hear a homonym, it immediately evokes the several meanings of that word. This obviously increases processing time and can lead to errors in comprehension. On the other hand, if a pretest indicates both meanings are known to be comparable, such an ambiguity could stimulate reversal.

If homonyms are to be used, the context of use within the advertising can be manipulated to enhance the probability of it being correctly encoded. A number of contextual clues can be included in the advertising copy to enhance the intended meaning. For example, a definition of the word could be worked into the copy, an example could be included, or a contextual description offered. Table 4.4 offers some examples of homonyms from actual headlines in print advertising, and should illustrate for the reader the potential problems in comprehension.

Antonymy

Antonymy is used for oppositeness of meaning. Words that are opposite in meaning are antonyms. While antonymy is often thought of as the opposite of synonymy, the status of the two are actually quite different. Osgood, Succi, and

TABLE 4.5

Impact of Antonyms on Message Comprehension

Condition	Example	Impact
different root	The dessert with a taste *surprise*	easiest to comprehend
negative prefix	The dessert with a taste *unexpected*	easier to comprehend
negative "not"	The dessert with a taste *not expected*	least easy to comprehend

Tannenbaum (1957), in their classic work on "semantic differential" scaling, found that antonyms may be classified into three major, universal categories of affective or connotative meaning: evaluative (represented by antonyms such as good-bad, happy-sad, beautiful-ugly); potency (antonyms such as strong-weak, brave-cowardly, hard-soft); and activity (antonyms such as fast-slow, tense-relaxed, hot-cold).

In considering antonyms and their impact on advertising messages, it is useful to understand that receivers are more disposed toward making favorable rather than unfavorable evaluations (Boucher and Osgood 1969). Perhaps because of this, there are many more favorable than unfavorable adjectives in, not only English, but almost all languages. While it is possible to create an antonym for a favorable adjective by adding a negative modifier, the resulting word is generally more difficult to use and comprehend than an antonym from an independent root. For example, if a copywriter were seeking an antonym for the word happy, sad should be preferred to unhappy.

Work by Salter and Haycock (1972) tends to support this notion. They asked subjects to think of synonyms for favorable adjectives and three antonyms: for example, if happy were the favorable adjective, a prefix was added for the antonym unhappy, not happy was the second, and a different root word, such as sad was the third. It was found that people were able to think of more synonyms for the favorable adjectives than any of their antonyms, followed by the antonyms with a different root. The antonyms created by the addition of a prefix or "not" were tied for least number of perceived synonyms.

When a different root antonym is difficult to imagine, the copywriter should probably use a prefix antonym rather than use "not." Sherman (1973) found that sentence comprehension was significantly faster and more accurate with prefix adjectives than with "not" adjectives. In terms of message processing, a sentence containing a prefix adjective reverses only the meaning of the word, while a "not" adjective requires the negative of the entire sentence. For example, a headline reading "The dessert with a taste unexpected" requires a two-step negation, but only for the antonym "expected." If the headline had been written "The dessert with a taste not expected," a receiver would first process the entire headline as "The dessert with a taste expected," and then negate the entire sentence. Overall, of course, it would have been better to use an antonym with a different root such as "The dessert with a taste surprise."

In order to maximize one's probability of correct message comprehension, these findings would seem to indicate that copy in advertising should avoid negatively modified adjectives, and use antonyms with different roots. Table 4.5 reviews this implication.

Hyponymy and Relational Opposites

Hyponymy and relational opposites are the names used for the notion of "inclusion" (hyponymy) and word pairs that exhibit the reversal of a relationship between items (relational opposites). These two semantic components are discussed only for the sake of completeness. While they offer additional insight into the relationships among words, they offer little direct application to the creation of advertising messages, with the exception of possible source attributions (for example, a sports figure as an "expert").

Some words do happen to be more "inclusive" than others. Lyons (1963) has termed this relationship between words that refer to a class and those words included in that class as hyponymy. Brown and green are colors; but beige and sienna are "brown." Complicating this "inclusive" relationship from a communications viewpoint is the fact that the same word could show up in several places in a hyponymous hierarchy. A copywriter again must be sure the meaning of such words are clear within the context of an advertisement. The word "man," for example, represents both a class and a component within that class:

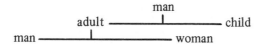

The idea of relational opposites, or "converseness," as Lyons (1963) referred to it, is a key to interference in reasoning (which is discussed in much greater detail later in this chapter). Examples of relational opposites would include: give-receive; buy-sell; husband-wife. One can see the obvious inference inherent in the use of one of these words. If A sells to B it follows that B buys from A; if A is B's husband, B is A's wife.

In the creation of advertising messages, one must keep in mind that an opposite will be implied when a relational opposite is used. The message point "our product is a cut *above* the others" implies other products are below our product. Fine, but one wouldn't want to say that a particular item in a product line is a cut above all others, because that would imply other items in the line were "below" the advertised item. Even if that were, in fact, the case, the advertiser would be unlikely to encourage bringing it up.

Word Usage

In the execution of advertising copy, the copywriter has the broad expanse of vocabulary to draw upon. Within this enormous set of words, given a particular circumstance, some words are better to use than others. Two word variables lead to a better understanding of which words are more likely to help generate the desired advertising response: the frequency of a word's use in everyday language, and whether it is concrete or abstract.

Word Frequency

The more frequently a word is used in print media, the more familiar that word should be to a receiver. It should follow, then, that the most familiar words would be more easily understood and remembered. In fact, there is an abundance of research in the psycholinguistic literature to support this notion. For example, Carroll (1971) reports very strong correlations between word frequency and familiarity—on the order of $r = .90+$.

Since word familiarity and word frequency are closely related, it should follow that perception is also related to word frequency. In perceptual recognition tasks,* it has repeatedly been found that high-frequency words are heard, read, and repeated faster and with fewer errors than are lower frequency words (cf. Paivio and O'Neil 1970). The implication of these findings for advertising is clear: higher frequency words used in advertising copy will result in a message more likely to be heard or read, and understood, by the receiver.

Perception of words has been found to be a good indication of how quickly those words will be cognitively processed. Since high-frequency words are perceived more quickly, it follows that they, too, should be easily and more quickly processed. Hence, advertising that uses more familiar words in its copy should be processed more easily. Additionally, the use of high-frequency words in advertising should tend to increase recall of that advertising. Most researchers have found a positive relationship between word frequency and recall in both short-

---

*As described by Paivio (1971), a subject is typically asked to read or repeat a message they have just been exposed to for the first time.

term and long-term memory tasks. Postman (1970) found that under both a short-term recall condition (30 seconds) and a long-term condition (7 days), high-frequency words were recalled significantly more often than either medium-frequency or low-frequency words; no difference was found between the recall of medium-frequency and low-frequency words.

The easier it is for a receiver to decode an advertising message, the more likely the receiver will be to encode the message as the desired advertising response. Once again, one finds that high-frequency words lead to an easier time of decoding messages. Perhaps this follows because high-frequency words correlate so highly with meaningfulness (cf. Klare 1968). Obviously, the more meaningful the words in an advertising message are to a receiver, the easier it will be to comprehend that message. A receiver in attempting to decode an advertising message must deal with both a denotative or explicit meaning of the words and connotative or implied meaning. Lowenthal (1969) has demonstrated that denotative meanings of high-frequency words are much easier to decode. There is plenty of evidence that word frequency may be related to the connotative meaning of words. For example, studies by Dixon and Dixon (1964) and Zajonc (1968) have indicated that low-frequency words are more likely than high-frequency words to be associated with negative feelings. This finding reinforces much of what was presented in the previous section on word meaning, where use of familiar (that is, high-frequency) words in advertising copy was encouraged.

Another consideration in the frequency of word use is the multiple meanings of some words. As pointed out by Slobin (1971), the more frequently a word is used, the more meanings it seems to have. Look in any dictionary and you will see many more listings under common than under uncommon words. For example, in one dictionary the word "case" has 23 meanings, "free" has 38, "take" 69 meanings, and so on. Given the large number of meanings for high-frequency words, in order to accurately comprehend a message, receivers must have a special way of attending to specific meanings of potentially ambiguous words, on the basis of how they are used. The word "taste," for example, has two clearly different meanings within the context of the sentences: "People have taste" and "Desserts have taste." When a receiver interprets these sentences, the correct meaning must be based upon the other words in the sentences, because there are no syntactic or positional cues. In fact, the syntactic structure of the two sentences is identical. This again underscores the point made repeatedly in the last section: words in advertising must be used in copy reflecting their common meaning if one is to maximize the potential for the correct advertising response.

Concrete versus Abstract Words

The attribute of concreteness versus abstractness in words provides an underlying dimension mediating the extent to which an object can be experienced by the senses. Concrete words are those that have clear, "real world" referents as opposed to vague, abstract referent. It is easier for most people, for example, to experience visual imagery in response to the word "beer" than to the word "beauty."

Many researchers, going all the way back to Stoke (1929), have demonstrated that concrete words are easier to learn than abstract words. Learning of the simplest kind, in which memorizing a single item involves a single transition, may be thought of as an all-or-nothing process. However, learning (in this case, recall) is not generally or even usually an all-or-nothing process. More often it involves a two-stage learning process (see Figure 4.2).

In two-stage learning, a word will initially be in an unlearned state and remain there until the first stage of learning is accomplished. If the probability of learning in this first stage is high, it will be easy; if it is low, learning will be more difficult and a number of trials (or exposures, in an advertising sense) may be needed before it is complete. The second stage of learning can occur on the same trial as the transfer from the first stage, but more often an intermediate state is reached first. From this intermediate state, additional trials (or exposure) are necessary before the second stage of learning is complete.

The reason for this discussion of learning in a section on the concreteness of words is that Humphreys and Yuille (in an unpublished study reported in Greeno et al. [1978]) found that with concrete words, learning occurred in essentially an all-or-nothing fashion, but a two-stage learning model was required for abstract word stimuli. An interpretation of these findings could be that concrete words, once a receiver succeeds in storing a representation of the word, are easier to retrieve, and, as a result, further learning is not needed. Following this line, advertising messages with concrete words would involve only one stage of learning, because the second would occur with a probability of 1.0 once the first stage was reached. As a result, concrete words are easlier to learn than abstract words.

Verbal stimuli in advertising are usually thought of in terms of initiating a verbal comprehension response of some sort; the verbal stimuli as a word, sentence, or large copy unit, is decoded and understood. But, verbal stimuli may simultaneously evoke visual imagery responses (as discussed later in this chapter). Indeed, the imagery value of a verbal stimulus has consistently been shown to have a more powerful influence on verbal learning than verbal comprehension factors, such as meaningfulness of the words (Paivio 1969, 1971; Hulse, Deese, and Egeth 1975). And Paivio, Yuille, and Madigan (1968) have demonstrated a powerful association between imagery arousing capacity and the concreteness or abstractness of words. In their study of 925 nouns, concreteness and imagery correlated at $r = .85$. This should really not be surprising, because both imagery arousing capacity and concreteness include degree of sensory experience as components of their operational definition.

In advertising, if verbally comprehended stimuli are recognized as favorable

FIGURE 4.2

Two Stage Word Learning Model

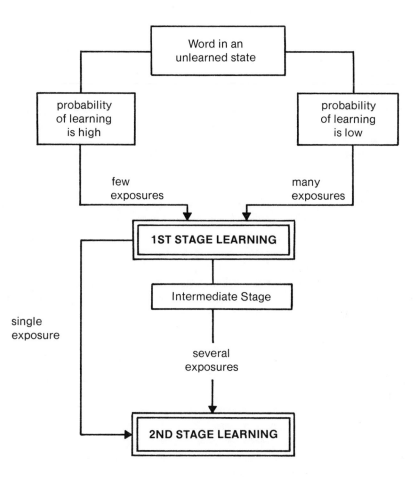

(for example, the word "good" versus the word "bad"), verbal reinforcement will occur; and likewise, if a visual imagery response is favorable (for example, a pleasant, perhaps personally involving mental picture), visual reinforcement will occur. There is a long history of evidence, beginning with a classic experiment by Staats and Staats (1957), that favorably evaluated words can function as verbal reinforcers. By associating objects or other words (for example, the name of a product) with these verbal reinforcers, attitudinal responses toward the object or word can be increased. Advertisers, of course, have always known this implicitly—hence their predilection for highly favorable words, such as "new" or "free," in copy. However, it has been shown by Paivio (1971) that the verbal learning superiority of concrete or high imagery value words occurs, regardless of their connotative value; that is, "good" words are learned just as well as "bad" words, providing their visual imagery values or concreteness are equivalent. This, at first, would seem to indicate that verbal reinforcement is not involved in verbal learning, but that some type of visual reinforcement, mediated through the word's evoked image, may be.

However, "learning" in verbal learning and imagery studies has invariably been defined in terms of recognition or recall. This can be contrasted with the type of affective learning involved in the Staats-type experiments, in which the dependent variable is an attitudinal or evaluative response. An important question for advertising is whether the imagery value of verbal stimuli relates to affective learning. Paivio's (1971) finding that imagery independently increases recognition and recall cannot be taken as evidence that imagery could also increase attitude, because the latter type of dependent variable has not been employed in imagery studies. In contrast with verbal learning researchers, who try to select connotatively neutral verbal stimuli, advertisers deliberately select affectively loaded verbal stimuli to describe products. If these affectively loaded stimuli not only produce verbal reinforcement (of the good type) but also visual reinforcement (of the pleasant, personally involving type of mental picture), then such stimuli may constitute extra reinforcement for affectively learned responses, such as attitude. A study by Rossiter and Percy (1978) has, in fact, demonstrated a positive relationship between concrete copy oriented advertising and a more favorable attitude toward the product advertised.

Overall, the literature on concrete and abstract words leads to the unmistakable conclusion that concrete words are more effective than abstract words in communication. Concrete words are better remembered, tend to be more meaningful to receivers, and, as a result, are better understood. The effectiveness of concrete words in comparison with abstract words, in increasing retention, has been found in both recognition and recall studies (cf. Paivio 1971). The whole notion of imagery just discussed helps one understand why concrete words seem to do so well in memory tasks. With this in mind, it would seem that advertising employing mnemonic devices along with concrete words in the copy should be exceptionally well recalled. Many studies in the psychology literature support this conclusion (for example, Bull and Wittrock 1973; Peterson and McGee 1974), as well as advertising-specific research done for such products as Chuck Wagon dog food, which employs perhaps the best known mnemonic in advertising.

SENTENCE STRUCTURE

Sentence meaning depends on more than just the component words making up that sentence or the order in which they are presented; it is also dependent on the sentence's overall structure. Current developments in linguistics have made it especially clear that sentences are far more than the simple sum of their parts. For example, most sentences are far too long for a receiver to wait until hearing or reading in their entirety before trying to interpret the meaning. The receiver must begin to formulate the meaning before the sentence is over; otherwise the object of the sentence would come too late to be of much help in interpreting the full meaning of the sentence. Read through several ads and notice how many are using short, "bullet"-type sentences, rather than long, involved sentences (such as the ones you have been reading in this text).

The synthesis involved in processing sentences would seem to be "local" at first, establishing the structure of a sentence a few words at a time. Each of these pieces is then integrated into a larger pattern, as the succeeding information and the receiver's cognitive resources permit. The truly remarkable aspect of this process is that, given the almost limitless possible interpretations of various groups of words (as opposed to single words), most people will come up with the same meaning for any one sentence. This suggests that a common set of cues exist for most people, which initiate this process in their mind when they hear or read a sentence. While one is not logically required to assume grammatical structure is directly relevant to cognition, there is considerable evidence to show that it does seem to govern perceptual segmentation and sustain recall (Neisser 1967). The importance of this to the creation of persuasive communication, particularly advertising, should be obvious. The ways in which sentences are composed for ad copy will bear directly on how a receiver will respond to that advertising.

Content Ambiguity

A receiver is usually successful in processing one part of a sentence before hearing or reading the rest. Following a procedure that tends to assign meaning to words used in the early copy first, the receiver utilizes experience, analyzing syntactic and semantic relations among the words, and integrating this information as quickly as possible in order to minimize the load on short-term memory. Sometimes, however, this strategy can go wrong. Consider the sentence:

John insisted on taking the plane to New York
even though it was quite heavy.

The phrase "taking the plane" is ambiguous in isolation, and, in fact, would most likely be interpreted to mean flying on an airplane rather than carrying a wood-working tool (Wason and Johnson-Laird 1972).

The way in which one interprets sentences (that is, by determining the meaning of sentence parts early) would lead to a false impression of the sentence's meaning initially, requiring subsequent correction once the entire sentence has been heard or read. But what if the receiver is less attentive to the end of the sentence? This is certainly possible, and it should alert the advertising copywriter to avoid ambiguous sentence parts, particularly in the development of important message points.

While the above example may seem a bit obvious and extreme, somewhat ambiguous headlines are not uncommon in advertising. Consider the following:

"Enjoy Europe's favorite water sport—Scotch and water"
"Not just another low calorie dessert, it's a low-calorie (Brand Name)"
"A low-calorie dessert with taste isn't fiction anymore"

Each of these examples represent copy adapted from the headlines of actual print advertisements. In each of these illustrations, a hearing or reading of the entire sentence is necessary for full and correct meaning, and, even then, a receiver may have to work hard for the correct interpretation. In the first example, the copywriter has used a play on words with the word "water"—but what if the receiver is uninterested in Europe or water sports? Chances are the receiver will not remain with the sentence past the initial (and for purposes of this message, incorrect) interpretation. In the second example, "not just another low calorie dessert" implies the product is not another low calorie dessert; but, in fact, that is exactly what the product is. And, in the last example, the advertiser is relying on a negative evaluation of all low-calorie desserts, coupled with an allusion to fiction, or an additional implication that other taste claims for low-calorie dessert products have been false; this certainly requires a good deal of effort in piecing together the expected interpretation of "*our* low-calorie dessert tastes great." In most advertising exposures, a receiver is unlikely to fully decode such copy.

When you are dealing with portions of sentences such as these, which may be interpreted in two or more ways, the resulting ambiguity could take one of two forms (or even a combination of the two): (1) *lexical ambiguity*, in which case a word in a sentence or a particular message point may be interpreted in more than one way; or (2) *syntactic ambiguity*, in which case a sentence itself can be organized in different ways. In either case, ambiguity will increase the difficulty of processing the message. In the case of lexical ambiguity, for example, the claim "a product with taste" may refer to either flavor or high standards.

The sentence would be expected to impose a relatively greater load on short-term memory, especially if subsequent copy made clear that the less usual frequent meaning of "high standards" was correct.

In cases of syntactic ambiguity, such as the phrase, "for racing engines," the word "racing" can function as either a verb or as a modifier. More than one interpretation would be possible. Suppose the ad was for a special 20W50 motor oil designed for high-performance engines. The receiver could understand that phrase to mean the oil was for engines used for racing, not for (the advertiser-intended reference to) fast, high-performance automobile engines. As a result, if the advertising is to be correctly received, both meanings must be remembered or referred to, once additional information is offered. As a result, the receiver is called upon to do more work than usual in processing the message, increasing the likelihood of misinterpretation or disinterest. If possible, as we discussed earlier, this should be avoided in persuasive communication.

This whole question of a receiver's ability to correctly handle ambiguous thoughts lies in the ability or inclination to retain alternative interpretations in short-term memory for final encoding of sentence meaning. In a study by Foss, Bever, and Silver (1968), they hypothesized that a receiver generally makes or retains only one interpretation of an ambiguous phrase, and that the one retained is the most likely or probable interpretation. This was tested in an experiment in which receivers were asked to decide upon the truth of a sentence relative to a pictured event (analogous to print advertising, for example). A sentence was presented, followed by a picture. If the sentence and picture matched, a "yes" response was given; if they didn't match, a "no" response was made. The dependent criterion was the response time for each sentence. For example, the sentence "The boy is looking up the street" is usually interpreted as a boy gazing toward one end of a street or road. When this sentence was followed by a picture of a boy standing in a road, a "yes" response occurred quickly. When the picture following the sentence showed a boy holding a map as if looking up an address, also a correct response, the time required to make the "yes" response was significantly greater. These results tend to confirm the hypothesis that the more probable interpretation of a sentence is the only one made and retained. When the less probable interpretation was required by the picture, the receiver appeared to backtrack in order to come up with an alternative interpretation, and then to decide if the picture and sentence match. If both interpretations had been carried in short-term memory, the response times in both cases should have been the same.

The implication of this finding for advertising communication is critical. It would appear that even when the visual elements in advertising reinforce a less probable interpretation of an ambiguous sentence, the overall effect on message processing is retarding. Recalling our first ambiguous example above, the ambiguity of the copy "Enjoy Europe's favorite water sport—Scotch and water" was reinforced visually by a full-page picture of a girl floating on a raft in a swimming pool. While such a play on words may be thought of as creative and interesting, here we have a case of both the copy and the visual elements implying the probable meaning of "water sport," when what was meant is the unlikely meaning of drinking! The receiver is quite obviously being asked to do too much in interpreting the meaning of this advertisement. One would expect the resulting impact of overloading the receiver's short-term memory to have a negative or null effect on communication and advertising response.

Content Comprehension

Looking next at sentence comprehension in advertising, it is generally thought that a sentence has been understood or comprehended when the receiver is able to use the information conveyed by the sentence in some appropriate way. Two considerations have been studied, which linguists and psychologists have shown to affect sentence comprehension: (1) whether a sentence is affirmative or negative, and (2) whether a sentence is presented in the active or passive voice.

In an experiment reported by Wason (1961), subjects were presented with simple affirmative or negative sentences and were asked to decide if each was true or false. The sentences used numbers ranging from two to nine in four types of sentences: (1) true affirmative of the type that states "four is an even number," (2) false affirmative of the type that states "three is an even number," (3) true negative of the type that states "four is not an odd number," and (4) false negative of the type that states "three is not an odd number." Results indicated that subjects took longer and made more errors with negative sentences than with positive statements. While this question of negative assertions is discussed in more detail in later sections, it appears from these findings that negative sentences are more difficult to process than affirmative sentences, primarily because of the conceptual way in which they were presented. One could conjecture that, in more usual situations, negative sentences could be processed as easily as affirmative sentences. In fact, Wason (1965) has shown this to be the case. As a result, in creating advertising or other persuasive communication, one could, no doubt, use negative sentences when appropriate, but only if the way they are presented is in a manner common to the way in which a receiver might be expected to use the same sentence (for example, "not just an ordinary Scotch").

Similar results have been found in experiments dealing with active versus passive sentence voice (following McMahon 1963) in which subjects were asked to determine whether a given sentence is true or false with respect to a specific picture of a situation (for review, see Slobin [1971]). In these studies by McMahon (1963), Gough (1965, 1966), and Slobin (1966), it was found that passive sentences took longer than active sentences to verify as true or false relative to a picture. For example, shown a picture of a car hitting a truck, a subject would be asked whether the statements "the car hit the truck" and "the truck was hit by the car" were true or false. It required significantly more time to judge the passive sentence correct than the active.

While there is no doubting these findings, as far as they go, one is cautioned against a blanket indictment of passive sentences as more difficult to process than active sentences, and hence to be avoided in message construction. Again, we find that common usage mitigates these results. Olson and Filby (1972) found that the important factor is the way in which receivers choose to remember the pictures (or by extension, early message points or sentence parts); that, in fact, passive sentences are not basically more complex than active sentences. If the pictures are encoded in a passive format, a passive sentence interpreting the picture will be readily processed. The critical concern should be understanding when a receiver would normally use a passive construction. Returning to Mc-Mahon's example of a picture showing a car hitting a truck, it would seem natural to use the active voice when the topic focus is the car (that is, the "doer" or active participant), while a passive voice construction would be more natural when the topic focus is the truck (that is, the "receiver" or passive participant in the situation). In advertising, for example, one might wish to focus on the source or the product.

In general, Olson and Filby (1972) found that when the sequential order of elements in a sentence is congruent with the sequential order of describing a picture, it is relatively easy to decide whether they match. On the other hand, when sequential orders do not match, more time is required to fully understand the meaning. This same kind of effect from syntactic mismatches was demonstrated with sentences by Wright (1969, 1972) and by Garrod and Trabasso (1973). This would indicate that sentence or copy congruence both within and between sentences in persuasive communication, as well as between copy and visual elements in advertisements and commercials, is essential for maximizing the overall comprehension of a message.

Since these studies suggest that the syntactic form of a sentence has no direct effect upon sentence processing, once the sentence has been encoded, an obvious question is whether it is, nonetheless, more difficult to encode passive sentences than active sentences. Slobin (1966), in a study of the time needed to decide whether a picture matched a previously heard sentence, presented subjects with reversible sentences, such as "The cat chased the dog" and nonreversible sentences, like "The boy watered the flowers." He found that, indeed, active sentences were easier to process than passive sentences, but only when nonreversible sentences were used; and furthermore, that nonreversible sentences in general, regardless of voice, were easier to process than reversible sentences. Glucksberg, Trabasso, and Wald (1973) found similar results in an extension of the Slobin study, plus the additional finding that receivers do not require longer to read and encode passive or reversible sentences. This led them to speculate that the differential difficulty of passive and reversible sentences is not in the sentence perception and encoding stage, but in the comparison stage, due entirely to the particular strategies the receivers use to compare the content of a picture with the information presented by a sentence. In other words, if a sentence is nonreversible, containing a verb and nouns reflected in the picture, then the picture and sentence will match, regardless of sentence voice.

What this means for the creation of advertising is a need to ensure compatibility between visual and written or audio components of an advertisement or commercial. The greater this compatibility, both between visual elements and the copy, and within and between the sentences comprising the copy, the more easily will comprehension of the entire communication follow. To the degree that passive or reversible sentences are used, this need for congruence increases. Overall, active nonreversible sentences should prove more efficacious for message comprehension.

We have seen, in reviewing a number of psycholinguistic experiments, that a negative need not always be more difficult than an affirmative sentence, and that a passive sentence need not always be more difficult to understand than an active sentence. Rather, when the communicative and linguistic contexts are appropriate, one linguistic construction is no more difficult to deal with (in terms of comprehension) than another. It seems that people prefer to describe certain types of situations using certain types of sentences, and when they are receivers in a communication situation, they tend to encode message material for comprehension according to habitual strategies. Effective communication in advertising requires an understanding of these strategies, and avoidance of any violation. Testing, of course, helps avoid these problems.

Content Memorability

The desirability of avoiding ambiguity and adhering to conventional meanings in the structuring of a message in order to maximize recall or memorability is illustrated by Thorndike's (1932) classic experiments on what he called "belongingness." In his experiments, subjects listened ten times to sentence sequences such as: Alfred Dukes and his sister worked sadly, Edward Davis and his brother argued rarely, Francis Bragg and his cousin played hard. Recall of the content of these sentences later showed that while subjects generally remembered Edward's last name, what he had done, and how, they almost never remembered his first name (or any of the words following "sadly," "rarely," "hard," and so on). There were no meaningful associations formed between sentences, because the words involved did not "belong" together. In other words, there is no syntactic structure relating the last word of one sentence with the first word of the next. This would seem to suggest that in order to maximize the probability of recall, the placement of a brand name in advertising communication should avoid becoming buried between sentences. A headline reading "Quality and value. Maxin gives you both" should be better recalled if written "Quality and value. You get both with Maxin."

The question of sentence structure and meaning is an important area in the study of psycholinguistics. Savin and Perchonock (1965) report an experiment that suggests that the number of words in a sentence is not the most important determiner of how much space it will occupy in memory, but rather the structure of the sentence. They read subjects a sentence, followed by a string of eight words. Each was asked to memorize the sentence verbatim and then recall as many of the words that followed as possible. The sentences themselves varied mainly in terms of syntactic structure. It was hypothesized that the fewer words a subject recalled after a sentence, the more space in short-term memory that sentence occupied.

The results clearly revealed that the more complex the structure of the sentence, the fewer words recalled following that sentence. An active declarative sentence, the simplest sentence type (for example, The boy hits the ball), occasioned the greatest number of recalled words. While this sentence is comprised of six words, a shorter but more complex sentence of only five words (What has the boy hit?) resulted in fewer recalled words. The reason for this seemingly counter-intuitive result is that a rather complex grammatical transformation must take place, in order for a receiver to encode a more difficult type of sentence, and this would be expected to occupy more of the available short-term memory space otherwise available for word recall.

In general, sentence difficulty was found to follow an active, passive, negative, passive negative ordering: the boy has hit the ball; the ball has been hit by the boy; the boy has not hit the ball; the ball has not been hit by the boy. In order to maximize memorability, message content should reflect less complex sentence structure. Even though, we have seen, the memorability of a single sentence may not be greatly affected, the information in subsequent sentences will. Examples of how these findings may be translated to advertising copy are illustrated in Table 4.6.

Another rather remarkable finding of the Savin and Perchonock (1965) study is the effect of emphasis or special stress in the reading of a sentence on the number of words recalled. The possible implications of these results on broadcast advertising could be significant. For example, they found that when the simple declarative sentence "The boy has hit the ball" is used, subjects remembered 5.27 of the 8 words that followed. But when the identical sentence was read with special stress on the word has (The boy *has* hit the ball), subjects were only able to remember 4.30 words. This would seem to suggest that, in terms of recall, more than sentence structure is involved; any special emphasis placed in an execution could quite possibly reduce recall of subsequent message points. This could be particularly critical if an emphatic lead-in was used, followed by the brand name or principal product benefit. These results indicate brand recall could suffer from such an emphasis in execution.

TABLE 4.6

Order of Difficulty in Sentence Structure for Learning
Typical Advertising Headlines

Sentence Structure	Headline
active[1]	"only one bank has offered CHECK INTEREST—1st National"
passive	"CHECK-INTEREST has been offered by only one bank—1st National"
negative	"other banks have not offered CHECK-INTEREST—only 1st National"
passive negative	"CHECK-INTEREST has not been offered by other banks—only 1st National"

[1]*Note*: order of difficulty follows how active (easiest to remember) to passive negative (hardest to remember).

Although this experiment suggests that the number of words in a sentence is less important than the sentence structure as far as memorability is concerned, Wearing (1973) has shown that the number of words contained in a sentence is an important variable, and that it may operate through the load placed at acquisition on short-term memory. Specifically, he found that both the total number of words (regardless of form or class) and total number of content words recalled correctly rose slightly from sentences of five words to sentences of seven words, dropped significantly from seven word to nine word sentences, then remained rather stable for sentences of more than nine words, though tending down (see Figure 4.3). Moreover, the recall of the sentence object was better than recall of the verb for all sentence lengths, increasing for sentences of nine words or more. (This verb-object difference in recall is interesting, given the much greater impact of verbs on reasoning, discussed below). So, while sentence structure is perhaps the most critical variable effecting the use of short-term memory (and hence recall) in the processing of the message content in advertising, sentence length, too, will have some effect. The optimum sentence length appears from these results to be somewhere around seven words. This would seem to be particularly appropriate in considering the length of both headlines and tag lines (or slogans) in advertising where specific recall is generally sought.

FIGURE 4.3

Relationship between Recall and Sentence Length
(Adapted from Wearing, 1973)

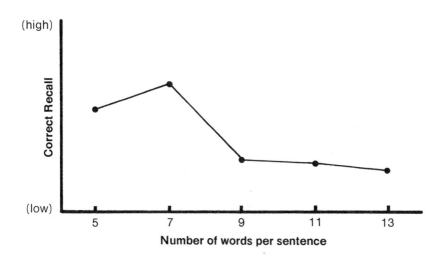

REASONING

The actual value of any persuasive communication is not realized until the receiver has fully encoded and correctly processed the message as the source intended it to be communicated. Judgments are made concerning the evaluative or affective aspects as well as the descriptive or denotative aspects of the information presented in a persuasive communication, and these judgments determine what the message communicates to the receiver. It is vitally important to the development of effective advertising communication that one understand the reasoning process of receivers and the different sets of assumptions that may lie under inferences based upon various types of message construction.

Abelson (1973) has reported a general theoretical approach that may lead to a much better understanding of the types of information (or advertising copy) that affect inferences in different situations, and of the contribution of cognitive consistency to these inferences. Elaborating on his earlier work (cf. Abelson and Reich 1969), he suggests that certain sets of sentences may be tied together by psychological elements, depending upon the subject, verb, and object to which they pertain. Such sentence sets are referred to by Abelson and Reich as "implicational molecules," and closely parallel typical rules of inference. These implicational molecules could be thought of as habitual ways of thinking or reasoning. For example, considering three general classes of variables, such as subject (S), behavior (B), and consequence (C), one implicational molecule that may obtain from this set could be: S does B; B causes C; S desires C.

Abelson and Reich (1969) hypothesize that an individual's cognitive structure may be composed of a number of such molecules, each pertaining to somewhat different classes of elements, connected by various types of verbs. If the relevant implicational molecules in a receiver's mind can be identified, the inferences the receiver will make from a particular message could be predicated by something they refer to as a "completion principle." Quite simply, this principle states that if a receiver is known to have the implicational molecule (S does B; B causes C; S desires C) and is told that using a particular product effectively solves a specific problem (for example, B causes C) and that everyone desires that specific problem solved (that is, S desires C), the receiver will infer that everyone is likely to use that particular product (that is, S does B). In other words, if an advertising message believably communicates that two out of three propositions from the receiver's implicational molecule are true, the third will also be presumed true, even though it is not explicitly stated.

The importance of this theory to the creation of effective advertising, particularly in what one says in the message, may be illustrated by considering the impact of a receiver's belief set on the encoding of a specific message. If one knows that a target receiver holds beliefs I and J, and believes that "if I, then J," following the completion principle just discussed would suggest that not only will belief in I affect beliefs in J, but beliefs in J will have a reciprocal effect upon beliefs in I. Advertising that addresses belief I or J in such a case will occasion the belief "if I, then J," even though this implication is not explicit in the advertising. It is obviously crucial to understand the relationships between receiver beliefs when one is going to include them as message points in persuasive communication. It is possible that certain beliefs could be incompatible with each other within the context of the advertised product or service.

Research has shown, for example, that most homemakers believe that a quick meal is easy, but not necessarily convenient. Convenience implies a lack of involvement in the preparation of the meal, while easy implies only a minimum of time. If one were to advertise a frozen entree as "easy and convenient," it should be expected that a homemaker receiving that message would infer that the product was also "quick" to prepare. But what if the cooking time were 50 minutes? The product is certainly "convenient;" all the homemaker must do is place the product in an oven for 50 minutes. However, it certainly isn't "quick" because the homemaker must wait almost an hour to serve it. As a result, advertising this product as "easy" (belief I in our discussion above) when homemakers believe that easy implies quick (if I, then J), would result in a miscommunication of the product's ultimate "convenience" benefit.

A problem in operationalizing or interpreting this formulation, though, could occur when different implicational molecules within a receiver's cognitive structure would suggest different implications for validity of a given proposition. Which implicational molecule would assume priority, and would this judgment require more internal processing? A second concern might be the degree to which a receiver is willing to generalize from specific copy points. The implicational molecules theoretically concern only broad conceptual propositions and not specific objects or events (Wyer 1974). In order to predict whether a receiver will accept an assertion made in a persuasive communication one must know both the implicational molecule the receiver is likely to utilize in processing the message and whether the receiver actually believes the information presented in the message.

Once more, one can see the importance of a full understanding of a potential receiver's attitudes and perceptions. Suppose, for example, that in promoting a line of products the manufacturer advertises one product (A, the top of the line) as containing one feature (X_1) and another product (B, another member of the line) as containing a second feature (X_2), with the hope of conveying the idea that the entire line is made up of high-quality products. For a receiver to accept this assertion would assume that it is consistent with an implicational molecule (A has X; A is similar to B) in which X is one of several general classes of quality. If the receiver does not feel that the specific information contained in the advertising about the quality features (X) of the products is sufficient to accept the general proposition of the molecule, it is unlikely the desired conclusion would be reached.

For example, the product line being advertised is a particular make of automobile, and the advertising features the top-of-the-line model, with all the extras, plus a mid-size "family" model (product A and B above). The top-of-the-line model is described in terms of its "smooth ride" (X_1) and "roominess" (X_2). Both are perceived to be component beliefs of "quality." Applying the implicational molecule (A has X; B has X; A is similar to B), a receiver would be likely to consider each a quality car, and, by extension, the line. However, if "roominess" was not to be a component of quality, the mid-size model would not be thought of as similar to the top-of-the-line model. As a result, the goal of communicating an image of quality for the entire line would not be satisfied.

General Inference

It should be clear that inference plays a significant part in the communication process. The better one understands how a receiver draws an inference (or makes a deduction) from a message, the better one will be able to ensure that the desired message is communicated. We have just seen how a receiver is likely to infer specific information from a message, based upon the extent to which that information is consistent with existing general attitudes or beliefs, using a set of informational molecules. While it is possible (and desirable) to know a great deal about the beliefs associated with a particular product category when creating advertising messages, in order to fully understand the probability of a correct inference being drawn from a message, it is necessary to have some feeling for how much supportive copy will be required in the message before a general proposition is accepted as valid. Some propositions may be accepted on the basis of very little evidence, requiring less "hard sell" in the message, while others may require a great deal of supportive evidence before they are believed.

Gilson and Abelson (1965) have looked at several possible influences on the acceptance of a general proposition: the total amount of information bearing upon it, the proportion of statements in the message that support the proposition, whether the verb connecting a sentence subject and object is manifest (for example, use or have) or subjective (for example, love or trust), and whether the information presented in the message was object-specific or subject-specific. They found that while the total amount of information presented, and thus the number of supporting claims, did not affect the acceptance of the general proposition, the proportion of supporting claims did have an effect. When most of the information presented was supportive of the desired proposition, it was almost universally accepted. But when only one-third of the information in the message was supportive, the general proposition desired was accepted only when the claims were object-specific (that is, when the evidence pertained to the sentence object) and the connecting verb was manifest. This would suggest, for example, that in advertising, which does not stress a number of product-specific claims, and therefore has a lower proportion of product information relative to general information, one must be careful to structure product claims so as to be object-specific with manifest verbs—for example, the product has feature X, the product does Y. This would tend to exclude product endorsements and other object-specific messages that utilize subjective verbs (such as, "Source A likes this product.") when most of the information contained in the message is not product supportive.

In general, Gilson and Abelson (1965) found that general propositions based upon manifest verb conditions (for example, buy, produce, have) are accepted much more frequently on the basis of object-specific message points than on the basis of subject-specific message points, and that propositions based upon subjective verbs (for example, hate, like, avoid) are unlikely to be accepted regardless of the type of evidence presented. The importance of verb effects upon what is communicated in advertising, or in any message, is discussed in greater detail in a later section.

These findings are, of course, important for the formulation of advertising messages, but equally so when considering measures of advertising evaluation. Consider the nature of a general proposition within the framework of a questionnaire designed to measure whether or not a receiver did indeed understand the message as it was intended to be communicated. Asking whether the receiver would now "buy" the product, having seen the advertising, calls for a reaction to a general proposition based upon a manifest verb. Following the conclusions of Gilson and Abelson, one could perhaps expect a more positive reaction to the advertising using this form of questioning than if one were to ask if the receiver now had a more favorable attitude toward the advertised product (a general proposition based upon a subjective verb), assuming the advertising being measured in each case conveyed object-specific information.

Inductive versus Deductive Inference

We have discussed how receivers use the information contained in the sentences that comprise an advertising message, in order to make subjective generalizations. The inference that follows these generalizations may be of two forms: inductive or deductive. Inductive inference follows from establishing an abstract generalization on the basis of one or more concrete instances. An example would be when a receiver attributes a "quality" image to a product, based upon concrete product attributes presented in the message. Deductive inference follows when an abstract generalization is used as evidence applied to a concrete case. They would occur, for example, when advertising featuring "glamorous" people and situations stimulated a receiver to give specific attributes to the product.

When inductive inference is desired, both Gilson and Abelson (1965) and Abelson and Kanouse (1966) found that there was a significantly greater tendency to generalize over sentence objects than over sentence subjects; or, as we have seen, object-specific evidence tends to produce greater agreement than subject-specific evidence with an inductive proposition. This would suggest that advertising designed to communicate the benefits of a full line of products, for example, should discuss specific items in that line as sentence objects rather than as sentence subjects.

Consider the following two sets of product claims which could be part of an advertising message (where A, B, and C represent items in a product line):

Subject-Specific Claims	Object-Specific Claims
Our A is liked by everyone	Everyone likes our A
Our B is liked by everyone	Everyone likes our A
Our C is liked by everyone	Everyone likes our A

If the Abelson and Kanouse (1966) findings hold, we would expect a receiver to be much more likely to reach the conclusion "Everyone buys our other products," once exposed to the object-specific message points than to reach the conclusion "Our other products are great," after exposure to the subject-specific message points, assuming there are other products D, E, . . . in the line.

Reporting on a similar study dealing with deductive inference, Abelson and Kanouse (1966) found that for the most part the results were exactly opposite those found for inductive inference. There was a significant tendency for subject-specific evidence rather than object-specific evidence to provide greater agreement with a proposition. In other words, an advertising message built upon subject-specific claims such as:

Young people use our product
Middle-aged people use our product
Old people use our product

should be easily generalized to "People like me use that product," while messages built upon object-specific claims such as:

People use products that do X
People use products that do Y
People use products that do Z
Our product does X, Y, and Z

would be much less likely to be easily generalized to "People like me use that product."

These rough examples illustrate the fact that receivers appear more willing to make inductive inferences when the supporting claims in a message bear on the object of the sentences, and more willing to make deductive inferences when

FIGURE 4.4

Inductive versus Deductive Roles Used in Drawing
Inference from Advertising

INDUCTIVE INFERENCE:

concrete copy points

receivers tend to generalize
over sentence **objects**

leading to abstract generalizations

"A car with an uncommon
blend of rare woods, exotic
metal and supple leather"

accept the hypothesis—
"Discriminating people buy"

DEDUCTIVE INFERENCE:

abstract copy points

receivers tend to generalize
over sentence **subjects**

leading to concrete generalizations

"Quality materials along with
pride in workmanship for a
truly fine car"

accept the hypothesis—
"A car for rich people"

the supporting claims bear on the sentence subjects. With this in mind, consider a typical advertising claim, such as "sold at fine stores everywhere." If the message points within the advertising tell the receivers that fine stores sell some products like ours, but not others (presumably only the best), the receiver would be expected to infer that "Fine stores sell products like those of the advertiser." However, if the advertising says some fine stores sell products like ours, while others do not, the receiver will be less likely to infer that "Fine stores sell products like those of the advertiser." In the first example the support bears on the sentence object (some products but not others) and in the second it bears on the sentence subject (some fine stores . . . while others do not).

On the other hand, when one wishes a deductive inference, if the advertising states only that "Fine stores sell products like ours" (which could be the case if this line were used as a tag to an advertisement or commercial that did not otherwise discuss where the product was sold), the receiver would be more likely to believe that a particular type of store (for example, a department store or jewelry store) sells "products like ours" than that fine stores in general sell the specific product advertised. These examples underscore why the importance of understanding how an inference will proceed is critical to the effective development of an advertising message. The basic rules used by receivers when drawing inductive or deductive inference are illustrated in Figure 4.4.

Kanouse (1972) provides three possible explanations for why inductive inference should proceed more readily from sentence objects than from sentence subjects, while deductive inference proceeds in an opposite fashion. First, and least compelling, is that the gramatical subject of a sentence is treated differently from the sentence object, either because it occurs first in the sentence, or for some other reason. The second, and more substantive explanation, derives from the homogeneous character of subject versus object classes. Sentence subjects, for example, tend to be less homogeneous or interchangeable as a class than sentence objects, thus making it easier to generalize to the more interchangeable objects. A final explanation offered by Kanouse is the possibility that perceived differences in the role of the subject versus the role of the object in a sentence underlies the generalization process. Whatever the explanation, the empirical evidence certainly indicates there are differences in inductive versus deductive generalizing over subject-versus object-specific, and in evaluating message copy in advertising these differences should be recognized.

Verb Effects

The nature of the verb used in a message, as already noted, has considerable effect on the persuasiveness of a communication. Abelson and Kanouse (1966) have shown, in addition, that when an inductive inference is sought from a given sentence, the type of verb form used is critical to the level of proposition acceptance. In fact, the results of both the Gilson and Abelson (1965) and Abelson and Kanouse (1966) studies find that inductive inference not only generates a significantly greater tendency for generalizing about sentence objects rather than sentence subjects, but also follows more easily when manifest verbs (such as use or have) rather than subjective verbs (such as like or hate) are used.

When subjective verbs were used in a sentence, a rather low level of agreement to any generalizations resulted, but when sentences containing manifest verbs were used, high agreement rates followed. Although some differences on the positive-negative dimension of the verb used were found—specifically that more positive verbs tended to elicit higher agreement than verbs describing negative feelings—those effects were minor compared with the semantic dimension of manifest versus subjective verb form.

Verb differences have also been found to be significant in determining the ease with which a deductive generalization is made. However, in this case, it is the positive-negative verb differences that are more important, not the manifest-subjective verb differences. Also, people are more likely to make a deductive inference when the verb provides a negative orientation of the subject of the sentence toward the object (Abelson and Kanouse 1966). If a source spokesperson in an advertisement or commercial were to say they "hated" doing a specific household job, the Abelson and Kanouse findings suggest the source would be perceived by the receivers as hating all household jobs—a deductive inference encouraged by the negative orientation provided by the verb "hate" for the subject spokesperson toward the object household jobs. On the other hand, if the spokesperson were to say that the spokesperson "loved" doing a specific job, the receivers would be reluctant to infer that the spokesperson "loved" doing all household jobs.

In addition, a slight tendency was noticed for receivers to agree with a deductive generalization when a verb is subjective rather than manifest. Again this is the opposite of the findings for inductive inference. So one finds that, while the pattern of results is the same, regardless of whether an inductive or deductive inference is sought, those verb differences that produce strong inductive inferences tend to produce weak deductive inferences, and vice versa, and also that the importance of the two semantic verb dimensions are exactly opposite.

Implied Quantifiers

In addition to the rather substantial verb differences affecting inference generally, there appears to be a pronounced effect on the implicit weight of the evidence offered in an advertising message as a result of the verb form used. In a study of the minimal amount of evidence a receiver felt was necessary to support a given message assertion, Abelson and Kanouse (1966) found that the amount of evidence required varied significantly with the type of verb used in the message sentence. Utilizing a scale of subjective quantifiers, such as "some," "many," or "all," they report that manifest verbs, which we have learned tend to occasion rather strong generalizing power, usually elicit lower implied quantifiers than subjective verbs, which we have seen tend to generate rather weak generalizing power. For example, a message copy point that reads "Football players *buy* our products" would be interpreted by a receiver as meaning football players buy only "a few" or "some" of the advertiser's product, while a similar message copy point that reads "Football players *love* our products" would be understood as meaning they love "most" or even "all" of the advertiser's products. The manifest verb "buy" implies a low quantifier; the subjective verb "love" implies a high quantifier.

The Abelson and Kanouse (1966) findings suggest that, not only do verbs differ systematically in the implicit quantifiers most receivers will attach to them, but that these implied quantifiers may, in fact, contribute to the way in which the message points communicated are processed, and affect the generalizations or conclusions reached (owing to the relationship between verb and generalizing power discussed in the last section). Kanouse (1968) has addressed exactly this point, suggesting that the reason some assertions are more readily agreed to than others is that some assertions are implicitly more general than others and that this is related to inductive versus deductive reasoning. For example, although the sentences "Modern women buy frozen food entrees" and "Traditional women avoid frozen food entrees" would seem to be equally unqualified and general, the first will be taken to mean modern women buy "some" frozen food entrees while traditional women avoid "all" frozen food entrees.

One could reason from this analysis that it should be easier to support an inductive inference in which the implied quantifier is "some" or "a few," rather than when it is "most" or "all," because only a few supportive points would be necessary to satisfy the inference. On the other hand, it should be easier to support a deductive inference in which the implied quantifier is "most" or "all," rather than "some" or "a few," because a single supportive point certainly falls within the category "all." In other words, inductively, it should be relatively easy to believably communicate "Modern women buy frozen food entrees" by supplying only one or two supporting message points, such as modern women buy frozen chicken breasts and pepper steak. However, it would be almost impossible to convince a receiver that "all" frozen entrees are avoided by traditional women without exhaustive supportive message points. Conversely, it should be equally true that it would be easier deductively to show that traditional women avoid a specific frozen entree (for, after all, it is implied that they avoid "all" of them) than to show that modern women buy a specific frozen entree (since it is implied that they only buy "some"). These points are summarized in Table 4.5.

TABLE 4.7

Verb Effects and Implied Quantifiers

	"Modern women *buy* frozen food entrees"	"Traditional women *avoid* frozen food entrees"
Verb form	manifest	subjective
Implied quantifier	some or a few	most or all
Inductive evidence	1-2 points	exhaustive
Deductive evidence	exhaustive	1-2 points

If it is true that the implied quantifier indicates the verb affect in generalized inferences, then once the quantifier is made explicit, one should expect the verb difference to disappear. Leaf (1969) tested this hypothesis and found that the effects of manifest versus subjective verb differences did, in fact, disappear when the quantifier was made explicit. However, positive versus negative verb differences, although somewhat lessened, did remain. Kanouse (1972) suggests that this could result because a negation affect toward an object may easily follow from a single negative salience while a single positive salience is rarely enough to ensure acceptance. For example, no matter how well liked a rich dessert may be, to a person on a diet the single negative of high calories is enough to override a considerable number of positive attributes.

As a result, suppose one were trying to generate agreement with an advertising message using a source spokesman discussing several message points which described attributes associated with the use of the advertised product. Evidence indicates that a receiver would be much more willing to believe that the source spokesperson dislikes something (for example, doing certain household tasks) if the spokesperson dislikes most (but not all) of the attributes presented. They would be considerably less likely to believe the spokesperson likes something (for example, using the advertised product) if the spokesperson does not like all of the attributes associated with it.

The importance of this distinction in the creation of advertising should be obvious. If an advertiser wishes a receiver to make a deductive inference about a popular source's use of a particular product, the advertiser will have an easier time of it if a negative scenario is developed and the quantifiers made explicit. In other words, if the quantifier is made explicit, and the verb form is positive, a single negative salience in the receiver's cognitive set will be enough for the receiver to disagree with the message conclusion. But, if the quantifier is made explicit and the verb form is negative, a great number of positive saliences would be required before the receiver would disagree with the message conclusion.

Negation

An important question to be asked when considering the use of negatives in advertising copy is whether or not receivers respond just as quickly to a negative proposition as they do to the same proposition positively stated. In an experiment reported by Wason (1961), the subjects were asked to provide a number between two and nine that would make one of four types of sentences either true or false, according to an oral instruction from the experimenter. The four sentence types are shown below.

Sentence Type	Example	Instruction
True affirmative:	"_____ is an even[a] number"	TRUE

Sentence Type	Example	Instruction
False affirmative:	"_____ is not an even number"	TRUE
True negative:	"_____ is an even number"	FALSE
False negative:	"_____ is not an even number"	FALSE

---

[a]In one-half of the trials the sentence read "odd" rather than "even."

Each response was timed from the presentation of the sentence through a number response. The results indicated that not only were the affirmative statements more quickly dealt with, they were also less likely to be in error.

While it is not particularly surprising that false negative conditions should prove the most difficult (containing, as they do, two negative components), what is surprising is that true negatives seem to be consistently more difficult for receivers than false affirmatives: that is, a sentence containing "not" which must be made true gives more trouble than an affirmative sentence that must be made false. Overall, the order from easiest to hardest was found to be true affirmative statments, false affirmative, false negative, and true negative. As Johnson-Laird and Tagart (1969) have noted, the negation of falsity does not seem to be psychologically equivalent to "truth."

A subsequent study by Wason and Jones (1963), as well as work by McMahon (1963), Gough (1965), and Slobin (1966) support this general finding that negative sentences are more difficult than affirmative sentences to understand, both in terms of the time required to process the information and the number of errors involved while processing. Additionally, these results tend to be invariant over repeated trials. The importance of these understandings to the creation of advertising should be clear: requiring a receiver to reason negatively will require more attention on the part of the receiver as well as a higher probability of reaching an incorrect conclusion. However, as was mentioned earlier in the discussion of how sentences are processed, although it is more difficult to reason quickly and correctly from a negative advertising message (more so, even, than merely requiring a false inference), if the representation of the message substance within the receiver's cognition is congruent with the manner in which the message is encoded, these effects will be minimized. In other words, if negative sentences are used in advertising, one must be certain the message is written in a way that reflects how consumers think. Again, this underscores the need to understand what receiver beliefs and attitudes are. For the interested reader, Clark (1969) discusses this whole question in detail.

Considering that evidence that is offered in support of a message, and whether it is positive or negative, Kanouse (1972) notes that verb differences again play a significant role, a role paralleling that already discussed in the section on inference and verb affects. "John buys a specific product" is seen by a receiver as a clear indication that John buys items from that product category, while "John hates a specific product" does not establish that he hates the category. Conversely, the negative evidence that "John does not buy a specific product" appears to be only weakly inconsistent with a statement that John buys items from this product category. But, similar evidence that he does not hate a specific product is very damaging to the general proposition that John hates items from this product category. Kanouse (1972) found that these verb differences (that is, manifest versus subjective acting, with either positive or negative evidence) occur regardless of the form of the desired conclusion: true affirmative, false negative, false affirmative, or true negative.

The context in which a negative sentence is received is, in fact, a critical mediator of the way in which reasoning follows. Denial tends to correct otherwise normative beliefs. For example, if an advertisement made the statement "Cleaning the floor wasn't hard today," it would make sense to a receiver only if cleaning the floor is generally perceived to be hard. This claim then functions to correct the perception that cleaning floors is hard in all cases, the assumption being that it is not hard when the advertised product is used.

While a particular copy point may suffer from the standpoint of believability if the belief attacked is firmly conditioned, the receiver should not have difficulty processing the message. Wason and Johnson-Laird (1972) review a number of experiments that tend to suggest that an affirmative preconception must be recovered before the meaning of a negative can be correctly understood. Because negation involves this extra mental step in reasoning, if such a preconception is not present within a receiver's set of beliefs, extra time will be required as the receiver consciously performs this task of affirmative construction. When a preconception is part of the receiver's cognition, this step goes unnoticed because it follows immediately upon message reception.

This whole problem of reasoning and the effects of negation may, in fact, rest in large part on the difficulty most people seem to have in believing that a negative can somehow become more so, or by a possible reluctance on their part to feel they can draw a correct conclusion from an assumption stated as a negative (Evans 1972). This seems to be particularly true of deductive inference. Apart from the generally accepted notion of the difficulty involved in understanding negative message components, there does not appear to be a great deal of difficulty in processing when a negative is used to deny an affirmative proposition; but when a negative is itself denied by an affirmative message point, the receiver tends to lose track of the argument.

When possible, it would seem best to just avoid negation in the writing of advertising copy because of the potential problems in processing the message.

MESSAGE CONGRUENCE WITH RECEIVER
BELIEFS AND ATTITUDES

The impact of message variables on response to advertising is probably more generally interrelated with other mediating variables than one finds with source, receiver, media, or scheduling variables. After all, it is the message itself that is the vehicle for the arguments contained in a persuasive communication. Nevertheless, perception of the source of these arguments, their compatibility with the attitudes and behavior of the receiver, how they are transmitted to the receiver, and toward what end, obviously mediate the effects of a message on advertising response.

The probability of a particular message being presented to a receiver, as well as the receiver attending to it, has a great deal to do with a certain level of de facto selectivity. While it has been pointed out in earlier chapters that evidence for a conscious selective exposure theory is weak (cf. McGuire 1973), there is overwhelming evidence to support the notion that whenever possible a receiver will tend to select the environment so that it will be compatible with the receiver's attitudes (Newcomb 1967). To the extent that a message is compatible with a receiver's environment, one should expect a greater or lesser probability of message attention. Further, Lowenthal (1969) has found that receivers tend to have a preference for messages that are strong consonant or weak dissonant as opposed to weak consonant or strong dissonant. In other words, one should expect greater attention to advertising that is strongly compatible with a receiver's belief and attitudes. When the message is not compatible with a receiver's beliefs and attitudes (for example, advertising for a product not used by the receiver), attention would be more likely only when the differences are not cognitively negative.

This functional approach to message reception would predict that if the topic of an advertisement or commercial is not ego-involving, the usefulness of the information provided in the message will probably become the primary mediator of attention. In this case, whether the information is supportive or not supportive of the receiver's beliefs and attitudes would be largely irrelevant, since there would be low involvement on the part of the receiver. While it is true that most people in everyday life are exposed de facto to disproportionate amounts of supportive messages, there is no support for the notion that they prefer to be exposed to supportive as opposed to nonsupportive messages. It is only when a receiver's beliefs or attitudes are challenged on an ego-involving issue (or when arguments have little actual utility) that the receiver will prefer supportive communication. Other factors too, although less prominent in the literature, also seem quite likely to enhance message attention: messages attributed to unusual, exotic, loud, or prestigious sources, and messages containing controversial, interesting, or surprising executional elements (Triandis 1971). Such devices, of course, are widespread in advertising.

In decoding advertising messages, the message must obviously be understandable to the receiver. The clearer and less likely a message is to place the receiver on the defensive, the greater the likelihood it will be decoded properly. Message differences affect encoding the desired response to the extent that they fit with the existing beliefs and values of the receiver. For example, a message that makes it clear that there will be some form of positive reinforcement following acceptance of the message's argument will stand a greater chance of positive response than one where a positive inference is more difficult.

The more frequently a message is repeated or presented to the receiver, the longer it is likely to be retained. In addition, Jones and Kohler (1958) have found that implausible dissonant and believable consonant messages tend to be better remembered than unbelievable consonant or plausible dissonant messages. They suggest that this may be because messages that are implausible or inconsistent with the receiver's beliefs and attitudes would tend to be difficult to refute or painful, and hence forgotten more readily. On the other hand, messages compatible with existing beliefs are reinforcing and useful to remember for future reference, while those messages generally consistent with the receiver's attitudes, but not believable (for example, advertising extolling the virtues of using a product category, but suggesting only one worthwhile brand), are useless and, as a result, more easily forgotten.

It should be clear from this discussion that an understanding of the environment in which a receiver behaves, along with a thorough understanding of their attitudes, is necessary for the successful implementation of a persuasive message, and that these understandings help one maximize the desired advertising response. Adoption of the argument contained in a message, a positive advertising response, is in the end most likely if the cognitive and affective components of the receiver's attitudes are consistent with that message.

VISUAL VERSUS VERBAL ELEMENTS IN THE MESSAGE

Advertising, in all media except radio, relies heavily on visual as well as verbal information to present the advertised product. While researchers have not been blind to the importance of visual information per se, visual information processing is not usually represented in models of advertising response. Studies of consumer spatial behavior in retail location research (for a review, see Reynolds and Wells [1977]), of packaging, and of the effects of illustration size in print advertising (for a review, see Hendon [1973]), have at least partially been concerned with consumer response to visual information. However, these studies have employed stimulus-response (S-R) designs of an input-output type, in which the nature of visual information processing has not been assessed.

The concept of information processing implies that something theoretically necessary, if not directly accessible, is going on inside the organism that operates on the incoming information and consequently affects the output response. Variables that tap these organismic processes constitute valid O-variables in the basic S-O-R paradigm assumed by most information-processing theorists. Most of the research on individual differences in visual information processing has been concerned with the mediating effects of these O-variables on verbal learning (item recall and recognition) and motor learning (performance improvement after visualized practice). However, Richardson (1977) speculates that visually oriented O-variables may also mediate the learning of affective (attitudinal) responses. But, no one has yet demonstrated visual mediation of affective learning empirically, nor developed a theoretical model that would predict it. This joint theoretical and empirical endeavor, however, would be highly relevant to advertising.

One O-variable that should be of interest to those creating advertising is visual imaging ability. Visual imaging ability may be colloquially defined as the individual tendency to "think in pictures" (Richardson 1977). Although everyone experiences pictorial imagery at some time or other, individuals vary widely in the extent to which they employ visual imagery as a habitual mode of thinking and simultaneously in the extent to which visual imagery occurs easily and spontaneously as a covert response to external stimuli (Paivio 1969; Richardson 1977).

Visual Stimuli

If verbal stimuli can elicit visual imagery responses (as discussed in the section on concrete versus abstract words), then visual stimuli should almost certainly do so. One may assume that the initial and primary reaction to a visual stimulus is some type of visual or iconic (picture-like) encoding, which one might think of as a visual imagery response. With visual stimuli, as with verbal stimuli, it is the subsequent responses that are in dispute. One school of thought acknowledges that the initial response to a visual stimulus may be a visual imagery response, but that the subsequent responses are verbal. That is, the receiver mentally "describes" or interprets the visual stimulus in verbal terms. The verbal response then provides the basis for further effects such as recall or recognition. The best known theory in this verbal coding school is the "verbal loop hypothesis" (Glanzer and Clark 1969). However, verbal labeling of this type would not be able to account for some visual recognition findings such as those of Shepard (1967).

He has suggested that visual imagery always occurs in response to visual stimuli. Shepard's experiment is interesting because, although it was conducted in the context of experimental psychology, the stimuli employed happened to be magazine advertisements. Subjects in the experiment studied 612 illustrated magazine advertisements at their leisure. They were given a recognition test on 68 pairs of ads in which the pairs consisted of one ad from the originally studied set, plus a new ad of the same type as the rest. The task was to identify which of each pair had been in the original set. On an immediate recognition test, subjects were 98.5 percent accurate. On a delayed test one week later subjects were still 90 percent accurate. Performance did not fall to the chance level (50 percent) until four months afterward.

This normal but amazing recognition feat implies that people store visual images of every visual stimulus they pay attention to. The alternative nonimagery explanation—that the subjects in Shepard's experiment generated verbal responses to the 612 advertisements, which later aided them in the recognition test—is hardly convincing because this would imply that the subjects could accurately recall a list of 612 words in one trial, which simply cannot be done. Visual imagery therefore seems to be an inevitable response to attended-to visual stimuli.

Initial imagery response can serve as an internal stimulus that triggers further visual imagery. If this imagery is favorable, visual reinforcement will occur. This view should be carefully distinguished from the imagery coding theory advanced by Bugelski (1970, 1977). Bugelski's imagery coding theory is the diametric opposite of the verbal coding theories of Glanzer and Clark (1969) in that it holds that all coding is imaginal. However, Bugelski is not referring to a picturelike visual image when he uses the term "image." Imagery as discussed in this section follows that of Richardson (1977), who defines visual imagery as a consciously experienced, quasi-perceptual event. Rossiter and Percy (1978), however, have suggested that visual imagery may also have reinforcing properties. In particular, subsequent visual imagery responses made to the initial iconic image are capable of assuming reinforcing qualities—hence their concept of visual reinforcement.

In their theory, visual content is hypothesized to be potentially as effective as verbal content in creating a favorable product attitude and persuading the consumer to purchase the product. Advertising may persuade consumers to buy products primarily by serving as a vehicle for price deals and sales promotions that operate directly on purchase behavior rather than on product attitude; most retail advertising is of this type. Alternatively, advertising may persuade consumers by creating or maintaining a favorable product attitude which then forms the basis for subsequent purchase behavior; this is the process underlying most consumer advertising. It is this attitudinal approach to advertising with which Rossiter and Percy were concerned.

Undoubtedly, the major trend in attitudinal approaches to advertising has been toward the multiattribute attitude models derived from social psychology (Fishbein and Ajzen 1975). Within the context of such belief-based attitude models, the only way to form or change attitude is to change beliefs, usually by providing verbal information directed to these beliefs. The reason why beliefs (cognitive) are capable of altering attitude (affect) is because of their own affective connotations. It is the affective or emotional feeling that accompanies the belief that is critical. In other words, it is the feeling of satisfaction that one feels in learning that a product possesses a particular attribute that increases one's attitude toward it, not the knowledge itself.

But there are ways other than through verbal beliefs that stimuli with favorable emotional consequences can be paired with a product. Visual imagery is one of these other ways. Auditory imagery, especially through the use of music in broadcast advertising, is another. Each is capable of increasing the receiver's overall evaluation of the advertised product (that is, product attitude).

Earlier it was mentioned that visual content could be especially capable of stimulating visual imagery (Rossiter and Percy 1978). Words and music can also stimulate visual imagery, as when one reads a book and imagines the characters and settings, or listens to a song. But pictures have the advantage of presenting visual images, already in appropriate modality, which the receiver-viewer may then internalize as a basis for personal imagery. Experiments by Shepard (1978) have shown that visual imagery can be as effective as an actual experience in guiding behavior. Thus, in an advertising context, one may "see" oneself behind the wheel of an attractively advertised automobile; "imagine" oneself drinking that refreshing looking bottle of soda, and so forth. The visual imagery derived in this manner may serve as a favorable unconditioned stimulus that increases our attitude response toward the product. Attitude can thereby be created or altered without any verbal belief process occurring and without the aid of advertising copy.

Advertisements entirely devoid of copy (other than the product name) are relatively rare, although campaigns, such as the primarily visual one for Marlboro, are a well-known exception. Even here, a belief-based attitude theorist may argue that such campaigns work, not through the visual imagery process just described, but through the ability of visual content to imply verbal beliefs. The "Marlboro man," for example, may lead consumers to experience subvocal verbal beliefs such as, "Marlboro is a cigarette for rugged people." This belief-based explanation was advanced in a study by Mitchell and Olson (1977), in which they found a picture of a kitten paired with a fictitious brand of bathroom tissue was more effective than an explicitly verbal claim in creating the belief that the brand was soft. However, the visual advertisement was also more effective in creating a favorable overall attitude (affective rating) toward the brand and it was by no means clear that this was achieved by operating first on the softness belief. It could have been at least partly the result of direct classical conditioning; that is, through a favorable emotional reaction to the kitten paired with the presumably originally neutral reaction to the bathroom tissue.

This "verbal loop" possibility, however, leads on to the notion of a "dual loop" theory in which both visual and verbal advertising content could influence attitude through the verbal belief process and the visual imagery process: a "visual loop" (see Figure 4.5). A feature of such a notion is that it predicts the visual loop is more likely to occur with visual content and the verbal loop is more likely to occur with verbal content (cf. Paivio 1979). This would seem to be a logical hypothesis, given the respective modality types of incoming stimuli.

Rossiter and Percy (1978) tested this theory by varying the relative salience or strength of the visual content and the verbal content in four advertisements. High visual emphasis (large picture relative to the ad as a whole as opposed to a small picture) was hypothesized to encourage the visual loop process, with visual

FIGURE 4.5

Visual and Verbal Loop Possibilities*

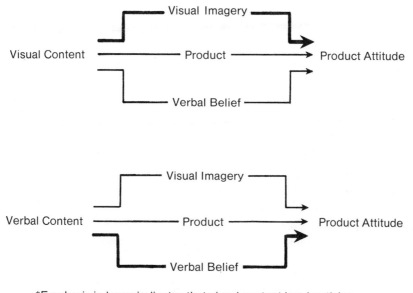

*Emphasis in loops indicates that visual content in advertising is more likely to stimulate the visual imagery loop, whereas verbal content in advertising is more likely to stimulate the verbal belief loop (see text).

imagery influencing product attitude. Strong verbal emphasis (explicit belief claims as opposed to vague ones) should encourage the verbal loop process, with verbal beliefs influencing product attitude.

The effect of the four advertising variations on product attitude are shown in Table 4.8. The results were exactly as predicted. The "superior" combination of high visual emphasis with explicit belief claims produced a mean product attitude rating of +5.95 (when a rating of just under zero would be expected for the brand names alone), whereas the "inferior" combination of low visual emphasis and implicit verbal claims produced a mean product attitude rating of only +2.07. The two "middle" combinations, which each contained only one of the hypothesized attitude increase components, produced nonsignificantly different mean product attitudes of +3.14 and +2.93; both of these were significantly lower than the superior combination. Use of a high visual emphasis to activate

TABLE 4.8

Product Attitude Scores by Type of Advertisement

Verbal Claims	Visual Emphasis		
	High	Low	Verbal Means
Explicit	+5.95 *	+3.14	(+4.54)
Implicit	+2.93	+2.07	(+2.50)
Visual Means	(+4.44)	(+2.60)	N = 88

*Product attitude was measured on a −12 to +12 scale. Significance levels for the mean differences are given in the text.

the visual imagery loop was almost equally as effective as use of explicit verbal claims to activate the verbal belief loop.

While these results may not be totally generalized to the extent that visually oriented advertising always is better than verbally oriented advertising, those creating print advertising should be aware that visual imagery can play a significant part in enhancing attitude for the advertised product.

The concept of visual reinforcement has provocative implications for advertising. Visual reinforcement resulting from visual imagery may explain the superior learning produced by television commercials, even when television commercials and print advertisements are apparently "equated" for visual and verbal content (Grass and Wallace 1974). The multiple visual stimuli provided in a television commercial video should produce multiple initial imagery responses and thus increase the amount of visual reinforcement experienced by the viewer.

Research to date has focused on positive visual reinforcement. However, one would predict that visual imagery can have negatively reinforcing and also punishing consequences for the affective learning of brand attitudes. Advertisements for pain relievers, for example, frequently employ the negative reinforcement principle. Negative verbal reinforcement from the copy or audio may be enhanced by negative visual reinforcement from the visual elements of the picture or video. Similarly, public service announcements entailing health warnings often employ the punishment principle. These too may be enhanced by visual imagery.

Visual reinforcement has many unrecognized applications in advertising and probably in other areas of marketing communication as well. Indeed, a visual or verbal stimulus that reaches the consumer may produce visual reinforcement.

FIGURE 4.6

Stereo Ad

The Stereo 648.
A nitty-gritty,
100% solid-state,
built-to-take-it,
100-watt receiver.

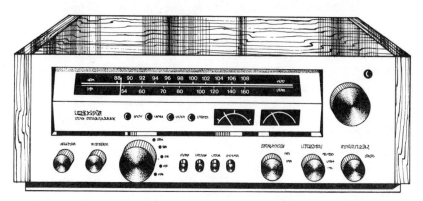

**WHILE LIMITED
SUPPLY LASTS**

$399

REGULARLY $449.95

Now while limited supplies last, get the Stereo 648 for only $399. Rugger quality in a 100% solid-state, com-compact 100-watt receiver. Heavier, more advanced toroidal-core transformer. Features four gang zink plated variable capacitors. Many of the features you'd expect to find on a more expensive radio. Go for quality. Get the Stereo 648 now while limited supply lasts. Only $399. And built to take it. **Stereo**

An Application

We have seen how important it is for the manager to understand the various effects of message structure in determining the correct creative strategy for the brand or product. It is most frequently put to the test in evaluating some form of rough execution. The manager is continuously called upon to review and approve storyboards and scripts for broadcast commercials, and layouts and copy for print advertisements. The rough print execution shown in Figure 4.6 represents a typical advertisement designed for a special price-off promotion. The manager must decide whether or not to use this advertisement in its present form, or order revisions (or perhaps a completely new execution).

While the advertisement itself appears to be a straightforward sales announcement, the price in the lower-left corner is not as potentially effective as it might have been in the headline. The headline, however, suffers from several problems the manager should recognize. Although the brand identification is up front, the entire headline is much too long for easy comprehension. Too many semantic, as well as memory encoding, complications can arise from such an overly long construction. Perhaps its most serious fault is that it strings a bundle of modifiers before the noun; and four of the six modifiers are compound adjectives, in themselves difficult to understand and discouraging to readership. Also, one might question the relevance of the modifier "nitty-gritty" to a stereo receiver; what does it mean in this context? It is unlikely to suppose the receiver will want to do the work required to find out. Finally, although it may be supposed that the target receivers will understand the rather technical body copy, nowhere does it provide support for the "built-to-take-it" claim. It is merely stated, and the receiver is asked to accept it at face value.

Because the layout and visual elements of this advertisement present the product and sale price clearly, the manager should not totally reject it. Rather, with corrections to the headline, and perhaps the inclusion of some support for the "built-to-take-it" claim in the body copy, the message of this advertisement could reasonably be expected to generate a positive behavioral intention response.

REVIEWING VARIABLE 3: MESSAGE STRATEGY

The overall objective of this chapter has been to provide the background necessary to evaluate the potential response to various advertising executions. Specifically, one should be able to:

1. Identify various message appeals
2. Compare the particular merits of various message appeals in maximizing response to advertising
3. Understand the effects of fear appeals in advertising

4. Know when to draw a conclusion explicitly for the receiver or leave it for the receiver to infer

5. Determine the number of message points best for memorability

6. Interpret the order of various message points, selecting the most appropriate order for a particular strategy

7. Understand the effect of syntax and grammar on the way in which a receiver will respond to advertising

8. Identify the potential problems in negative message construction

9. Understand the effect of visual imagery advertising

KEY CONCEPTS

Ethos, Pathos, Logos

Emotional Appeals

Logical Appeals

Positive versus Negative Appeals

Implicit versus Explicit Conclusions

Refutational Appeals

Distraction

Repetition

Message Content

Order Effects

Counter-arguing

Primary-Receiver Effects

Receiver Attention

Conclusions

Sentence Structure

Content Ambiguity

Comprehension

Content Memorability

Reasoning

Inductive Inference

Deductive Inference

Verb Effects

Negation

Visual Imagery

5

MEDIA SELECTION

Theories of communication that follow Lasswell's (1948) analysis in terms of who says what to whom, how, and with what effect generally specify the "how" as having to do with channel factors such as the media of the modality through which a message is presented (for example, auditory versus visual). These communication's channels are the means through which a single or multiple source conveys a message to one or more receivers, and might be thought of in broad terms as either interpersonal means or mass media vehicles of communication.

The obvious channel variables belong to mass media: all of those vehicles that transmit messages involving some mechanism to reach a broad range of receivers, who are frequently widely diverse and spread out. Newspapers, magazines, film, radio, and television are all examples of mass media. Interpersonal channels tend to be two-way face-to-face interactions, such as word-of-mouth communication. While it may be that interpersonal channels are of little concern in a study of advertising communication, the reader is reminded of the discussion in chapter 2 dealing with multi-step concepts of communication; individual receivers can assume an important role in effectively relaying an advertiser's message. Although the thrust of this chapter deals with mass media and its mediating affects on the advertising response, the interrelationship between interpersonal and mass media variables is not ignored.

In the interpersonal communication situation, the source and channel can be the same individual, or the individual who is the communication channel may only be a mediator. This would, in fact, be the case in a multi-step communication in which an advertiser seeks out opinion leaders as target audience receivers in the expectation that they will then communicate the advertiser's message to other individuals. The actual source of the message would be the original advertising situation, although the perceived source at the second step would be the more credible (from the receiver's viewpoint) opinion leader. With mass media, of course, the source is usually perceived as distinct from the channel, although McLuhan (1964; McLuhan and Fiore 1967) has taken the position that the medium through which a message is communicated has significant impact.

Rogers (1962) has noted mass media variables are effective in changing cognitions, or one's knowledge about a subject, but interpersonal channels of communication tend to be more effective when the goal of a communication is to change attitude. Frey (1966) has reported that when people are asked what prompted their adoption of a new idea, they are more likely to recall a recent conversation with a neighbor (interpersonal) than a radio program heard several months before (mass media). It would appear that media variables are not in themselves an optimum channel for change in buyer behavior, although little basic research on the issue is to be found in the literature. McGuire (1968c) remarks that this area of neglect on the part of social psychologists both surprises and bothers communications practitioners (such as those in the business of advertising) who, because of the lack of any organized body of knowledge, must make very expensive decisions regarding "media mix" on the basis of intuition and folklore.

In this chapter, we shall consider the effectiveness of mass media, media variables and their relationship to other channel factors, the modality of media variables, with emphasis on the question of the relative effectiveness of the written versus the spoken word, and considerations in planning the selection of media and media vehicles to meet particular strategic objectives.

Part I
Media Variable Characteristics

The nature of media variables might be thought of as classified into two segments, following Deutschmann's (1957) description of "public" channels: assembled and nonassembled. For example, assembled media variables would include movie theater audiences, or from an advertising standpoint, billboard advertising in places such as municipal auditoriums or stadiums. More familiar would be nonassembled media variables such as in-home radio listening or television viewing. This classification attempts to take into consideration the motivations and activity of the source and receiver in the communications situation. Overall, it is a rather simple dichotomy, but one easily enlarged or complicated. At what point does a medium take on the characteristics of an assembled media variable? The size of the group of receivers involved is, of course, a factor, as are the motives or goals of the assembly (cf. Blumer 1946) and the relationships among the receivers. The problem could become as complex as one desires. It seems more appropriate, particularly for the purpose of a text on advertising and communication, to treat media variables as a whole, contrasted with face-to-face communication.

Within this class of media variables, however, a number of more common-sense characteristics are evident. Schramm (1973) offers six contrasts of mass media variables along with face-to-face communication following such earlier thinking of Heider and his contemporaries as "naive psychology" and the works of Cantril and Allport (1935), Lazarsfeld (1940), and Lazarsfeld and Merton (1948): the senses affected; the opportunity for feedback; the amount of receiver control; the type of message-coding; the multiplicative power; and the power of message preservation.

Whenever anything is interposed in communication, some restriction is put on the use of the senses (a point discussed in some detail in the section dealing with modality). It is therefore essential to understand how different senses handle different communication situations in response to advertising. Television utilizes both eyes and ears; radio only the ear, and print media only the eye. Face-to-face communication can, of course, stimulate all the senses. But, for advertising communication, it is clear that one characteristic of media important to effective persuasibility is its utilization of the senses.

The second characteristic, opportunity for feedback, is of course maximal in face-to-face communication: but, it occurs in mass media as well. Recalling our discussion of the basic notion of a two-step process in communication from chapter 2, we saw that feedback is not only assumed, but could possibly be anticipated and influence a priori an advertisement or other communication. Although in practice feedback with mass media is restricted in terms of quality and speed, it is not unusual to pretest the communication in a laboratory situation or among a smaller group of target receivers. This, of course, is common practice in the development of advertising, as is a certain amount of postcommunication feedback. In fact, coupon advertising in print media and telephone or mail-in offers in broadcast media could be considered a measure of feedback.

The amount of receiver control is a more discriminating characteristic in mass media. A receiver reading a magazine or newspaper has the opportunity to pace himself, to study points of particular interest, or reread an entire piece if it is desirable or helpful. A receiver in a face-to-face communication has somewhat less control, although if attending fully, the receiver could always ask the source to go over a point again, or to provide more clarification. A listener to radio or a viewer of television has no such control. The receiver may not attend to the message, or may even turn it off, but has no control over the pace of the communication, and no ability to see or hear the message again. Schramm (1973) suggests that this is one of the reasons why television advertising has drawn more complaints than newspaper advertising. Overall, the more control exercised by the receiver, the more effective is learning; the more control exercised by the source of the message, the more effective is persuasion. Once again, we are confronted with a complex situation. To maximize one stage of message processing adversely effects another. For example, choosing a print media would tend to increase the probability of learning through more receiver control, but lessen the probability of persuasion (which would be more likely if a broadcast medium had been chosen).

The type of message-coding, as remarked by Schramm (1973), considers the availability of nonverbal information to the receiver; below we shall consider the use of media as a form of nonverbal communication. Obviously, face-to-face communication offers the highest probability for the effects of nonverbal encoding of cultural reaction, gestures, or body movement. To a lesser degree, television would follow; then radio and print media. While this point will be discussed further in a later section dealing with the modality of media, it should be noted that print media tends to be encoded in orthographic signs enabling one to abstract easily; broadcast media more easily permits one to concretize. From an advertising standpoint, the question of what one is attempting to accomplish through the buyer response hierarchy by an advertising communication involves consideration of how the message will be encoded, and as such, what constitutes the most effective media mix.

Consideration of the multiplicative power of a medium is less a conceptual than practical question. All mass media, compared with face-to-face communication, has the ability to reach great numbers of people over vast distances. This ability to multiply a message, however, may not always be efficient from an advertising strategy viewpoint. Certain print media cannot be directed specifically at particular regional segments; very little remains in the way of network radio, although one could probably accomplish a near-network coverage through local spot placements of an advertising message. So, while mass media enjoys a strong multiplicative power, it may sometime prove to be too much for a particular program of communication, thus affecting media selection.

Schramm's (1973) final point, that of the power of message preservation, is again a rather obvious classification criterion. Without recording equipment, broadcast media are evanescent. And, although in advertising one attempts to overcome this problem through increased frequency of presentation, the message is never really available for study. Print media, of course, offers a certain permanence for a communication.

Finally, in addition to the above characteristics for classifying media variables, we would like to suggest another: the inherent use of proxemics associated with the use of a medium. While perhaps an extension of the availability of nonverbal information, the proxemics involved in communication are interesting in themselves. Hall (1959, 1966) has suggested that different cultures use the senses to distinguish between one space or distance and another. The specific distance chosen depends on the transaction; the relationship of the interacting individuals, how they feel, and what they are doing. By extension, this relationship could be applied to the source of a communication or the medium of transmission and the receiver.

Mass media, to the extent that they are presented to a receiver, must intrude somewhere in the receiver's proximate space (see Table 5.1). Print media would generally find themselves within a receiver's "personal distance" close phase (1½ to 2½ feet). This is a term Hediger (1961) used to designate the distance consistently separating the members of noncontact species—a sort of protective bubble that a person maintains between the self and others. Entering this space, print media perhaps enjoy a certain amount of "closeness" with the receiver. Radio, on the other hand, can easily find itself in any of the four proximate spaces: intimate, up to 18 inches; personal, up to 4 feet; social, up to 12 feet; or public, where the important sensory shifts occur well outside the receiver's circle of movement. This could be quite important to the type of advertising communication carried on radio. A message seeking a certain level of involvement on the part of a receiver may be more consonant with the expected advertising response if one could be assured it would be received within the intimate or personal space of the receiver. If, for example, the radio is on while a homemaker is going about household chores, it is unlikely it would fall within the homemaker's personal or intimate space. On the other hand, if the radio is in the hands of a teenager, the likelihood is great that it will not be far from the teenager's ear. In the case of television, it would almost certainly fall within the receiver's social distance. While voice levels are normal, a proxemic feature of social distance in its far phase is that it can be used to insulate or screen an individual from others; it permits them to be uninvolved. This distance makes it

TABLE 5.1

Receiver Proximate Space

Space	Phase	Description
Intimate	close: under 6 in.	soft whisper; top secret
	far: 6–18 in.	audible whisper; very confidential
Personal	close: 1½–2½ ft.	soft voice; confidential
	far: 2½–4 ft.	soft voice; personal subject matter
Social	close: 4–7 ft.	full voice; nonpersonal information
	far: 7–12 ft.	full voice; public information for others to hear
Public	close: 12–25 ft.	loud voice; talking to group
	far: 25 ft. or more	shouting; hailing

possible for a receiver's attention to wander without a commitment to the medium.

So, it would seem that mass media could be classified according to its probably proxemic relationship to a receiver. And, as we have discovered, this could have significant impact on the mediating effect of mass media on the buyer response hierarchy. This would seem to be an area in which some experimentation and research is called for, if we are to fully understand the relationships between mass media variables and persuasibility.

EFFECTS OF MEDIA VARIABLES

While the effects of media variables are many, there is really no generally accepted theoretical schema available for classifying them. Hovland (1954) reached this conclusion some time ago, and little has evolved since to dispel that notion. However, Lazarsfeld (1963) has suggested a number of dimensions, which have been elaborated upon by Weiss (1969), that could at least be seen as providing a framework for a general empirically derived organization of the effects of media variables: dimensions such as the nature of the effective stimuli, the social unit affected, the temporal extent of the effect, or the type of effect.

Generalized Media Effects

In considering the nature of media variable effects, one must question what is to be understood as the effective agent when it is said that mass media or a particular medium has certain effects. This could mean the various media characteristics as we have discussed them in the last section; or one could perhaps consider the mere existence of one or more media, the various programs or communication messages usually associated with a specific medium, or even a specific factor within a communication itself. For example, it would take the unavailability of an existing media, or the appearance of a new one to make the obvious point that attention to one medium takes time away from another. Or, more generally, that attention to mass media at all takes time away from other pursuits (a charge frequently leveled at television, particularly in relation to children). From an advertising standpoint, media availability is of course a central issue, as is a certain compatibility between an advertising communication and the program environment (both issues independent of the "target audience" or receivers associated with a particular media or program).

The intrinsic characteristics of a medium may relate to other sorts of effects, providing a basis for intermedia differences in effect. This is often confounding within receivers, for the manner by which a particular medium conveys its content may be more or less appealing than another, depending on situational considerations. As a result, these situational considerations have a mediating affect on the time spent with a particular medium by the receiver. The more appealing under the circumstance, the more time a receiver will spend with it, and hence its effect on overall allocation of the receiver's time will be greater. Some understanding of these situational considerations, which would seem logically correlated with life-style and personality variables, are as necessary to effective media planning in advertising as the more traditional gross measures of media reach and frequency, impact or continuity (which are discussed in more detail in the section on media selection).

Unfortunately, attempts to assess the less obvious intermedia differences by studying their normal impact in actual reader, listener, or viewer use faces serious methodological difficulties. It is difficult to distinguish whether it is receiver characteristics or media characteristics, for example, that would be responsible for differences in attraction to a medium overall or in various situations. Lazarsfeld (1940) argued some time ago that only after it is known who each medium reaches, and why people are attracted to it, does it make any sense to compare the effects of media. It is the "why" component of this analysis that is usually lacking in most advertising media scheduling, although a great deal of money and effort is devoted to whom a particular medium reaches. This, perhaps, helps to explain why media scheduling, as practiced by most advertisers and their agencies, is not terribly efficient in reaching the most persuadable receivers, thus seriously affecting the probability of success for an advertising communication achieving its desired response objective.

Differences between media, at least in their short-term effectiveness, may be a result of differences in their social contexts of reception; in other words, who is generally present when the media is viewed, listened to, or read, may contribute to media variable effects. In an old study by Cantril and Allport (1935), they suggested that radio as a communication's media could have an advantage over print media precisely because people listen to radio and imagine themselves to be members of a wider audience of simultaneous listeners. The reception of an advertising communication could also certainly be tempered by such an analysis. For example, advertising viewed on television could be received in a number of social contexts: at home with family, alone, or with friends; or possibly at someone else's home or at a neighborhood bar. The environment in which a communication is received certainly mediates the effect of the media.

There also seems to be degrees of "trust" attached to different media in different situations. To the extent that this occurs, the medium becomes a level of the source of the communication (see chapter 3, "Source Factors"), although it remains a dimension of intermedia difference in effect. Weiss (1969) reports that a number of studies in various countries have sought evidence on the relative trust accorded mass media, by asking people which they would be most likely to believe if different media carried conflicting reports of a specific event, or by asking people to evaluate the general reliability of a medium as a news source. Overall, he finds that the primary broadcast medium of the day (radio in the past, and television now) has been viewed more favorably as a reliable source of news than newspapers, even among young people and children. The difference, of course, could in part be a function of the extent to which each medium is generally used as a news source. But, also involved are questions of modality (addressed in more detail in the section on modality below), particularly the attractiveness and compellingness of the visual dimension provided by television, as well as the temporal priority and continuous "up-to-dateness" of broadcast media with respect to print. In addition, Carter and Greenberg (1965) have shown that the perception of newspapers is one of taking a clearly more biased or partisan stand on issues. However, with recent exposure of network television abuses in selective reporting and even staging of news events, this distinction may now be blurred. Also, one must be careful in drawing conclusions from these results as evidence of the differential effectiveness of media in other communication situations as well: other dimensions may be mediating other choices. For example, MacLean (1954) studied two lists of categories: one appropriate to newspapers and one to radio. Subjects were asked to rate which radio category they would listen to, and which newspaper category they would read that day. There was relatively little correlation between radio and newspaper categories that one might expect to be intercorrelated or thought to be media counterparts

of each other, such as "service" or "public affairs" and the entertainment categories. These decisions are again quite possibly situationally based.

The Nature of Media Effects

The nature of media effects, in addition to mediating advertising response,
are reflected in a number of psychological dimensions. Any communication, advertising or otherwise, over a particular medium will be received and acted upon
conditioned by one or all of these dimensions; however, there is no implied
hierarchy of the dimensions.

Identification with a particular medium is particularly central to any interpretation of effect which is based on the media's role as a contributor to outside or vicarious experiences. Under specific circumstances, certain media may
be more conducive to source identification or persuasibility (again independent
of the media acting as a level of source). For example, if one were to advertise a
product for which a strong group usage image was considered important, the extent to which a target receiver found it easier to identify with a medium as a
transmitter of, or reflection of, the receiver's feelings, that medium should be
used as the message channel. This follows from Weiss's (1969) notion that identification with a medium is often taken to include or imply a kind of "as if" experience, in which the receiver's imagination assumes the personality and role of
one of the participants in a communication; and this is more or less likely depending on the media involved.

In considering the normative dimension, one is reminded of the frequent
charge leveled at television—that it generally degrades public taste or panders to
its most common level, failing to "upgrade" the audience's cultural interests, and
so on. And, coincident with this is the more specific charge that television advertising "insults" the viewer's intelligence. Clearly, whether real or not, there are
selected norms against which media effects are considered. It may be easier for
certain receivers to remark on having seen an advertisement for a particular
product in a high-status print media than to reveal seeing it advertised on television. Similar arguments are available in discussing how the values associated
with a particular medium effects a communication carried within it. Broadcast
media, because of their ability to reach great numbers of people, obviously have
a greater opportunity to influence personal or social values, as well as ethical or
moral views, or attitudes toward life. Associations of advertising communication
with media necessarily impart experiences, a carryover effect of those values that
may be attached to the media. To the extent that these values are operative in
media, they will effect how a message is processed and the likelihood of achieving
the desired response objective.

Turning next to the emotional arousal possibilities attendant to media, one
is dealing with particular perceptual and cognitive understandings of media: such

things as the mood evoked and the perceived pattern of the media or its general theme. One might merely enjoy watching television more than reading a magazine or newspaper. This could form the basis for perceiving an emotionally satisfying similarity in the communication experiences collected by that media. For example, enjoyment of a particular television program could precipitate greater enjoyment of an advertisement within that program, as opposed to another program or media. The experience would be similar, although the detail of the communication would differ (that is, program content versus advertisement).

It is also possible to consider both a cognitive and affective nature in the effect of media. Exposure to media obviously makes people aware, and people's evaluations of what they are made aware of cue responses conditioned by their earlier learned predispositions. More important, from a practical advertising standpoint, is the receiver's overt behavior. The allocation of discretionary time to various activities mediates the receiver's use of media. The way in which media fit into the everyday lives of people is affected by the extent to which a particular medium requires the exclusive attention of the receiver, as well as by kinds of activities with which that medium are comparable. For example, Weiss (1969) points out that although the introduction of television reduced the time people spent on other media, their total time devoted to all media actually increased.

In advertising, a great deal of effort is spent in an attempt to position a particular product or service as compatible with existing receiver attitudes toward an end of holding current brand users and attracting new users away from other brands or product alternatives. The effect of media on the success of this effort is rarely measurable in any tangible sense. While product success is ultimately measured in terms of sales, relating this to the advertising campaigns and the media used is not a suitable criterion for evaluating their effectiveness. Unfortunately, there are too many confounding variables in the marketing mix to control for, thus making it too difficult to determine the specific contribution of the advertising itself. As a result, the effectiveness of the media in contributing to positive behavior through an appropriate advertising response is often measured in terms of one of the response objectives, or such scheduling effects as salient awareness of a brand name, recall of specific sales message points, evaluations of the characteristics of a brand, and expressed interest in purchase.

This whole question of the relationship between sales and advertising or media effectiveness has been put into somewhat better perspective by Bauer (1964). He reminds us that even when a campaign is highly successful on the practical grounds of dollar increment in sales, this may mean no more than an increase of about one percent in a brand's current share of a high-turnover consumer product category. Considering that in terms of the total population of consuming households this may only represent a behavioral change in one-half of one percent, the probability of successfully measuring that change and attributing it to an effective use of media or a highly persuasive message is remote.

And to further complicate the matter, Bauer (1964) suggests that a campaign may be highly successful financially even though it positively affected fewer people in terms of a specific advertising response than it alienated. The next section will discuss in more detail the widely held notion that the measured impact of mass media in persuasion is slight.

Measured Media Effect

In discussing measurements of the effectiveness of mass media, it should be noted that frequently the intention of effectiveness is no more than exposure to or recall of a communication message. When it comes to more stringent criteria, such as attitude or behavioral change (the goal of the buyer response hierarchy), the efforts of advertising and market researchers, as well as researchers in the area of political behavior, to measure such change has been embarrassing. As McGuire (1969a) points out, there is little evidence of attitude change, much less change in gross behavior, such as buying a particular brand or product, in the results of their labor. In fact, he mentions some results that even suggest mass media campaigns could have quite the opposite effect; Belson (1956), for example, found that television programs designed to enhance the viewers' confidence in their ability to speak French had precisely the opposite effect. Such results have, of course, befuddled those in the business of advertising and communication. They have tended to rationalize the problem by pointing out that these are effects other than attitudinal change that flow from mass media, or that the attitudinal effects are of a much more subtle nature than originally supposed.

McGuire (1969a) reviews eight "reinterpretations" of what he calls the communication researchers' considerable ingenuity in suggesting possible excuses that would permit them to maintain the hypothesis that the media really are effective in changing attitudes and behavior. We shall look at each, and how they may be of interest to those in the business of selecting a medium and creating advertising.

The first argument, which, he remarks, makes up in plausibility for what it lacks in profundity, is that the media actually are effective in changing attitudes and behavior, but that poor measures fail to pick up the produced change. As we commented above in discussing Bauer's (1964) analysis of the sales to advertising relationship, this is indeed a "plausible" explanation. But, even more to the point, most research conducted on the effects of advertising in changing attitude and behavior in the market rely on very crude attitude scales, assuming any research is done at all prior to the running of an advertising campaign in the media. And, even rarer is a longitudinal study that tracks attitude (although many panels exist for tracking longitudinal behavior). The fact that fluctuations in the use of advertising and various media and media weight does relate in a positive way to brand awareness (easily measured and important to both message processing and advertising response objectives), and this in turn to actual product use, does imply a certain effect on changing attitude and behavior through mass media. Plus, one is reminded of McGuire's (1972) own formulation of the probability of successful persuasibility through his information-processing paradigm. In considering a straightforward situation in which the persuasive effectiveness of an advertising campaign in the media markets compared with sales in nonmedia markets, the probability that a sizable difference in sales (that is, behavior) will be found is proportional to the joint probability that all behavioral steps of the information paradigm occur. This means that even with an even chance of each step occurring, the probability of success is about one chance in a hundred (and as he reminds us, anything like a .5 probability for any step with an advertising campaign is hardly likely). As a result, he remarks: "The wonder is not that advertising campaigns have so little effect but that they have any discernible effect at all." Given this, a strong argument seems to exist for thinking that most survey methodology will have a difficult time isolating statistically significant changes of less than one percent. However, one is cautioned that this argument is less appropriate to a new product or rapidly changing product category, in which greater fluctuations in share would be expected.

A second "reinterpretation" is that such a degree of selective exposure occurs that the receiver tends to receive only information supporting preexisting conceptions. Recalling the section in chapter 2 on selectivity and persuasibility, there is no evidence that this phenomenon of selective exposure is real. Therefore, on this point, we must agree that no reasonable explanation for the lack of measurable difference in attitude or behavior may be supported.

A third explanation is that one is often dealing with media effects in situations in which cancellation is likely to occur. In other words, the media weight or amount spent for one brand in a product category is quite likely to be very similar to that of other major brands in the same category. As a result, some communication researchers have suggested that receivers would tend to be exposed to messages for all brands more or less equally, assuming, of course, a common audience and no selective exposure. If this argument is followed, one could conclude that for every receiver convinced in switching to brand A from brand B, another is convinced in switching from brand B to brand A, while the majority remain unpersuaded. In effect, the comparable advertising for various brands tend to cancel each other out. This is reasonable, on first reading, but it completely neutralized all the other mediating variables effecting advertising response. And, as McGuire (1969a) remarks, this explanation fails to account for the difficulty in demonstrating the effectiveness of mass media public service campaigns, when there is no exposure to the opposition side. A close correlate to this explanation is a fourth possibility: that the media do not make converts, but do solidify one's preexisting preferences. In this case, one would argue the necessity of mass media advertising to insure canceling the effects of competitive advertising. However, once again, there is more to the dynamic of advertising communication than this simple formulation. To be sure, there is certainly a maintenance effect to media advertising, but the general lack of any measurable shifts in attitude or behavior is not sustained by this rather delicate balance among competitive advertising pressures.

A fifth contention is that it is too hard a test of mass media to evaluate their effectiveness in terms of behavioral or attitudinal change when one is dealing with highly salient and entrenched beliefs. This is a frequent argument among those engaged in research on electioneering. Yet, it is certainly a contemporary shibboleth that candidates for public office, particularly presidential candidates, are "packaged" by the media (cf. McGuinnis's *The Selling of the President*). And, there does not seem to be any greater effect when the message is dealing with less weighty issues, such as what brand of a particular product the receiver should buy, or what service he should subscribe to.

The sixth point offered by McGuire (1969a) has less application to product advertising than to political campaigns or other more galvanizing issues. In order to handle the mildly embarrassing finding that those who expose themselves most to this type of mass media communication show less opinion change than those who are not exposed, researchers argue that those who expose themselves most to mass media in these situations are better informed, more highly educated, more stable individuals who enter the opinion arena with more firmly formulated opinions. While this may in fact be true, many other receiver characteristics mediate response to advertising, and it is doubtful that these particular sample biases are sufficiently large to account for the differences in opinion change noted. This sort of post hoc reasoning, while perhaps applicable in these severe instances, does little to "explain" the general lack of measured media effect in changing attitudes and behavior.

The two remaining "reinterpretations" are more concerned with rather complex theorizing about social and cognitive processes. The first of these is the two-step model of communication discussed in chapter 2 (cf. Katz 1957). One recalls that according to this notion, mass media advertising communication directly effects only so-called "opinion leaders" who subsequently influence others through word-of-mouth communication. As a result, to measure the true effectiveness of attitudinal or behavioral change, one must rely on the effectiveness of the opinion leaders in transferring the desired message, and here one finds it difficult to gather accurate measures. The final saving explanation is that mass media may not change opinions on given issues, but do affect the relative salience of the current issues (Berelson 1942; McPhee 1952). Taking this tack, assuming one understood what existing positive saliences were in terms of attitude and behavior within a product category, increased usage could be effected by associating one's brand with these favorable saliences through advertising. If this were truly an explanation for the seemingly low correlation between mass media communication and attitude or behavior change, it would imply that, generally, advertisers are unsuccessful in stressing appropriate saliences.

Whatever the reason, there is no getting around the point that mass media effects in changing attitudes or behavior are seldom measured. In an analysis of Nielsen retail index data for a period of several years for a number of different brands (Peckham 1975), it was found that for most brands that have been on the market for a number of years (say 12 to 15 years or more) the change in advertising share required to produce an additional one percentage point gain in market share was 20 percent. This is an incredible amount of change for a competitive market, and one not likely to be cost-efficient. For newer established brands that have been in the market some two to five years, the relationship is not quite so severe; a change of about five percent in advertising share is required to produce a one percent increase in market share. These empirical results could be seen as supporting the belief that changes in attitude and behavior do indeed occur as the result of mass media, but that the changes are generally slight (and hence difficult to measure), unless major dislocations in the relative share of competitive advertising expenditure are present.

A final consideration of this question involves the traditionally passive nature of most measures of attitude and behavior change resulting from mass media. Such measures rarely address either message processing or advertising response objectives: they usually assess some general measure of recall or expressed intention, inferring from those results the effectiveness of the communication. Aside from the fact that actual attitudinal or behavioral change has not been a focus of the measure, Wright (1976) suggests that, in most studies, the environment in which the subjects are placed has not been constructed purposefully. In particular, he finds little effort has been made to match the environment of a postexposure measurement of product evaluations or preference (reflective of a change in attitude) with that which the subject acting as a real-world consumer would be likely to face. If an actual behavioral change or attitudinal change occurs as the result of an advertising communication, efforts to measure that change should try to match the measurement environment with anticipated real-world decision environment on factors important to that process. Of course, this presupposes one understands the consumer choice process involved, and can effectively simulate the appropriate environment. Wright (1976) recommends using an active evaluation on choice task as the context for postexposure measures of mass media advertising effects since the ultimate goal of such advertising communication is to influence the choice the receiver makes. He cautions that if the measurement environment creates controlled conditions unrepresentative of the real-world decision process of consumers, such measures of postexposure effectiveness on attitude or behavior change could be unsteadying.

In addition, one should understand that the majority of research on the question of mass media effectiveness in changing attitudes or behavior is conducted through field research rather than research in a laboratory setting. Hovland (1959) has pointed out that research on attitude change tends to show a large amount of attitude change occurring in laboratory situations, while relatively little tends to occur in field studies. This suggests a possibility of certain methodological problems in the manner in which mass media research is conducted—problems beyond those considered above by McGuire (1969a) and Wright (1976). For example, field studies of mass media advertising effect usually take place days or even weeks after the message appeared in print or on broadcast media (with the exception of recall measures, which are generally taken 24 hours or so after exposure).

In summary, any measured effect of mass media in changing attitudes and behavior is rarely documented. While a number of explanations are offered for this disquieting result, little actual research has been directed at coming up with a satisfactory explanation. With the incredible amount of money spent each year for advertising in mass media, it does not seem too demanding to hope for some media-sponsored or advertiser-sponsored efforts toward a better understanding of this dilemma. On the one hand, millions are spent on an effort to change attitudes and behavior through advertising; on the other, one cannot demonstrate that it is money well spent.

Modality Effect

Much of the recent interest in the question of whether auditory or visual modes of communication are most effective stems from work among communication researchers in the area of information processing, and critical to this work is an understanding of the internal channels of message encoding and transmission. Laming (1973) suggests that this process involves an initial encoding of a message into a suitable form of signal that is passed physically through some transmission channel to a receptor that then performs the inverse transformation (decoding) on the received signal to recover the original message. This encoding is necessary in order to convert the message into an acceptable form for internal transmission and processing. It is desirable, when considering the sensory modes involved in a communication, to match the message to the statistical properties of the channel. While it is beyond the scope of this book to detail the mathematical theory underlying these statistical properties (the interested reader will find a review of several models in Laming [1973]), work by Jacobson (1951), Pierce and Karlin (1957), and others, suggest that the maximum input from reading is probably somewhat less than that for hearing.

The process of encoding may be thought of as being so arranged as to achieve the theoretical maximum efficiency of internal transmission for processing. This formulation is based on two assertions: (a) the receiver's performance involves, formally, the transmission of messages through a channel of limited capacity; and (b) the limitation on the speed of performance (Laming 1973). Jacobson (1950) estimates that these channels of transmission can handle only one percent of the information that can be taken in by the ear. Shannon (1949) has established through a series of theorems that an appropriate coding system always exists, although it may not necessarily be a simple one. It will depend on the probabilities of stimuli rather than their identities, and moreover, in a discontinuous fashion. This limitation on transmission capacity implies that prior to the critical section of the central nervous system at which performance is limited, there must be some quite flexible mechanism shaping the neural signals so as to ensure their optimum onward transmission. The effect this has on communication modality may be understood by considering that when the combined input from two senses exceeds the amount of information the central nervous system can handle, conditions of interference are set up; and unfortunately, it would seem that this means interference between channels may occur at any rate of presentation except a very slow one.

It is important to bear in mind at this point that the neural channels from the sense receptors are clearly separate. Broadbent (1958) speculated that the selective process involved in handling interference between channels could be explained in terms of a one-channel model of information processing. In modifying this model, Travers (1964) provided for a series of "compressions" of information, first by the sense organs involved and the peripheral nervous system, then by recoding and categorizing of the input. Then, he assumes a short-term memory of two to three seconds that can store information from one channel, while another channel is discharging through some gatekeeping and organizing mechanism.

Thus, it appears that consideration of a neural transmission model does not lead to any invariant measure of any aspect of receiver performance. Differences in speed or reaction to a stimulus mode are related to differences in the discriminability of the stimuli and to subtle relations between stimuli and responses compatibility which have no natural representation within the framework of an ideal internal transmission model.

The modality question in terms of impact on persuasibility generally concerns whether the written or the spoken word is more effective: visual versus auditory. As we have discussed, there should be no commonality of neural transmission, so one is dealing strictly with modal effect. Overall, the finding has been that when a persuasive communication is presented in either a spoken or written form, the spoken word has had more persuasive impact. This result is somewhat surprising, since a significant body of research (see McGuire 1969a) has generally found that comprehension is greater with reading than hearing. Since it would be reasonable to assume that, all other influences held constant, comprehension should be positively related to persuasive impact, one must conclude that other stages in message processing have a greater persuasive impact in the hearing than in the reading situation. While the likely candidate is encoding, the difference in effect must be overwhelming, in order to counter the opposite tendency in comprehension.

One would also expect certain conditions in various mediating variables to influence the persuasive impact of particular communication modes. For example, the relationship of the receiver and source has been discussed in terms of a message's mode of communication, as has the influence of the source alone. Male sources have been shown to be perceived as more credible when heard than when attributed to written messages (Whittaker and Meade 1967). May (1965) has pointed out that individual receiver differences enter into the relative ability to learn from different modes.

Schramm (1973) has suggested that the learning effectiveness of different modes and combinations of modes seems to depend more on how they are used, and for whom, than on the mode itself. As a result, he concludes that there is no particular magic in multimedia presentations as such. Hartman (1961) goes even further, pointing out that when conditions for interference are present (that is, in any but a very measured presentation through multiple modes), the inclusion of too much may actually produce inferior learning, because the receiver's attention is divided and optimal learning is not possible in any of the channels. The implications for advertising are significant, considering the vast utilization of television, a bimodal medium. The tradition of message construction in television advertising is to place the majority of the information in the verbal audio mode and to use the visual mode to attract attention and illustrate the message. However, pictures often distract more than they illustrate; and attention-getting devices are of value only if they do not interfere with learning. Too often, the visual component of a commercial is not properly related to the audio track and a real barrier to effective communication is created by a tendency to focus attention on the visual when the message to be learned has been coded in the audio. This, of course, underscores the need to evaluate all advertising executions in terms of what the advertisement communicates.

PERSONAL VERSUS MASS MEDIA IMPACT

Interpersonal and mass media communication channels are indeed different, but as Katz (1957) and others imply with their two-step models of communication, the roles of each are potentially complementary. For example, in interpersonal communication, the source and the channel could be the same individual. But, if an advertiser wished to communicate first with so-called opinion leaders, in hope that they would then communicate, on an interpersonal level, the advertiser's message, the opinion leader becomes more a channel and less a source for the communication (or, more correctly, a secondary source transmitter). This whole notion of a two-step flow of communication rests on the belief that interpersonal communication between a receiver and someone the receiver knows or identifies with carries more persuasive impact than mass media.

A great deal of the basis for this belief comes from the fact that, in most situations, interpersonal communication involves two-way channels, with the receiver able to communicate back to the source, while mass media, of course, offers little opportunity for immediate feedback. This inherent superiority in effecting more persuasible communication is well documented, and McGuire (1969a) offers a review of five variables possibly responsible.

Active participation

The amount of active participation on the part of the receiver is quite naturally greater in interpersonal communication than in mass media. As a result, the receiver is more restrained in actively disagreeing with the source individual than the receiver would be when seeing or hearing the same message in mass media. In fact, advertising response is accelerated to a point that the receiver is more likely to make a decision and publicly state it, thus reinforcing the induced attitude or behavior change. An interpersonal situation is likely to find the receiver more aware of the social consequences of a decision among peers because of greater participation, facilitating an attitude or behavior change on the part of the receiver (Bennett 1955; Zajonc 1968). This is a well-known principle in personal selling: involving the receiver (or prospect) and forcing commitment. Mass media generally lacks this ability to involve the receiver actively in the communication in order to accelerate advertising response.

Feedback

As we have already discussed in a number of contexts, interpersonal communication enjoys the advantage of more immediate feedback from the receiver to the source. This permits the source to judge the relative impact of the message through not only verbal response from the receiver, but nonverbal communication as well (cf. Rosenthal 1967). Once again, these are well-known principles in personal selling. The effective salesperson adjusts the message and delivery to suit the particular requirements and reactions of the audience. With mass media, even when efforts are made to secure feedback on the communication's effectiveness in an advertisement, the ability to respond quickly and individually is missing. Practitioners, of course, attempt to anticipate reactions a priori (either through some pretesting procedures, audience research, or, more often, their supposed "knowledge of the market"), but the nature of large and diverse audiences make this a difficult and inexact task.

Commonality of interest

This point deals with the source-receiver relationship, as it was discussed in chapter 3. It suggests a probability of greater empathy with the personal source, while minimizing the tendency for mass media sources to be perceived as more prestigious. This makes a certain amount of intuitive good sense, if one considers it more likely that a given message is persuasible when the source is directly presented to a receiver's senses than when it is presented indirectly through print or broadcast media. Appealing as this notion may be, there does not seem to be any consistent literature to support it; nevertheless, it offers a possible explanation for the apparent superiority of interpersonal communication on persuasibility.

Attention factors

It could be that interpersonal communication is more likely to be attended to than mass media. Ignoring such claims as "selective attention," which have been discussed early as unlikely in any event (cf. McGuire 1968c), it is still socially easier to leave the room during a commercial break seeking something to eat, or to divert one's attention to some other stimulus in the presence of mass media than it would be to disengage another person when the person is talking with you. And, as McGuire notes (1969a), the attention advantage of interpersonal communication obtains even on a more passive, less psychodynamically interesting basis: the wanderings of attention deriving from the simple weakness of the flesh, such as boredom, fatigue, and intellectually limited attention, are more likely to interfere with a receiver's reception of mass media communication. The demands of courtesy and the efforts of the communicator in interpersonal communication will, in all probability, minimize such inattention, permitting the receiver a more solid potential for advertising response.

Social context

While less interesting from an advertising viewpoint, there is some suggestion that the social environment in which one receives a message mediates its impact. For example, it has been found that a compactly seated audience shows less opinion change than one more scattered, even though these same audiences exhibit no appreciable differences in the enjoyment of or learning of message content (Furbay 1965). This is a finding that should be instructive to those who rely on "theater audience" measures of advertising persuasibility: the context of the test could very well effect the resulting measures. Also, though not conclusive, there is some evidence that a counter-norm communication is resisted more strenuously among an attitudinally homogeneous group, than in the presence of a more heterogeneous group. Again, the importance of this finding would seem great on so-called "disaster check" focus groups, in which subjects thought to be of like mind are used to ensure that no serious problems exist with a given advertising execution prior to final production. Aside from the more conceptual problems with this approach to advertising pretesting, the problem of the social context of the presentation looms significant. In both of these cases, one would anticipate lower than actual indications of persuasibility.

The literature on diffusion of innovation (for example, Rogers 1962; Weiss 1969) also seems to indicate a greater role for interpersonal communication in influencing the diffusion of innovation within a society. While some productive roles are noted for mass media communications, particularly in developing countries or among less elite populations when the source is a high status government organization, personal influence remains overwhelmingly the more important factor in the learning of new techniques.

Part II
Mass Media Planning
in Advertising

The entire area of media planning is something of an enigma. While it is clear that the objective in advertising media planning is to deliver a creative message to a group of target receivers in an efficient manner, there seems to be little consensus as to how one goes about the task. In part, this may be a function of the lack of explicit media behavior data available for most target receivers. Planners attempt to match available media behavior profiles they feel reflect those of the target receivers; but the problem, of course, is that they rarely have media behavior for a desired group of receivers, but only for a general group.

Next, a planner usually worries about how those media that seem to generally qualify as reaching the target receiver may perform against a series of artificial constraints in so-called reach and frequency efficiencies per dollar spent. In other words, which media are cheaper in delivering the desired reach and frequency against the desired audience? Although in principle not unreasonable, a media's reach and frequency will have been estimated against a target whose actual media behavior is unknown. And, compounding this problem, almost all available media data is averaged (usually over four-week units), totally confounding any analysis of real exposure effects. As a result, it is difficult to empirically support any particular media planning decisions against other reasonable alternatives: one simply changes one's assumptions.

In this chapter, the media planning process is reviewed as it is generally followed in advertising. Two basic approaches are found in media planning: (1) in the majority of cases, media planners concern themselves with how mass media, such as newspapers, magazines, radio or television and media vehicles (the specific stations and publications) are exposed to receivers; (2) in the others, planners concern themselves with how receivers make themselves available to mass media. All, however, use the same constructs and the same syndicated research data. The media planning process is outlined in Figure 5.1.

Once the general marketing problem is presented, media planners may draw on existing background knowledge that supports the advertising strategy, specific brand strategy, and creative strategy. Each of these areas has obvious mediating effects on eventual media decisions. For example, if the advertising strategy is built on a particular formulation of the market place, an understanding of this competitive environment would perhaps suggest tighter media-oriented target receiver definitions; the brand marketing strategy could be regional in nature, with attending media considerations; and the creative strategy has par-

FIGURE 5.1

The Media Planning Process

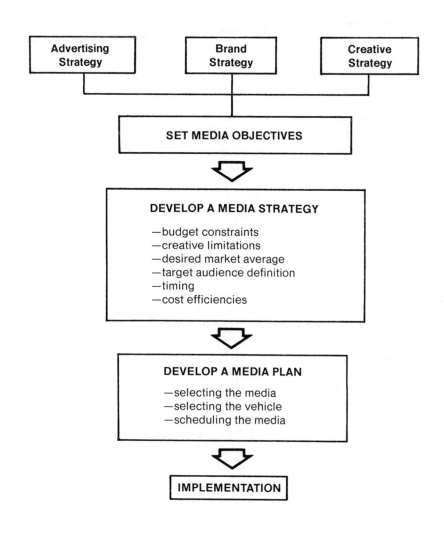

ticular modal concerns (for example, print versus broadcast), which must be addressed with media.

Using this knowledge as background, a planner can begin to address specific media approaches to help meet advertising, marketing, and creative objectives. A strategy incorporating these objectives is developed in which practical options for accomplishing them are spelled out. Now, the media planner should be in a position to study the best media alternatives that could play a role in achieving the strategic objectives. After the media selection is made, intramedia (or vehicle) selections must be considered. These are aimed at selecting one or more vehicles that effectively reaches an optimum number of prospects, generally by following four principles (Sissors and Petray 1976): (a) an optimum amount of frequency (or repetition); (b) at the lowest cost-per-thousand prospects reached (called a CPM analysis of cost-efficiency); (c) with a miniimum of waste (nonprospects); (d) within a specified budget. The rub comes, as we have mentioned, in obtaining anything like an actual accounting of all but the last of these principles. Finally, a schedule is developed which allocates the selected media vehicles over the length of time covered by the original budget.

One might legitimately ask whether there is ever such a thing as an optimum or "best" media strategy—one that is generally applicable to most advertising situations. The answer is no. Everyone has different ideas about the marketing objectives for their products, so media alternatives available to meet those objectives may be different. A media plan is developed specifically to meet the needs of an advertiser at a given point in time following the marketing and advertising strategy then advanced.

Even when considering strategy for a single brand, the selection of specific media varies as a function of how the target audience definition is viewed; and in addition, those involved in the media decision (advertiser, agency account personnel, media planners) all tend to have their own subjective evaluation of the desirability of using particular media or specific vehicles. To a large extent, these decisions are based upon someone's perception of the editorial or programing impact of certain media vehicles as more compatible with their view of the target receivers' probable tastes. The same audience data may be used by everyone involved in media planning, but the variations in interpretive "weighting" applied to the figures used for classifying the delivery of specific media vehicles by audience type are as numerous as practitioners.

It would be easy to get the impression that an incredible amount of advertising dollars is spent almost at whim, since there seems to be such an endless list of acceptable alternatives in media planning. The fact of the matter is, though, that most of this variation is found within classes of media vehicles that deliver essentially the same audience profile. One does not usually find arguments made for including an automotive specialty book in a plan for a baby-care product rather than a women's service magazine on the grounds that, after all, some women with babies are interested in cars. More likely, you will find arguments being made for one versus another women's service magazine (such as *Ladies Home Journal* and *Redbook*), or a women's service magazine versus a home magazine (such as *Better Homes & Gardens*), all with essentially a strong under 35 female readership. Unless one has a good set of primary research data relating specific media behavior to specific receivers of interest, the insensitive nature of available audience research data will continue to encourage wide speculations on appropriate media plans.

DETERMINING MEDIA OBJECTIVES AND STRATEGY

Ideally, the development of media objectives and strategy is a natural outgrowth of a consideration of the other four independent mediating variables: knowledge of the receiver, source, message, and scheduling. By providing a target receiver oriented perception of the brand and product category (for example, through segmentation research), media objectives and strategy will be better oriented toward maximizing agreed upon advertising and marketing strategy; questions of creative unit, and one hopes editorial or program environment, are answered by the creative strategy; and consideration of the desired advertising response will help guide scheduling. For example, the objective of the advertising may be to make as many people as possible aware of a new brand (an awareness response), suggesting one maximize reach, or the number of receivers exposed at least once to the message. Alternatively, the objective may be to explain the need for the new brand (a cognitive response), perhaps suggesting one maximize frequency, or the number of times a receiver will be exposed to a message.

Media decisions, just as all other decisions in the creation and delivery of an advertising communication, should be considered within the broad context of these mediating variables and how each decision will ultimately affect the desired advertising response. In setting media objectives, one should be concerned with maximizing the probability of achieving the desired advertising response, selecting strategies for fulfilling those objectives. Typically, however, media objectives are more likely to be chosen on product usage criteria. For example, if one were introducing a new frozen food product, it would not be unusual for a media planner to consider alternative objectives, such as:

a. Buying media against heavy frozen food users

b. Buying and scheduling media in a similar pattern to that of leading frozen food advertiser

c. Concentrating media in high category development (CDI) areas

d. Setting a minimum level of expenditure based on competitive share-of-advertising to share-of-market ratios for category leaders

e. Attempting to achieve a message frequency twice that of the leading frozen food advertiser (sacrificing reach).

As one can see, the principle thrust of these alternative media objectives is against existing market behavior. Little concern has been shown for what impact an effective implementation of these objectives might have on particular advertising responses.

It is often hypothesized that heavy users of a product should be most likely to try a new product in that category. But, what if heavy users tend to be brand loyal? What if a fresh understanding of attitudes toward category behavior has been developed, and the creative message for a brand is designed to expand category usage? Obviously if either were the case, it should most certainly temper the final choice of media objectives; and, if the information were available, in all likelihood it would. Unfortunately, the orientation, in practice, would still be against marketing objectives rather than maximizing communication. While one should certainly not ignore the marketing considerations, they must be viewed within the framework of stimulating the desired advertising response kneaded by the independent mediating variables.

Constraints on Strategic Development

Major constraints placed upon the determination of media objectives and strategy center around the size of the advertising budget and the accepted creative strategy. While it is possible to set media objectives and strategy in line with an advertiser's marketing and communication goals, and to let these objectives and strategies serve as a guide in setting a budget, as a rule, the money available for media is established long before any consideration has been given to media goals, forcing one to set media objectives and subsequent strategy within those bounds. Constrained by this limitation, choice of media and the depth of impact needed are directly affected and frequently compromised. For example, television is more expensive than print, and could be sacrificed in a media plan if reasonable levels of impact on target receivers cannot be affected.

When an advertising media budget is insufficient to realistically meet the intended marketing and communication goals of an advertiser, a number of alternatives present themselves: (a) the marketing or communication goals may have to be modified to conform to the budget; (b) discounts may be obtainable through selected media vehicles; (c) scheduling could provide for longer hiatus periods or modified reach and frequency objectives; (d) or finally, the advertiser may be better advised to forgo advertising completely, until the advertiser can afford a meaningful plan.

More often than not, however, a media planner is forced to live within the budget constraints set by the advertiser and meet the original objective, even when the budget is known to be inadequate. This is a particularly prevalent occurrence when a small- to medium-sized company, unaccustomed to large advertising expenditures, decides to introduce a new product in competition with heavily advertised alternatives. Rarely is the company prepared to make the necessary budgetary commitment to adequately support a new product introduction.

The influence of creative strategy on establishing media objectives and strategy is most clearly evident in a priori creative decisions to use television or print. These decisions, from a creative viewpoint, may have been predicated on a need to demonstrate a product in use (which would generally require the use of television), or the need for a refutational strategy (which usually requires print execution—see chapter 4, "Message Strategy"). More subtle creative constraints on media decisions involve specific creative execution: such things as 30 second versus 60 second commercial lengths, page size in print, two-page spreads, and color versus black and white.

Finally, a number of minor constraints may also figure in setting media objectives and strategy. The nature of the product or brand to be advertised could have strategic implication because of seasonality or other unique usage characteristics. For example, although beer may be advertised in the winter, it is more heavily advertised in the summer. If broadcast media are used, it would be important to consider the fact that summer media habits are different from winter media habits, because people are outdoors more often. Other products may be directed toward very specific audiences: teenagers or older adults, tennis players, golf players, skiers. Each of these audiences would raise the question of whether to use general media or specific media. While 96 percent of the readers of *Tennis* magazine may play tennis, only 5 percent of all tennis players may read *Tennis* magazine; on the other hand, 95 percent of all tennis players may watch television, but most of the people who watch television don't play tennis. These types of factors must be considered when attempting to optimize media objectives and strategy.

Past use of media by an advertiser often leads to habitual behaviors. Large corporate media buys frequently restrict the availability of media and program or vehicle selection for one or more of the company's brands (particularly a smaller or less significant brand). For example, a large package goods company with many brands (like General Foods or Procter and Gamble) will make a major media buy, and then allot time or space to various brands. Even when a company's brands are assigned to different advertising agencies, a single "agency of record" will be selected to place all of the company's advertising. While certain cost efficiences are certainly realized by the company, this can frequently be inefficient for specific brands.

Competitive activity in media use and spending levels frequently affect how media decisions are made; such things as share-of-market and share-of-advertising ratios often affect the setting of media objectives and strategy. It is always good practice to study the strategies of competitiors before planning one's own. However, this should not override the critical importance of setting media goals to maximize efficiency in satisfying the desired advertising response. Unfortunately, the general constraints on media objectives and strategy rarely involve considerations of their effect on advertising response.

Specifying Receivers

In its broadest terms, media objectives and strategy should consider to whom the advertising message is directed. This is, of course, essential to achieving proper advertising objectives, as both media variables and receiver variables are important mediators of advertising response. Most media objectives and strategies will, for obvious reasons, include some statement indicating where the receivers are to be found geographically. Unfortunately, most media plans will then go no further in defining the sought after receivers than to describe them roughly in demographic terms, or possibly some gross behavioral measurement, such as usage. As will be pointed out in some detail later in a discussion of media and media vehicle selection, while this is certainly a convenient way to describe the target receivers, it approaches the question more in terms of market rather than communication considerations.

Media planners are admonished to be as specific as possible in their definitions, because vague or subjective evaluations cannot be translated to syndicated media research data for "efficiency" analysis, and it is thought that this could lead to wasted exposure on individuals who would never buy a given product or brand under any circumstances. Yet, that is exactly what occurs when target receiver definitions are based primarily on demographic characteristics. However, because the "validity" of any given media plan is evaluated against that demographic definition, it is thought to be correct. True, with a well executed media plan, one will have delivered a set of receivers as demographically defined by the media objectives and strategy. But, since demographic characteristics are notoriously poor predictors of the receivers one is actually hoping will respond to one's advertising, there is no way of knowing for sure if the plan delivered the actual receivers desired (at least not efficiently).

Another consideration related to receivers and setting media objectives and strategy is some specification of the coverage levels desired. In other words, how many of the desired receivers should we attempt to reach with a specific media plan? While 100 percent coverage would be ideal from a practical standpoint, finding every receiver one would like is almost impossible. The limited task of reaching very high coverage levels in selected markets can also be a tedious and expensive effort, even assuming one knew, from a communication standpoint, to whom one wished to present the message.

Most media have significantly overlapping audiences, so, as you buy more and more media to increase reach, the majority of your money is doing nothing more than reaching the same people over and over again (increasing frequency). In trying to reach more receivers, the media planner would again almost certainly be constrained largely to demographic definitions. But, suppose the advertiser had primary research available relating receivers and media behavior, and it was known that the target receivers tended to consume particular media and selected media vehicles. This would certainly improve one's chance of effectively increasing reach.

Coverage using the major media vehicle alternatives available may only constitute about 40 percent of the receivers, but reaching the remainder with more select media could be much too expensive. Still, it would be important to establish a coverage goal, for selection and use of media will necessarily be based upon it. The usual factor affecting frequency goals (discussed below) also play a part; and one would hope that consideration of the effects of coverage on expected advertising response would be included.

Continuity

Another important component of media objectives and strategy is how the media and media vehicle selection should be scheduled. While the details of scheduling are left to a later chapter, some discussion as it relates to media objectives and strategy will be useful at this point. A number of marketing considerations legitimately play a role here. For example, some products have definite sales volume peaks during the year, and it would make sense to concentrate advertising during those times (unless, of course, one's strategy were to expand usage during off-peak periods). Other products, while exhibiting certain predictable high and low seasonal fluctuations in sales, may require a continuous program of advertising. An illustration of this may be found with frozen products, which generally slacken off in sales during the warmer months. Nonetheless, one would not wish to eliminate summer advertising, although the media strategy might well recommend a somewhat lighter schedule for the summer months (perhaps in line with an overall advertising strategy calling only for "reminder" advertising during the slower summer period).

The introduction of a new product would also be a case in which marketing variables are critical to the continuity of a media plan. Advertising cannot break until distribution is achieved. At that point, a heavy introduction period is usually scheduled, followed by a more normal sustaining level for the remainder of the year. However, a new product may not roll-out nationally, but in a series of regional introductions, as manufacturing capabilities and distribution are obtained. This would have obvious implications on the continuity of a total media program, necessitating regional or "spot" analysis of the schedules.

And, in addition, to these market considerations, there are a number of communication-oriented questions that must be considered. A major question is: What is the effect of repetition on advertising response for a particular product or brand? If, for example, an awareness advertising response is the primary communication objective, is it more effective to run continuous advertising at moderate levels, high-level advertising with periodic hiatuses, or as much pressure as possible in a short period of time, with the hope that the initial levels of awareness and trial generated will be sustained over time at a reasonably high level? This and other important questions are addressed later, in the chapter on media scheduling.

Reach and Frequency

It is important, when considering media objectives and strategy, to determine whether one is primarily interested in maximizing either reach or frequency, and the level of each desired. When a media planner selects media or specific media vehicles, the planner is, in effect, choosing those that will deliver a given number of desired receivers; and reach and frequency are the two principal measures of a media schedule's delivery. Reach may be defined as the number of receivers reached (or more correctly, presented) by a media vehicle at least once during some specified time period—typically, four weeks. Frequency may be defined as the average number of times each receiver reached is exposed to the vehicle. Given a constant amount of money, it should be obvious that an increase in reach will mean a decrease in frequency, and vice versa. Therefore, in setting objectives and planning strategy, one must generally settle for maximizing one or the other, rather than both.

It should be equally clear that the concepts of reach and frequency cannot really be treated separately. The nature of mass media makes it all but impossible to develop any reasonably large media schedule that does not present the advertiser's message to at least some receivers more than once. Even if the advertisement was placed only in a single magazine or newspaper, there is a good probability a few receivers would be exposed to it more than once (as they looked through the magazine or newspaper on several occasions). Only in broadcast media does a single insertion generally mean a receiver will be afforded only one opportunity for exposure. But, even here, duplication is almost guaranteed if more than one vehicle within the medium is selected.

The specific levels of reach and frequency considered by media objectives and strategy have an important effect on subsequent selection of media or media vehicle. Network television, for example, when purchased as a program or set of programs, tends to provide a very high frequency level. This level, however, will tend to drop off significantly if scattered buys on network television are made, when the time purchased is distributed over a number of different shows. When daytime television is included as part of a media mix, it will usually produce higher frequency levels than prime time. If one includes radio in the mix, higher frequency levels would again be expected. Magazines, on the other hand, apart from any repeat exposure possible from a single issue, tend to build frequency much slower than other media.

This leads one quickly to two specific strategy questions: How much reach, and how much frequency, are necessary for an effective media plan? Once again one finds that in practice there are few rules to follow, and as a result, a great deal of "expert judgment" is permitted to condition the choice. Still, a few guidelines may be presented, which reflect some of the more general experiential maxims of media planning. For example, when a medium reaches 70 percent of the target receivers, it becomes increasingly difficult to inexpensively add any more reach. A goal of 100 percent reach would be all but impossible to attain, however desirable, in any but the most concentrated and easily identified group of receivers (a situation that usually recommends a direct mail campaign). One might consider building reach by selecting a variety of different vehicles, but, because of duplication in reach among most media vehicles that would be expected to reach the same target receivers, there are likely to be few new receivers added with each new vehicle; frequency would tend to increase with very little increase in reach. As a result, it is often too costly to go beyond certain levels in building reach. Considerable early attention must go into a study of the size of a market and the characteristics of the target receivers, in order to provide reasonable estimates of the probability of attaining various reach levels without adding more frequency (unless, of course, one is also interested in high frequency).

Another guideline to establishing appropriate levels of reach may involve the advertiser's marketing plan. If the marketing objective is to build a franchise through the addition of new customers (as opposed to increasing usage among current users), the media strategy must then consider where these new customers are to be found. If they are supposed to come from a competitor's customers, or from new segments of the market attitudinally or behaviorally disposed toward use, the reach level will be predicted on some estimate of the size of those groups and the probability of converting them to customers—the lower this probability, the higher the required reach level.

Finally, the level of reach may depend on the required level of frequency. One guideline followed in this case is the expected response of the receiver to the advertiser's message. It has been suggested, for example, that it is necessary to see a persuasive advertisement three times in order to understand fully the message (Krugman 1972). While this would seem to obviously imply an effort to maximize frequency at exactly three, the matter is not quite so simple, as Krugman notes. Being presented a message three times (which is what a frequency of three as measured by syndicated media research would mean) does not necessarily mean that the receiver attended to the message three times. And, even if an actual frequency of three might optimize desired advertising response, there is no empirical way of knowing how many media "exposures" are necessary to generate actual receiver attention (at least with usually available media research data). In addition, as is noted later in the chapter on media scheduling, a schedule with a reported average frequency of three will be one to which, in reality, most of the receivers are actually exposed fewer than the expected three times.

In practice, though, a media planner will try to match the frequency levels of competitive alternatives to the advertised brand, especially the category leaders. When a brand is being advertised in well-developed markets (markets with high CDI, or category development index) where there is a lot of competitive advertising pressure, frequency levels are usually established to be at least as large as the competitors', or equal to or better than the frequency level of the number one market share competitor. The assumption in this reasoning is that greater frequencies are required in order to maximize the probability of receiver attention within the high level of competitive "nosie" (that is, other advertising).

One reason for looking at competitive reach and frequency when developing one's own media objectives and strategy is that, to some extent, the competitor's advertising strategy will be revealed. As a result, it is not unusual to take competitive strategies into account, probing for weaknesses to be exploited. An example of a competitive reach and frequency analysis is illustrated in Table 5.2.

What these data reveal is that brand B is spending much more than the other two major brands in the category in order to maintain a superior position in both reach and frequency. In addition, all three brands spend more heavily in the fourth quarter. Another brand looking to effectively compete in this market, especially if brand B is the major factor in the marketplace, must seriously consider meeting brand B spending in order to effectively gain a "share-of-voice" with consumers. And assuming the reason for the heavier media expenditures in the fourth quarter is because of a seasonal sales factor, it would make good sense, particularly for a new product, to outspend brand B in this last quarter.

All of this analysis, of course, assumes the advertiser can afford the spending levels involved, and is desirous of a strong run at the market leader. If less money is available, a more discrete media strategy will be necessary, possibly aimed at the other brands; or, a less general, more segmented approach to the market may be considered. In any event, a review of competitive reach and frequency will help the media planner more realistically appraise the plan's potential for success.

Overall, in considerations of reach and frequency for media objectives and strategy, most media planners adopt a rather simple strategy. In areas of high category development (CDI), they will seek to maximize reach when there is low brand development (BDI) for the advertiser, and to maximize frequency when there is a high BDI for the advertised brand. Their thinking follows from the general notion that one is seeking more triers of the advertised brand in low BDI areas and more frequent use of the advertised brand in high BDI areas. In low category development areas, media planners usually seek to maximize reach regardless of brand development, on the assumption that more people must be made aware of the brand. This thinking is summarized in Table 5.3.

Media planners, in dealing with this trade-off between reach and frequency, employ a concept called "effective reach." The underlying assumption of effective reach is that more than one exposure to an advertising communication

TABLE 5.2

Hypothetical Reach and Frequency Analysis

	1st Qt. Reach	Freq.	2nd Qt. Reach	Freq.	3rd Qt. Reach	Freq.	4th Qt. Reach	Freq.
Brand A	56	2.3	58	2.4	52	2.7	62	2.6
Brand B	83	4.1	81	4.0	87	4.9	92	6.0
Brand C	61	3.0	60	3.5	72	3.8	75	4.7

will probably be necessary to achieve the desired advertising response. How many exposures are necessary for a receiver to attend to a message, to adequately decode and then encode the desired response? Unfortunately, there is a considerable lack of empirical evidence in this area.

TABLE 5.3

Category and Brand Development Considerations in Reach and Frequency Objectives

Category Development	Brand Development	Reach and Frequency Objective
high CDI	low BDI	maximize reach
	high BDI	maximize frequency
low CDI	low BDI	maximize reach
	high BDI	maximize reach

Nevertheless, most advertising agencies will utilize certain "rules of thumb" in assessing effective reach. A typical cumulative reach function is shown in Figure 5.2. It is generally conceded that the rate of accumulated reach will begin to decline at the point where the frequency level begins to impact the response to advertising. Most agencies think of three exposures as the minimum level of frequency for effective reach. The upper level is less well defined, but is thought to be that point at which the message is no longer effective. Remember that Krugman (1972) argues that this point is, in fact, no more than three exposures. But, as was pointed out earlier, it may take a number of media exposures before a receiver becomes involved with a message.

In the current scheme of media planning, consideration of reach and frequency is perhaps the only area of media objective and strategy development where attention is drawn to the ability of mass media to mediate "persuasion" through exposure value, and hence the principles of advertising response. More often, however, those setting media objectives and strategy concern themselves with pragmatic budget and marketing constraints, thus encouraging a great deal of subjective evaluation in the actual use of media.

FIGURE 5.2

Cumulative Reach Function

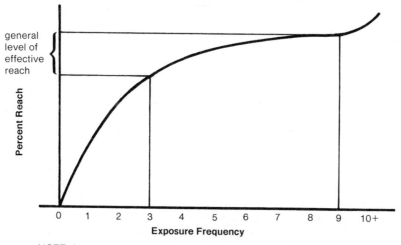

NOTE: At some point in time, increased frequency may stimulate a more
rapid increase in reach, but at this point the cost inefficiencies
are severe.

SELECTING MEDIA

Although a number of general criteria are available to the media planner
for use in the selection of specific media as the planner attempts to satisfy the
media objectives that have been established for a particular brand and the strategy
developed for its execution (several of which are discussed below), surprisingly
little is a result of research reported in the behavioral science literature. Among
those few examples that are available, however, indications are that print media
seem to more positively affect cognitive responses (that is, "thinking"). For example, Coffin (1975) has reported that the effects of print media, particularly
magazines, will tend to be more enduring than broadcast media. This may be
attributed to the higher probability of expected exposure to a persuasive message among magazine readers who will generally look through a single magazine a

single magazine a number of times. Krugman (1972) has found that cognitive arousal tends to be greater for advertising in magazines than for television commercials, and he has hypothesized that print media in general is more involving than broadcast media (Krugman 1967).

In a highly controlled test between a print versus radio execution of the same persuasive message, Wright (1974a) found significantly more total cognitive responses for the print execution—more support arguments or favorable inferences, and less source derogation. When the female subjects involved in the experiment were cued that they would be asked to evaluate the product being advertised, counter-arguing or unfavorable influence from the print message increased; it did not increase for the radio message. On the other hand, over a period of time, the radio message showed greater potential for both increases and decreases in various cognitive responses, compared with the print message. This, perhaps, follows from the more rapid rate of transmission for broadcast media, which could inhibit both the amount and variability of response activity, offered immediately upon hearing the message. This would provide relatively more opportunity over a period of time, for increases in cognitive responses to occur. While interaction between both content involvement and delayed (two days) cognitive responses were found with the radio message, no such delayed interactions were noted for the print message.

Considering the more traditional means of media comparison, one is struck by the obvious difficulty to be expected in cross media evaluations. A receiver does not "use" different media in the same way; nor does the receiver "expect" the same things from different media. As we have already seen, the modality of a persuasive message significantly affects the response to the advertising. A receiver watching television is not the same as one reading a magazine, just as the reader of a newspaper is not the same as a motorist passing a billboard. Even when the same message is presented in all four media, and, in fact, it is the same receiver in each case, the environmental and situational considerations mediating the reception of the message will vary significantly.

Nevertheless, a standard "measure" in cross media comparisons is audience size, without regard to (1) the condition of the receiver in the delivered audience, or (2) whether, in fact, the receiver is there at all. A Nielsen audimeter (source of television "ratings"), for example, records only the time a television set is turned on, not whether someone is actually watching. Thinking only of this one point (audience size), the reader should understand that syndicated mass media audience measurement can both overestimate and underestimate the size of the actual audience of receivers delivered—overestimate when magazine subscribers fail to read an issue or television viewers are distracted, and underestimate when magazine pass-along or word-of-mouth communication extend the reach of a particular media.

While all of the various criteria of mass media discrimination discussed earlier in this chapter are applicable to any mass media selection decision (and, in fact, should be considered), certain factors tend to be considered more than others. Crane (1972), for example, suggests there are at least seven dimensions characteristic of media choice: audience selectivity, existence in space or time, permanence, intrusiveness, concurrent symbol systems, sensory modality, and universality. In actual practice, the first three would be considered by a media planner in one fashion or another. "Intrusiveness" and "concurrent symbol systems" would be more likely to be subsumed by all involved in media selection approval (that is, the advertiser and agency account, media, and creative people) in their subjective evaluations. It is unlikely that the last two dimensions, although of obvious significance, would be a part of any conscious evaluation on the part of the media planner, although modality would no doubt temper all the others. These factors do enter into or affect media selection decisions, although rarely as a considered whole, or as mediators of advertising response. Their likely effects are discussed below.

Audience selectivity

Although, to a great extent, mass versus select audience choice is a media vehicle selection criterion (discussed later), it is also applicable as a media choice factor. The basic question of mass audience selectivity turns on one's knowledge of the media behavior of the target receivers, and how many "nontarget" receivers one is willing to buy. If, as is usually the case, very little is known of target receiver's specific media behavior, a mass audience medium, such as network television, mass interest magazines, or, on a local basis, newspapers, is selected. However, special interest media, such as opinion journals or classical FM radio could be selected, if specific information about one's target receivers suggest they consumed these media more often than other mass media. The more general the nature of one's information about his target receivers, the more likely a mass audience medium will be selected, on the theory that the probability of finding the desired target receivers will be greater than with more select audience media with comparable audience demographic profiles. One advertising medium, direct mail, as Crane (1972) mentions, can, in theory, collect an audience completely congruent with any target market segment, leaving no one out and including no one not desired; however, the use of direct mail has many practical limitations.

Existence in space or time

In an obvious relationship to modality, print media may be shown to occupy space, tending to spread audience delivery out over a period of time, while broadcast media occupy only the time a message is carried. Because print media occupy space, they may be presented to the receiver at the receiver's own pace, meshing with the receiver's ability to absorb the message. If one is considering a persuasive message requiring a great deal of detail in the copy—detail that may not be readily grasped with a single exposure—selecting print media rather than broadcast would seem the best course. The same would be true if a refutational strategy designed to reduce high negative salience were needed. On the other hand, if awareness were a principal goal of an advertising campaign, broadcast media may be more appropriate, because of their ability to stimulate both auditory and visual memory keys during the time of presentation.

Permanence

Closely related to media's existence in space or time is the permanence with which a message is held by a medium. Again, the relationship with modality is obvious: print media provide a permanent record of a persuasive advertising message, retrievable at a receiver's whim for the receiver's own purposes. Although not in the market for a particular product when first reading a periodical, a receiver may return to that vehicle "seeking out" information from the advertising at a later date, if the receiver enters the market. This would be particularly true of select audience print media. Broadcast media are not permanent in this same sense, occupying as they do only an allocation of time. However, utilizing music or other message variable techniques, it is possible to make a broadcast message more permanent by stimulating postexposure rehearsal. Coincident with this, broadcast media may be more likely to stimulate larger audiences through word-of-mouth carry-over effects than print (although magazines and other print media do have an advantage in possible pass-along).

Intrusiveness

Intrusiveness involves the ability of a medium to reach receivers who are not actively seeking information, or who may, in fact, be likely to avoid it. While this factor is strongly interrelated with the message itself, certain media, in themselves, effect independent mediation of the advertising response. For example, there is a certain voluntary action associated with newspaper or magazine readership—perhaps even more than with broadcast media. The receiver typically goes to print media for purposes other than persuasion. Involvement with a particular mass medium may facilitate attention to a particular persuasive advertising message because of viewer-reader-listener compatibility with the medium (and with the message). In general, mass media, such as print and broadcast, would be considered intrusive, while such media options as telephone Yellow Pages or catalogs would not be considered intrusive. The nature of one's communication problem should dictate the potential of nonintrusive media.

Concurrent symbol systems

Another consideration in the selection of media, although less likely to be directly involved in media thinking than with creative strategy, is the difference in the number of simultaneous symbol systems a medium can transmit. Print provides the ability to present an advertising message using both words and pictures, along with good control of color reproduction (in magazines) for hue, saturation, and intensity (a critical consideration for the so-called "beauty shot," particularly with food products). Radio offers both words and sound, varying on three auditory dimensions of tone, timbre, and volume, but subject to differing degrees of broadcast and reaction interference. Television, of course, employs all of these components, adding to them motion. As one might expect, however, in utilizing all these components television cannot meet the same high standards possible in other media for each separate component. If a specific component of an execution is to be maximized, an appropriate media selection should be made, where the component will benefit most. Overall, however, television tends to be the favorite media choice of creative people because it does permit the user so many creative options.

Sensory modality and universality

Sensory modality, as remarked earlier, tends to be reflected in other dimensions of Crane's formulation for media choice selection. The modality of a media selection has obvious significance which has already been examined in some detail in the last chapter and elsewhere. The notion of universality is Crane's final media selection factor, although in practice it would have little considered effect on media choice. He points out that, while speech is universally available to potential receivers regardless of their position in time or space, printed messages are possible only after an alphabet has been developed and people taught how to read. There is no doubt this is true, or that it provides an interesting print-broadcast media distinction. Yet, it is a distinction hardly relevant to the day-to-day practice of media selection.

More important to actual media selection (in the minds of most media practitioners) is the size of the audience delivered by any particular media. As outlined in Figure 5.3, all media provide both national and local audience delivery. The directional arrows reflect the historical development of a media's audience; either from national to local, or local to national. Broadcast networks traditionally provided only national audience delivery, while local stations offered spot or regional coverage; national magazines historically offered only national audience delivery, but in recent years have added editions providing regional audience delivery. Newspapers, on the other hand, were traditionally local, but now band together in offering package deals for groups of major

FIGURE 5.3

Media Audience Selection

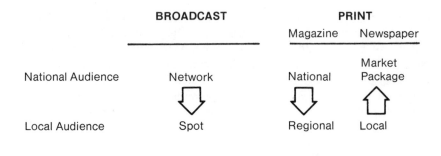

markets. The guidelines for media selection based upon specific audience delivery are provided by the media objective and strategy.

Despite the fact that reliable intermedia comparisons are difficult, requiring as we have seen the weighing of numerous factors, sometimes present, sometimes absent, with both positive and negative effects depending upon particular circumstances, all media will point to a wide range of "studies" and syndicated research data to show that they offer more potential for reaching your required target receivers than other media alternatives. The fact is that any medium has about as many reasons for inclusion in a media plan as it has limitations, depending on the situation (see Sissors and Petray 1976). As a result, too often deciding which media present the strongest argument in meeting a specific set of objectives and strategies involves a great deal of subjective judgment about the so-called "data" available. Some models do exist which include provisions for dealing with media selection, usually as a means of fulfilling some "objective function" (for example, MEDIAC, which is discussed more fully in the next chapter), but they utilize as input this same data. The task of media selection (without such a model) generally results from the conscious consideration of audience delivery size, some concern over the selectivity of the audience delivered and the media's relationship to space and time, all kneaded by feeling, intuitions, experience, and above all, cost. Serious consideration of the effects of a selected media on advertising response as such is, unfortunately, not likely.

SELECTING MEDIA VEHICLES

Attention is certainly paid to the selection of media in implementing a set of media objectives and strategies; however, the bulk of a media planner's efforts go into the selection of media vehicles within the selected media. Nearly all of the determinants of media objectives and strategies, as well as the criteria of media choice just discussed, enter in some way into the media vehicle selection decision. If print media are a part of one's plan, which magazine or newspaper should be selected; if broadcast, what television shows or radio stations?

Crane (1972) suggests that the media planner must answer five questions in making the selection decision: exposure versus impact, reach versus frequency, continuity versus massed frequency, select versus mass audience, and the degree of choice. Answers to the first four of Crane's questions should be available from the media objectives and strategy; yet, in addition, each candidate media vehicle would still need to be evaluated on its performance in delivering the answer to each question. The fifth question is more unique to the media vehicle selection decision. For example, Crane reminds us of the conjecture that the more freedom a receiver has to reject or ignore a media vehicle, the more impact the vehicles he does select will be likely to have. Additionally, there are those who feel that media vehicles a receiver must pay for are more likely to be attended to (for example, read in the case of print), and that print vehicles purchased at a newsstand are more likely to be read than those subscribed to and delivered by mail. This latter point, however, is probably as often not true as true, yet it seems to survive as contemporary wisdom among many media planners.

While these questions of Crane's are no doubt considered in some form or other by media planners in most of their media vehicle selection decisions (with the possible exception of degree of choice), one is more likely to find such decisions made on the basis of a number of specific factors, all by now familiar to the reader. Within the parameter of a particular set of media objectives and strategies, some of the more important factors considered in selecting the particular vehicles to be included in a media schedule are outlined in Table 5.4. The factors themselves are divided into two groups: (a) those that lend themselves easily to measurement, and as such are readily available through syndicated media research data or from the media; and (b) those that tend to be more subjective, and, as a result, are much more difficult to measure. Unfortunately, those that are most difficult to measure also are those most directly affecting advertising.

Easily Measured Factors

The size of the audience a particular media vehicle can deliver is an important criterion in selection, aside from the obvious consideration of potential

TABLE 5.4

Media Vehicle Factors

Easily Measured Factors	Difficult to Measure Factors
audience size	exposure value
timing of delivery	reception value
audience characteristics	yielding value
geographic distribution	(cost)
(cost)	

numbers of receivers. As it happens, there tends to be a general relationship between size of audience delivered and corresponding levels of reach and frequency. Larger audience size usually translates to greater reach and less average frequency while smaller audience size generally means less reach and greater average frequency. Even when gross audience size figures for two or more potential media schedules are similar, this generalization will tend to hold, a function of the component vehicle audience delivery. For example, Table 5.5 illustrates four hypothetical media schedules, each accounting for 60 percent of the total market. If one assumes a random pattern of duplicated reach among the various vehicles (which, if anything, would underestimate the actual reach and frequency pattern), one notices that reach increases with the size of the largest vehicle in a schedule. Although each schedule delivers an audience of identical size, the schedule comprised of three vehicles each delivering 20 percent of the market tends to provide lower levels of reach than any of the two vehicle schedules (all with at least one vehicle delivering more than 20 percent). For the two vehicle schedules—it should be remembered that the media vehicles considered in each schedule are different from one another—the larger a single vehicle audience size, the greater the reach. Recalling our earlier discussion of reach and frequency, it is not surprising to also find just the opposite effect on average frequency; frequency tends to decrease with the size of the largest vehicle in a schedule.

As a result, if the media objectives and strategy indicate one should maximize the level of reach, media vehicles would be selected which deliver larger audiences. If frequency is to be maximized, media vehicles with generally smaller audience delivery would usually be selected. But, as with most things, this general rule does not always hold. If the media chosen comprise highly specialized vehicles (*Ski Magazine* or *ART News*), there will be less of a tendency for over-

TABLE 5.5

Timing of Four Hypothetical Schedules

| Schedule | Audience Size | | | Reach | Frequency |
	Vehicle 1	Vehicle 2	Vehicle 3		
1	20%	20%	20%	lowest	highest
2	30%	30%	—	low	high
3	40%	20%	—	high	low
4	50%	10%	—	highest	lowest

lap in receiver coverage, resulting in less duplication of reach and higher overall levels, regardless of the size of the largest vehicle.

In discussing the selection of media, it was pointed out that print media tend to occupy space in unspecified units of time, while broadcast media occupy a specific unit of time. These same general principles mediate the selection of media vehicles also, particularly when the timing of a persuasive message's delivery is critical to overall advertising strategy. For example, a campaign's timing may require specific months, weeks, days, or even hours to be effective. Media vehicles must be selected that reflect these known temporal considerations. A campaign designed for maximum efficiency seen during the morning hours prior to shopping for groceries would be unlikely to include an evening newspaper in its schedule, if a morning paper were available.

For a great many products, the characteristics of the audience delivered by a medium become more important than either timing or size. In fact, the less general a product's appeal, the more critical the audience profile of the media vehicle considered. The more that is known about the characteristics of the desired target receivers, and the more that is known about the characteristics of specific media vehicles (in other than demographic terms), the better one will be able to attain media and advertising objectives. However, this is not the sort of data usually available in any detail, and although easily measured, usually isn't. Those who take the trouble to develop this information, though, have a significant competitive advantage in being better able to more efficiently select media vehicles and to assess their impact on the desired advertising response.

A final consideration in media vehicle selection, which is also easy to measure, is geographic distribution. Frequently taken for granted, the physical location of one's desired receiver is not always coincident with the physical distribution of the advertised product. Efficient use of media, in that case, would not usually include reaching receivers, regardless of their potential, if there is no way for them to buy the product (unless, of course, it is less expensive to include them within a schedule's reach than it is to purposefully exclude them). The allocation of media dollars through media vehicles selected on a regional or geographic basis can make sense in a number of circumstances. Areas with strong distribution or high sales volume are frequently given "heavy-up" advertising schedules; even in areas of poor distribution or sales volume, if potential is strong, one's strategy may call for increased expenditures so as to exploit the potential. Extra advertising effort may be required to offset intense competitive activity in certain areas. It is not, for example, unusual for a company to roll out a new brand or product on a regional rather than national basis. This requires media vehicles offering appropriate regional coverage for the new brand or product, as well as the ability to counter increased advertising pressure by existing competition. Often climatic differences, too, may prove to be important in the way a media schedule is built, requiring media vehicles capable of placing certain geographic emphasis in particular areas at different times during the year.

Any number of other geographic considerations could be a part of the media objectives and strategy, each demanding special attention be given to those media vehicles appropriate to the applicable areas. Rather than a network broadcast buy, the advertiser may wish to concentrate efforts in the top 20 markets—still a "national" plan, but one requiring heavy use of spot television and local radio. Even scheduling network broadcasting can have geographic consequences, depending on (for example) the metropolitan versus nonmetropolitan skew of the desired target receivers. Depending on the media objectives and strategies, the geographic distribution of media vehicles can be an important criterion of vehicle selection.

Factors that are Difficult to Measure

While data on the audience a media vehicle will deliver is easy to come by, this is not necessarily the audience it will deliver for a specific advertisement or commercial. This is an important distinction to understand, reflected in a factor known as the "exposure value" of a media vehicle. An exposure value represents the intrusive ability of a particular medium to present persuasive messages to a receiver within the audiences it delivers. It is wholly a function of the normal reading or viewing pattern of a media vehicle's audience, and has nothing to do with the stopping power of any individual advertisement or commercial. Understanding the exposure value of media vehicles is critical to efficient vehicle selection as well as to providing an estimate of the presentation potential required for message processing and ultimate advertising response. But the difficulty involved in developing a truly objective measure of a vehicle's exposure makes inter-vehicle comparisons difficult.

Media vehicle selection should be based upon more than exposure value. Also considered should be a vehicle's ability to attract the attention of a desired target receiver, and to provide an environment in which the target receiver will feel motivated to comply with the advertising. Although there are no explicit measures of the reception or potential response value of individual media vehicles, a number of factors are known to mediate their effect. Table 5.6 compares five such factors and how they could affect the selection of media vehicles based upon their probability of positively influencing advertising's reception and ultimate response.

The prior exposure of a media vehicle's audience to an advertising campaign will tend to familiarize those receivers with the advertising, and slightly increase the probability of reception, especially if several different executions are involved. If one were interested in maximizing attention through media vehicle selection, the vehicles should, if possible, be vehicles that have previously been used. If an attitudinal or behavioral response is to be maximized, as we have noticed so often before, the opposite would be true. Prior experience of receivers with an advertising campaign over any substantial period of time will

TABLE 5.6

Factors Affecting Reception and Response

Factors	Reception	Response
1. Prior exposure of audience to campaign	Reception levels raise slightly with prior exposure, particularly if executions are different.	Exposure over time tends to encourage well-defined ideas; as opinions polarize there is less opportunity to effect a positive response with additional exposure.
2. Category exclusivity for communication or advertising subject	Reception levels are generally higher with a monopoly of communication about the product class.	The fewer the competing messages, the better the chances for a positive response.
3. Receiver involvement	Advertising appealing to specific receiver-involved groups will attract greater reception in media with group-specific audience.	Opportunity for group identification provided by specialized vehicles increases a positive response.
4. Delivery timing	Reception is a function of the time of day or day of week exposure takes place.	Exposure compatibility with receiver behavioral mode or mood maximizes positive response by taking advantage of the receiver's frame of mind at certain moments.
5. Reproduction quality	Generally, the better the reproduction, the greater the probability of reception.	Subtle influence on response by enhancing source credibility

tend to establish well-defined feelings, thus lessening the likelihood of changing attitude or behavior through response to the advertising. In this case, to increase the probability of a positive response, media vehicles should be chosen that have not been used, or used as extensively, in the past.

The extent to which a particular media vehicle has exclusive coverage of an area of communication will tend to have positive effects on both reception and response to advertising. More attention than usual could be expected with fewer competing messages, as well as a better opportunity for one's advertising to persuade. A similar positive benefit for both reception and the desired response is associated with a receiver's involvement with media vehicles. For example, the opportunity for source identification provided by specialized vehicles should enhance the ability of a persuasive message to attract more attention among targeted receivers and increase the probability that the communication will prove persuasive. The quality of reproduction afforded by different media vehicles will also have an effect on the ability of an advertisement or commercial to attract attention and persuade, as will the timing of a message's delivery to take advantage of the attitudinal or behavioral circumstance of a receiver at certain moments. In maximizing the positive effects of a media vehicle selection decision each of these factors must be weighed. The more information a media planner is able to collect on the behavior of various media vehicles in relation to these factors, the better position the planner will be in to most efficiently execute a brand's media objectives and strategies.

One final consideration, which is both easy and difficult to measure, is the cost of individual media vehicles. While it is true that a cost figure is always available in some form for any particular media vehicle under any given circumstance, the fact that costs can vary in so many ways makes it quite difficult to arrive at any fixed cost estimates. Most media have rather complex rate structures, based on time or unit of space required, type of reproduction desired, and more. One would expect to pay more for a 60-second commercial spot than for a 30-second spot, but not all 60-second or 30-second time spots are equal. Contracts with broadcast media generally depend on the length of the contract, the ratings of the show involved, as well as the total amount of money the advertiser is spending with the network. And, it is important to understand that this total represents not just the spending for a specific brand, but the total spending for all brands owned by a single corporation or holding company. Similar conditions apply to the cost of print media as well.

All of this, and more, must be considered from a pragmatic standpoint when a media vehicle selection is made. Ideally, what one is seeking is some measure of the cost per desired target receiver as a function of a media vehicle's intrinsic abilities to effect the desired advertising response (quite aside from any consideration of the actual persuasive message involved). Such a measure, of course, is not precisely possible. In its stead, media planners use common measures of the cost per thousand people or the cost per thousand probable target receivers (based upon audience characteristics) in the audience a vehicle reportedly delivers. The unrelatedness of these available cost measures to the more important, but difficult to measure, advertising response effects of media vehicles leads to a great deal of subjective judgment in selection. A more disciplined framework within which to make these judgments is discussed in the next section.

Framework of Vehicle Selection

The number of considerations necessary in making media vehicle selection decisions are, as we have seen, many and varied. The need for some systematic procedure in approaching this selection problem exists because of the complexity of these varied factors, and because of the fact that many of the more important factors do not lend themselves easily (if at all) to direct measurement. A framework is needed to help organize the important influences upon the selection process, and to provide a means of efficiently handling inter-vehicle comparisons. The procedure outlined in Figure 5.4 illustrates how one might approach this problem.

Each media vehicle one may consider has a certain audience size. But as we have noted, the exposure value, or number of people it actually delivers for an advertisement, is somewhat less than this figure, and varies from media to media and vehicle to vehicle. One's first task is to assess the exposure value of each vehicle, and determine the probable size of the exposed audience. Next, this exposed audience is evaluated for its probable effect on the desired advertising response (awareness, cognitive, affective, or conative objective). A weighted probability is then attached to the exposed audience, providing what one might call a "persuasible" audience, or the number of receivers likely to change their response to the advertising as a result of exposure in this vehicle to a persuasive message for a particular brand. Next, these receivers are profiled to determine how closely their characteristics match those of the desired target receivers (remembering that although we have just qualified this audience as highly persuasible, this is only from a media vehicle standpoint, not potential use). This provides one with the proportion of the persuasible audience also likely to have the characteristics of the desired target receivers. However, depending upon how general one's information is about the desired target receivers, only a proportion of those with the desired characteristics will actually be probable target receivers. This would be especially true if all one had available was demographic or usage data. The more detailed correlates one has with media behavior, of course, the better the planner will be able to establish the correctness of the audience or probable target receivers. Dividing the cost per thousand delivered audience by the probable target receivers will provide a relative measure of a media vehicle's efficiency in delivering the desired receivers with a maximum probability of

FIGURE 5.4

A Framework for Media Vehicle Selection

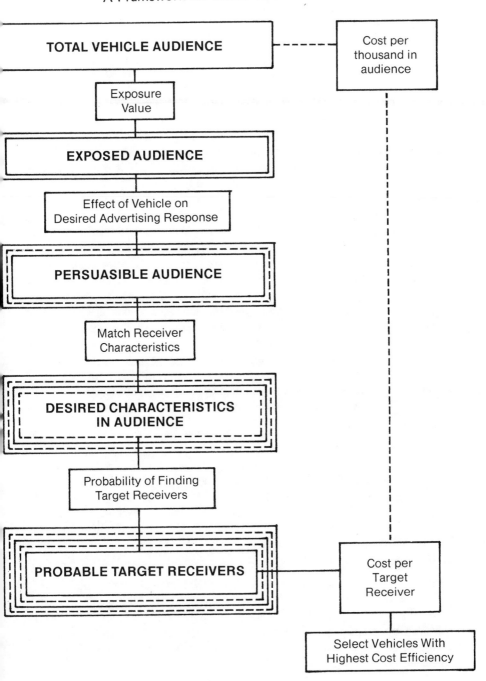

effecting the desired advertising response. Those media vehicles with high cost efficiencies should then be selected for inclusion in the media schedule.

An Application

As we have pointed out throughout this chapter, it is difficult to develop and implement truly effective media objectives and strategy relying only upon syndicated research. An excellent way in which to secure the primary media behavior information required for planning, as well as a detailed understanding of the potential target, is through an attitudinally based segmentation study, as discussed in chapter 2. The media planning application presented in this section makes use of data from such a segmentation study.

A number of questions asked in an attitudinally based segmentation study of meal planning and food choice were designed to determine certain general media behavior characteristics. The questions asked dealt with the frequency of viewing television within each part of the day (for example, early morning versus prime versus late movies), the receiver's favorite type of television programming, frequency of listening to radio within parts of the day, and regularity of reading various types of magazines. In addition, standard demographic and behavior questions were asked which were compatible with those included in syndicated media research. As the reader will recall from chapter 2, this permits correlating an attitudinally developed target audience definition with available syndicated media research data for vehicle selection.

Initially, a factor analysis of the media behavior questions was conducted in order to establish if any logical groupings of generalized media behavior occur. The results of this analysis indicated:

1. The frequency of television viewing may be described for three quite natural dimensions: (a) daytime and early fringe, (b) prime time, and (c) late night talk shows and movies.

2. The frequency of radio listening is a single factor, indicating that one either does or does not listen to radio a little versus a lot, rather than (for example) listening a lot in the morning but only a little in the evening.

3. The regularity of magazine reading is divided into two dimensions: (a) women's service, home, and general magazines, and (b) special interest and news magazines.

What this analysis provided the media planner was those dimensions upon which one should look for receiver differences, and within which strategic development and vehicle selection should be evaluated. In applying this analysis to differences between the prime prospect target receiver segments (that is, the prime segments provided by the attitudinal segmentation) and the nonprospects, two important media behavior differences were noted:

1. Prime prospects were significantly more likely to watch late night television than nonprospects.

2. Prime prospects were much more likely to be regular readers of women's service, home, and general magazines.

These important understandings provided the media planner with a set of vehicle selection criteria that would increase the likelihood of reaching probable target receivers. As a result, the media plan should include late fringe television programming and women's service, home, or general magazines.

The final step in utilizing the segmentation study results for setting media objectives and strategy involved an automatic interaction detection or A.I.D. analysis (Sonquist and Morgan 1969) of all those questions reflecting data available from syndicated media research. An A.I.D. analysis essentially scans all of the available data, finding that point that does the best job of discriminating a desired subpopulation from the remaining members. One could think of the results as providing the best question you could ask someone in order to maximize your chances of classifying the person as either belonging or not belonging to the desired subpopulation. The program then continues, finding the question you would next most want to ask to further increase your likelihood of correctly classifying a target prospect, and so on.

Results of this analysis are shown in Figure 5.5. While prime prospects made up 17 percent of the total population, among those who serve product A versus those who don't, 27 percent versus 5 percent are prime prospects. The next most important criterion was income. Among those making over $15,000 who also serve product A, 44 percent are prime prospects; among those who make less than $15,000 and serve product A, but who also live in metropolitan areas and serve product B, 32 percent are prime prospects. These findings are represented by the heavy line in Figure 5.5, and reflect the best possible target receiver definition.

With this information in hand, the media planner is able to: (1) formulate a media strategy that positively weights vehicles within late fringe television and women's service, home, and general magazines; and (2) seek to reach homemakers who serve product A and have family incomes over $15,000 or live in metropolitan areas and serve product B, if their incomes are under $15,000. In addition, a "heavy-up" media schedule (that is, more money would be spent) was planned in Region IV, which represented the Northeast, for media vehicles likely to reach product A servers with incomes over $15,000 (a finding also indicated by the A.I.D. analysis).

Using this strategy, media vehicles were selected within the framework outlined in Figure 5.4. As the reader should now understand, this was possible only because primary research was conducted to enable the media planner to match audience characteristics of vehicles more likely to deliver a persuadable audience (because prime prospects are more likely to use those vehicles) with

FIGURE 5.5

A.I.D. Analysis of Media for Prime Segment

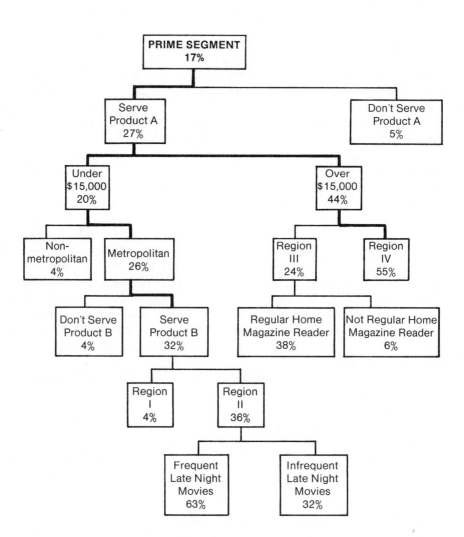

those characteristics most likely to describe a prime prospect. Without this information, the media planner would of necessity rely on a more general, and probably demographically oriented, target receiver definition, choosing media and particular vehicles based upon general competitive behavior.

REVIEWING VARIABLE 4: MEDIA SELECTION

The overall objective of this chapter has been to provide an overview of the media selection process, providing the background necessary to make effective media judgments. Specifically, one should be able to:

1. Contrast the important differences between mass media and interpersonal communication
2. Identify the important characteristics of media
3. Distinguish between the various effects of media on response to advertising
4. Understand the difficulty and limitation associated with attempts at measuring media effectiveness
5. Illustrate the general media planning process in advertising
6. Understand the constraints placed on strategic media planning for advertising
7. Distinguish between reach and frequency and their effect on strategy
8. Determine the reasoning behind specific media selection
9. Distinguish between media selection and media vehicle selection
10. Illustrate a framework for media vehicle selection
11. Understand the effects of specific media strategy decisions on potential response to advertising

KEY CONCEPTS

Mass Media	Constraints on Media Strategy
Interpersonal Communication	Receiver Identification
Channels	Continuity
Media Characteristics	Reach
Proximate Space	Frequency
Media Effects	Media Selection
Measured Media Effect	Audience Selectivity
Modality Effect	Existence in Space or Time
Message-Coding	Intrusiveness
Personal versus Mass Media Impact	Concurrent Symbol Systems
Media Planning Process	Sensory Modality
Objectivity and Strategy	Media Vehicle Selection

6

SCHEDULING STRATEGY

Although the actual media schedule is largely prepared by media practitioners, important inputs to the strategy that underlies a schedule will be the responsibility of advertising and brand managers, as will be the final approval of the schedule's ability to meet the advertising and marketing strategies formulated for the product. A key element in developing an efficient strategy for media scheduling is a clear understanding of the desired postcommunication effects embodied in the specific objectives of a communication effort. This can involve the general subject matter (for example, in most advertising, a purchase decision; or in the case of public service advertising, voting or health checkups), as well as the appropriate advertising response, which may range from a simple goal of name registration when the communication is designed to generate heightened awareness among target receivers through a favorable attitude toward the subject of the communication or a specific behavior, such as an actual purchase. In effect, scheduling strategy must account for those factors having to do with the anticipated impact of the communication.

One type of factor that has been thoroughly researched and has both practical importance and general theoretical relevance is the wearout or satiation of a particular piece of advertising over a period of time. As far as the temporal effect on the persistence of retained advertising effects goes, there seems to be little doubt that a steady decay of an induced attitude or behavioral change (as the result of a single communication without reinforcement) would be expected over a period of time. While there is a great deal of empirical evidence for such decay, under certain conditions one may also find evidence for an increase in a particular advertising response, as time passes, after receipt of a specific persuasive communication.

These postcommunication affects are discussed in this chapter. In addition, the usefulness of models as an aid in determining scheduling strategy is presented, along with various means of setting advertising budgets, which generally provide the cost parameters for any scheduling strategy.

POSTCOMMUNICATION AFFECTS

In attempting to understand the likely persistence effects of a persuasive communication, it becomes important to consider the patterns and underlying pressures occasioned by temporal decay in message retention. Assuming a single exposure to a particular communication message, one would reasonably expect to find a steady decay, in an Ebbinghaus fashion, of any induced opinion change, due to message yielding over a period of time prior to any actual buyer response. Even if multiple exposures are attended to, a certain harmonic decay over a period of time would be expected. The factors mediating this decay are well discussed in the literature on learning (cf. the Hilgard and Bower 1975 review of various theories of learning). For example, Freud supposed that forgetting resulted from an active repression of certain materials in the unconscious (Robinson 1932), while Thorndike (1932), in anticipating a more behaviorist viewpoint, felt forgetting takes place in the absence of practice. From a much more strongly behaviorist position, Guthrie (1952) describes forgetting as due to the learning of new responses that replace old responses, although there are some who feel that time alone, not intervening events, accounts for forgetting. However, the most credible theory for forgetting appears to be the so-called "interference" theory.

Interference theory is closely tied into the functionalist's analysis of negative transfer and interference (Hilgard and Bower 1975). Most learning theorists appear to subscribe to this theory, and the bulk of the empirical evidence seems to support it. The basic notion of interference theory is credited to McGaugh (1932), although later formulations by Postman (1971) provide a more cogent exposition. It is an association theory that states that once an association is learned and stored in long-term memory, forgetting is a function of a declining accessibility or likelihood of retrieval because of competing associations. For example, employing the usual notation A-B to represent an associative bond between A and B established by some past training, if recall of such an association A-B shows measurable decay over a period of time, this is not because of an inherent attrition of the association, but rather the introduction of alternative associations A-C or A-D. As a result, when one attempts to measure the recall strength of the A-B association, a receiver may be more cognitive of A-C or A-D associations, temporarily displacing the A-B association at the time of recall. It would be assumed, in this case, that the A-C or A-D associations came from learning that occurred either before the A-B learning took place (proactive interference) or after the A-B learning, but before the recall test (retroactive interference). A number of studies confirming the expectations of intereference theory along these lines are reported by Postman (1971).

Applying this to a typical advertising situation, one can see that an advertised association A-B, where A is a particular product and B is a specific brand, could be interfered with over a period of time by other associations of the product A with competitive brands C and D. Thus, if a receiver is asked (as is frequently the case in 24 hour recall testing) if the receiver recalls seeing advertising for product-brand A-B, the receiver may be likely to recall only A-C or A-D product-brand advertising associations—perhaps because of their heavier exposure. The receiver has not "forgotten" your advertising; it has merely been "interfered" with by competitive advertising. This argues for maintaining competitive pressure if brand recall is a desired advertising response. It also suggests why it is frequently difficult to elicit high recall scores for a single exposure of a new execution within an existing campaign. The product-brand association for the new execution is "interfered" with by a proactive interference of the existing association created by the ongoing advertising.

Of the two interference explanations, proactive interference is considered the most powerful. In reviewing a number of studies of proactive sources of interference in forgetting, Underwood (1957) pointed out a cumulative effect on forgetting ranging from a high of around 75 percent to 80 percent recall after 24 hours when receivers were exposed to only one list of associations, to a low of 10 percent to 20 percent under multiple list-learning conditions. The more lists a receiver was asked to learn, the less likely the receiver was to recall the last list 24 hours later. This generalization was rather convincingly demonstrated in an experiment reported by Keppel, Postman, and Zavortink (1968). Subjects in the test were asked to learn and recall 36 successive lists of A-B, C-D relations in sets of 10 at 48 hour intervals. Each new session began with a recall test of the previously learned list, followed by the learning of a new list (where learning was defined as a perfect recitation of the list). Results indicated a dramatic decrease in recall from 70 percent on the first list after 48 hours, to about 5 percent on the last 2 lists. Additional experiments by Underwood and Postman (1960) embellish this general finding of a powerful underlying mechanism of proactive interference, demonstrating that new material that clashes with prior verbal habits tends to be forgotten more readily, usually being distorted in the direction of agreement with prior habits or associations. For example, this would tend to suggest that new advertising that significantly departs from earlier, well-learned formats, should tend to show greater decay in message recall than new, but essentially familiar, advertising.

This speculation is given some foundation in the findings of a study by Coleman (1962). He took 24 word passages from a book and scrambled the words in a random order. A subject was asked to study the scrambled passage and to recall exactly what it was the subject had just read, in the scrambled order. The words, in the order in which they were recalled by the subject, were then presented as a passage to a second subject to read, learn, and subsequently remember. This process was repeated through a series of 16 subjects, and Coleman found that, at each step, the word order was distorted more and more from the original scrambled order to an order more consistent with sensible English sentences. The effects of prior verbal learning indeed have a critical impact on recall. Continuing with our example of new advertising that significantly departs from an existing campaign, one can see how difficult it would be to expect receivers who are quite familiar with an existing campaign to score well on a single exposure 24-hour recall test. Such tests generally rely on brand cues to prompt recall, and tend to discount anyone recalling copy points specifically associated with another campaign. But, as the Underwood and Postman and the Coleman studies show, one should expect such incorrect recall because of the strong influence of prior brand-advertising associations. Receivers have not necessarily failed to learn or forgotten the new advertising. It is simply overshadowed by the proactive interference of earlier, more familiar advertising.

The persistence effects of accumulated learning or recall is another serious inhibitor to high recall of unfamiliar advertising. If one considers a simple declarative statement of the form subject-verb-object (such as brand A has attribute X), this may be thought of as establishing labeled functional connections between groups of semantic concepts which are instantiated by these specific words (Hilgard and Bower 1975). These semantic concepts may now be considered triple associations similar to the dual A–B associations discussed up until this point, except that there are very real semantic and syntactic constraints (as illustrated in the message content section of chapter 4) that must apply if meaningful as opposed to nonsense statements are to be studied. Assuming such an associative triplet (S–V–O), consider interference occasioned by a change in the subject or predicate of the sentence: $S_1-V_2O_2$ or $S_2-V_1O_1$. In either event, one would expect an associative loss between the original subject and predicate when recall testing cues either the subject or object. For example, if the clause "brand A has attribute X" appears in one advertisement and the claim "brand A has attribute Y" appears in a second, following the notion of retroactive interference one would expect a loss of the original association between the brand and Attribute X, assuming the predicate "has attribute Y" is not considered a paraphrase of the predicate "has attribute X." Because interference appears to occur at the level of conceptual meaning, predicates that are perceived to be paraphrases of one another will tend to associate in a common manner with sentence subjects; and conversely, subjects of different statements that are perceived to be similar by receivers will associate in a like manner with sentence predicates (Anderson and Carter 1972).

Applying this reasoning to advertising, one can see how an advantage may be realized in campaign awareness, even when specific message point recall appears to suffer. If several executions of an advertising strategy are created for a specific campaign, or if a new execution is developed to extend an existing campaign, if one wishes to facilitate conceptual associations with the advertised brand, one need only vary the support statements in the various executions within a common cognitive environment. To the extent that the supporting message points are considered conceptually equivalent reinforcements of the message subject—the advertised brand in this example—overall meaning and understanding should be increased over a period of time. However, while overall campaign recall is enhanced, specific recall of copy points will probably suffer from interference. To the extent that an advertiser is interested in promoting a general concept comprised of a number of alternative supporting message points (all conceptually compatible), there will be a high level of positive transfer from one execution to another even though one is interfering with verbatim recall. Unfortunately, if too literal an importance is placed on the verbatim recall of specific executions in a campaign extension, or other new but generally similar advertising, under most day-after-recall scoring schemes, such advertising will appear to score quite low—this despite the fact that overall comprehension of the brand message will have been enhanced.

Decayed Impact Over a Period of Time

Given that there would seem to be a steady decay in any communication message, understanding of the extent to which an advertising response is retained for future buyer response becomes a major concern. The relationship between the general phenomenon of forgetting and the decay of opinion or attitude change induced by a persuasive communication is of particular interest. While some work has been done in the areas of suggestibility and conformity, the bulk of research has been done with persistence of induced attitude change within a persuasibility context. In all cases, as expected, decay appears to follow a negatively decelerating forgetting curve of the type originally suggested by Ebbinghaus (1885). However, there does not appear to be any consensus as to the rate of decay in induced attitude change.

In one of the earliest studies of the persistence of induced persuasion, Peterson and Thurstone (1933) found a wide range of resulting rates, ranging from no persistence through complete persistence, even after several months. Other studies have provided no evidence of a persistence effect (Eberhaud and Bauer 1941; and Sims 1938, in studies of somewhat controversial material) or just the opposite with complete persistence of the original yielding, even after ten months (Smith 1943). A more general finding, however, has been that there is a substantial (but not complete) persistence of any induced attitude change over a period of several months. Hall (1938) estimates that a rough figure from summarizing the early literature would be that the response induced by the average persuasive communication exhibits a half-life of about six months. A more recent review by Watts and McGuire (1964) finds that about 60 percent of initial yielding has decayed within six weeks; and interestingly, that some of these results suggest a rectilinear rather than a negatively decelerated curve over the six-week period.

The wide range of results reported in the literature might suggest that there is no general decay curve applicable to the problem of temporal decay in induced attitude change. However, McGuire (1972) has speculated that the results could be summarized as indicating a negatively accelerated decay curve for attitudinal response, similar in shape to the Ebbinghaus-type retention curve for recall of message content discussed above. He also suggests that the onset of this decay curve would not begin until some time after the communication message is presented to the receiver, following an initial short-term increase in impact similar to the so-called reminiscence phenonmenon in learning. The actual rate of decay would then be a function of the various environmental and cognitive constraints on the communication experience. For example, to the extent that the persistence of an attitudinal response is a function of the persuasive material in the message, then the factors affecting the receiver's rate of forgetting (such as intelligence) would also affect the rate of decay in that response.

In addition to the general shape of the curve describing the decay of induced attitude change over a period of time, one must be concerned with how that curve is affected by the interaction of other communication variables. Each of the variables discussed in the last four chapters has some affect on the persistence of a response to advertising. Following the sleeper effect described by Hovland and Weiss (1951), one would expect the persuasive impact of a given message to decay more rapidly, when it is attributed to a positive source than when it is attributed to a negative source. Cohen (1957) has found that the cognitive needs of a receiver affect the persistence of induced attitude change, and Watts (1967), among others, has pointed out that active involvement with a communication on the part of the receiver also enhances retention. There appears to be some indication that a more complex or subtle message induces more persistent attitude change than that induced by a more straightforward message (McGuire 1960a), and the interactive effect of media variables over a period of time are well established: the media schedule and the advertising medium itself interact with the persistence effects in advertising communications.

Retention of Induced Yielding

It should be clear that the discussion thus far assumes that retention of message content is essential for persistence of an attitudinal response to advertising (in fact, it is an underlying assumption of most day-after-recall and post-communication awareness and attitude studies). But one should ask if this need necessarily be the case. Must a receiver retain the content of the persuasive message that originally induced the response and the initial attitude change; or, once absorbed, can the message content be forgotten, while the new attitude remains?

To the extent that induced attitude change remains functionally dependent upon the material used to produce it, as the original message content is forgotten the receiver's attitude will tend to return to its precommunication level. McGuire (1960b) has hypothesized that a receiver's attitude at any point in time represents a sort-of "least-squares" equilibrium among all of the various contending influences on attitude. When confronted with a new piece of information via a persuasive communication, the receiver adjusts to this new influence. But when the receiver leaves the communication situation and the new information becomes less salient, the receiver's attitude will drift back in the direction of the original belief.

As one can see, this notion of whether opinion change is functionally autonomous or dependent upon the recall of the message points that produced it requires one to accept an initiating role for the message content in originally producing an attitude shift. Unfortunately, the obtained relationship between initial learning of message content and initial yielding tends to be surprisingly small. McGuire (1957) found a biserial correlation as high as +0.50, and Janis and Rife (1959) one of +0.21, between immediate recall and immediate yielding, but many other studies have found insignificant (Haskins 1964), or , under certain circumstances, even negative relationships (Hovland, Lumsdaine, and Sheffield 1949). Results are even less impressive from studies of the relationship between content recall and delayed change.

In an order effects study, Miller and Campbell, (1959) tested a number of hypotheses that immediate message learning and attitude change would decay as a learning theory interpretation of attitude would predict. Four test conditions were utilized in testing a relative recency hypothesis for two competing persuasive messages: (1) the second message immediately following the first and an immediate measurement; (2) the second message immediately following the first, but a one week delay until measurement; (3) a delay of one week between messages, with an immediate measurement following the second message; and (4) a delay of one week between the messages and an additional one week delay before measurement. As summarized in Table 6.1, based upon an assumed negatively accelerated decay curve, the largest relative receiving effect was predicted for condition 3, moderate recency effects for conditions 4 and 1, and the smallest recency effect for condition 2. The results were almost exactly as predicted for both content learning and attitude change. Yet, even though the correlations between immediate change and message content recall were quite positive (+0.38), the correlations between delayed attitude change and delayed content recall were highly negative (-0.45). Insko (1964), in a similar study, obtained almost exactly the same results, using a free recall technique rather than the multiple choice recall procedure of Miller and Campbell. Wilson and Miller (1968) also found similar decreases in recency effects over a period of time, although they failed to demonstrate any increases in recency effect for recall as the interval between messages increased. The empirical evidence appears to offer little

TABLE 6.1

Predicted Decay Effects Assuming an Ebbinghaus-type
Forgetting Curve for Two Competing Persuasive Messages
(Adapted from Miller and Campbell, 1959)

	Description	Prediction
Condition 1	second message immediately follows first, with an immediate measurement	moderate recency effect
Condition 2	second message immediately follows first, one week delay until measurement	slight recency effect
Condition 3	delay of one week between messages, with immediate measurement following the second message	strong recency effect
Condition 4	delay of one week between messages, with additional one week delay before measurement	moderate recency effect

support for a functional relationship between content recall and the persistence of induced attitude change.

In the experiment by Watts and McGuire (1964) mentioned earlier, they found that while recall of most aspects of message content exhibit the expected negatively decelerated decay curve, attitude change "forgetting" almost always followed a more rectilinear curve, suggesting at least some autonomy from content recall. Attitude change and various aspects of recall were measured immediately, and after one, two, and six weeks. It was found that recall of ever having heard a message on the topic of the communication was positively related to the level of response the first week after the communication, but that after six weeks, this same relationship had become strongly negative. Furthermore, more persistent attitude change was found to be functionally dependent upon recall of the specific arguments used in the message and the side taken. Watts and McGuire speculate that a discounting cue type of sleeper effect (discussed more fully in the section on "Increased Impact over a Period of Time," below) could be responsible for these results. Receivers who are not able to recall even the subject of a communication immediately after exposure to it have quite likely misperceived the message completely. Those receivers who are not able to recall the message subject after a passage of time are more likely receivers who have merely forgotten it, although they initially encoded it correctly. Those receivers could be subject to a sleeper effect, initially discounting the specific arguments of the message, because they remember them as being part of a persuasive communication. This discounting effect would be expected to decay over a period of time, permitting the persuasive impact of the still retained message content to surface, free of the persuasive communication situation. McGuire (1969a) has concluded that the results of the Watts and McGuire experiments suggest that immediate response is proportioned to the amount of message learning, and that the persistence of that attitude change continues to be positively related to recall of the specifics of the message argument, but that the induced attitude change tends to become functionally autonomous of, and even negatively related to, general recall of the communication situation.

Note the importance their conclusion has for day-after-recall testing or other postcommunication measures. Almost all such tests require an awareness cue for inclusion in the so-called recall audience. If McGuire's hypothesis holds, many receivers who retain good specific message recall and induced opinion change could be excluded from the recall measure, for failure to remember "seeing or hearing" advertising for the topic (that is, for discounting the communication situation or source of the message).

Retention of Cognitive Response

Rather than measuring learning by the traditional rote playback of message content, some researchers are proposing one look at the total cognitive response involved in a communication situation. Greenwald (1968), for example, has hypothesized that rehearsal and learning of cognitive responses to persuasive communication may provide a basis for explaining the persistence effects of persuasive communication in terms of cognitive learning, and that this may be more fundamental to persuasion than mere learning of communication content. Wright (1974b) feels that the traditional view of comprehension of a persuasion communication involves no more than a successful initial decoding of the message, but message learning requires the receiver to relate new information to an already existing belief structure. In this sense, a successful persuasive message is one that increases the probability of the receiver relating the advertised product or service to the receiver's existing belief structure on subsequent exposure to either additional advertising or during purchase situations. This means that, rather than evoking a playback of message content, one must alter cognition in a direction positively related to buyer response. Comprehension, in this new sense, is an active process, as receivers generate new beliefs in the course of processing information and engaging beliefs from long-term memory.

While the idea that cognitive responses to persuasive communication are important mediators of attitude has been tentatively expressed for some time (cf. Hovland, Lumsdaine, and Sheffield 1949), only recently has an attempt been made to actually measure the impact of cognitive activity on the persistence of an attitudinal response. Greenwald (1968) looked at both immediate and delayed measure of attitude following exposure to a persuasive communication and found that the best predictor of opinion was the cognitive responses (that is, "thoughts") elicited during the actual presentation of the message, followed by an index of retained cognitive response after one week; and significantly, no correlation between recall of the message content and attitude change was noted. Calder, Insko, and Yandel (1974), in employing a similar measure of cognitive response, found significant evidence that the number of supportive message points in communication, whether they were positive or negative, influence the type of cognitive response generated by a receiver, and that these were monotonically related to the persistence of yielding. Wright (1973) used four measures of cognitive response to an advertisement and found that those responses that tended to be receiver generated rather than merely recall of the advertising were more highly related to message persuasion.

These and other results provide a strong basis for believing that cognitive activity in response to persuasive communication and retention are important functional dependent mediators of immediate and persistent induced attitude change, and that mere recall of message content tends to be autonomous of persistence in response to advertising. Additionally, there appears to be some evidence that when these initial thoughts are negative (for example, in counterarguing or source derogation), they may restrict initial positive yielding, but that over a period of time, these negative thoughts are discounted and a more positive attitude change develops.

Increased Impact over a Period of Time

Although the typical retention curve in both learning theory and induced persuasion would seem to be a negatively accelerating decay curve of the Ebbinghaus-type, certain exceptions have been noted. Specifically, research in the area of the delayed-action attitude impact of persuasive communication has frequently shown a greater impact with the passage of time than immediately after presentation. Early evidence of this increased impact over a period of time was reported by Hovland, Lumsdaine, and Sheffield (1949), following their studies during World War II. Attitudes were measured shortly after or some 11 weeks later, of soldiers who either did or did not view the propaganda film, *Battle of Britain*. They found that the difference between the control and test groups was significantly greater with the passage of time, leading to speculation in a number of areas for an explanation of possible delayed-action effects in persuasion.

An explanation that was originally given only passing mention by the Hovland group has since received perhaps the greatest attention, and is today probably the most generally favored interpretation of increasing persuasive impact over a period of time: the discounting-cue hypothesis, or the so-called "sleeper effect." This hypothesis suggests that if the persuasive content of a message is presented to a receiver juxtaposed with a potential discounting cue (that is, some aspect of the message that causes the communication to be immediately discounted or resisted), its initial impact will be influenced by that cue, but, with the passage of time, the cue will tend to be forgotten or dissociated from the content of the message. As a result, the persuasive impact of the message content will gradually take hold and reduce a positive attitude change. For example, in advertising, if a particularly biased source is perceived in a message (such as the American Dairy Association encouraging the consumption of milk), initial measures of attitude change will likely reflect this source bias by discounting the message content. Over a period of time, however, the source of the message will become less associated with the actual message content, so that subsequent measures of attitude change will reflect the influence of the persuasive arguments.

Considering our example, if an advertisement or commercial from the American Dairy Association extolls the health benefits of drinking milk, a post-communication measure of attitude toward drinking milk would perhaps not indicate any positive attitude shift, because the receiver assumes this would quite naturally be the ADA's position, and remains unconvinced. Some time later, however, it is likely that the receiver will have dissociated the positive health benefits argued for in the message from the actual source of the communication—an advertisement of the American Dairy Association. Measures of attitude toward drinking milk taken at that time would be expected to show a positive increase over the immediate postcommunication measure. In fact, it should be pointed out that the evidence available seems to indicate that a source, if it is perceived as a discounting cue, will be more likely dissociated from the message over a period of time than actually "forgotten" (Kelman and Hovland 1953), although, as McGuire (1964) has shown, there is a possibility that over a period of time a receiver shows less of a tendency to readily associate a message and a source. While this example, along with most of the substantial research on the discounting-cue hypothesis, utilizes a negative source as the discounting cue, other types of cues are possible (Weiss 1953; Holt and Watts 1973).

A second hypothesis originally offered by the Hovland group concerned the possibility that when a persuasive message is built upon a complex or subtle argument, it may take some time for the full implication of the message to be absorbed by the receiver's cognitive system. In other words, the initially learned content of a persuasive communication would influence immediate attitude change, but the full impact of the message would not be felt for some time, perhaps not until the content learned from the message becomes relevant to some new situation (such as a delayed measure of attitude change or an opportunity for actual behavioral change). Although the easily learned components of the message would be expected to decay, given this explanation, any subsequent increase in the persuasive impact of the message would reflect the learning of more subtle arguments that were retained by the receiver, but which required more time to be well formed within the receiver's cognitive structure. This hypothesis is in line with McGuire's (1960b) notion of cognitive inertia, in which information from a persuasive message would be expected to make itself felt for a considerable period of time. As a result, if one attempts to measure the full impact of a rather complex or subtle message immediately after exposure, the implications of the more oblique message points will not have had a chance to fully impact the reasoning process. Only after time has permitted a full cognitive understanding of the arguments used can the full impact of the message filter down to the more remote implications. Delayed attitude effects that follow this "filtering" suggestion were also found by Cohen (1957), in his work with confusingly ordered messages (information before need arousal); by Stotland, Katz, and Patchen (1959) for complex antiprejudice messages that employed a subtle, case-history, self-insight communication; and in McGuire's (1960a) work on the filtering down of message impact when dealing with one issue on logically related, but unmentioned derivations.

Possible implications for advertising follow quite easily from this explanation. It is not at all unusual for certain advertising strategies to require a complex or detailed message in order to reasonably expect to communicate the features of a new or difficult to use product or service. To the extent that this cognitive filtering process occurs, it would require time, as well as the probability of multiple exposure, to adequately impact attitude change. Any immediate postcommunication tests of persuasive impact in such a case would not be appropriate, since it would not be accounting for the potential increase in persuasive impact over a period of time as the message detail has a chance to be fully processed into cognition.

A third possible explanation for increased impact over a period of time from persuasive messages, and one closely related to the discounting-cue hypothesis, is the "Bartlett" effect, following a delayed-action effect prediction offered by Bartlett (1932), for one-sided arguments in which many qualifications or reservations are included against the main argument. He speculated that the qualifying details would be more readily forgotten than the main argument, precipitating a delayed-action effect on attitude change as the main content of the message assumes more dominance. Some evidence to support this hypothesis was found by Papageorgis (1963), who tested the "Bartlett" effect on qualified and unqualified messages with measures of attitude change taken immediately, and at 2, 14, and 41 days after presentation. Significant increases in persuasive impact were noted in both recall and attitude change for up to 14 days, with a predicted greater decay in several cases for the qualified message units. If the

"Bartlett" effect holds generally for qualified messages, this could have a significant impact on the desired effect of such things as federally mandated "corrective" advertising, since it would appear that the imposed qualities in the advertiser's message would tend to be forgotten while the original message is maintained, continuing to influence advertising response.

Satiation Effects: Wearout

The discussion so far has centered on the phenomenon of "forgetting" and its impact on postcommunication effects. A parallel question concerns the effect of repetition or multiple exposure of a persuasive communication on advertising response. The work of Ebbinghaus (1885), in addition to suggesting the decreasing function of forgetting curves already discussed, also dealt with the effect of repetition on both acquisition and memory. Some of his findings indicated a logarithmically increasing acquisition curve, along with early indication of a satiation point he referred to as "overlearning," or repetition beyond the point of perfect learning. Similar findings are reported in the more recent work of Craig, Sternthal, and Olshan (1972). In a study of the effects of a 100 percent learning condition versus 200 percent and 300 percent learning conditions (7 versus 14 and 21 exposures) for 12 print advertisements, they found that although both "over learning" conditions generated more advertising brand recall after 28 days than the 100 percent learning conditions, 200 percent learning provided greater recall than the 300 percent learning, resulting in an overall nonmonotonic inverted U-shaped repetition function.

In an early effort to measure the effects of repetition and forgetting over a period of time for advertising communication, Strong (1974) tested a number of print advertisements within four simulated magazine environments and found that four weekly exposures generated a higher level of recall than four consecutive exposures at a single reading, four daily exposures, or four monthly exposures. This, too, represents a nonmonotonic inverted U-shaped function, suggesting a satiation point for both the number of exposures (as discussed above) and the timing of the exposures. Similar studies by both Zielske (1959) and Strong (1974) also noted significant effects associated between the repetition of an advertising message and the timing of those repetitions. Such findings suggest that not only does recall decay in an Ebbinghaus fashion for a single exposure, but that the compounding harmonic effect of the decay following each exposure may be maximized over an entire exposure pattern when careful attention is paid to the time lag between exposures.

This means that "wearout" of advertising or other communications could conceivably be an inverse function of the timing of the exposures. For example, if one considers three exposures (reminiscent of Krugman's notion of three exposures effectiveness [1972]) sufficient for establishing recall at its maximum level, then one should expect a satiation or wearout effect to begin, and recall to decay from that point. But, suppose the time between exposures were doubled, say from an original biweekly to a monthly schedule. One could reasonably expect a certain amount of decay to set in following the first exposure, with subsequent recall measured at week four to be significantly less for the monthly schedule than for the biweekly schedule. At week six, however, some of the awareness will be recovered with the second exposure of the monthly schedule, even though one would still expect it to be somewhat less than the level of awareness generated by the third exposure of the biweekly schedule. From this point on, though, the monthly schedule will improve, while the biweekly schedule suffers from satiation, even with additional exposures. This is hypothesized because the monthly scehdule permitted a regeneration of recall for the advertising, thus postponing satiation beyond the third exposure. While this is only speculation, and the timing of the exposures (biweekly versus monthly) in this example serve only as a discussion point, the implications seem reasonable from the empirical evidence cited above. The hypothesized predictions are illustrated in Figure 6.1.

In a study of the effects of pooling commercials, Wallace (1970) reported results that could be construed as support for this hypothesis. When the same

FIGURE 6.1

Hypothesized Prediction of Advertising Recall Assuming an Inverse Relationship between "Wearout" and Exposure Timing

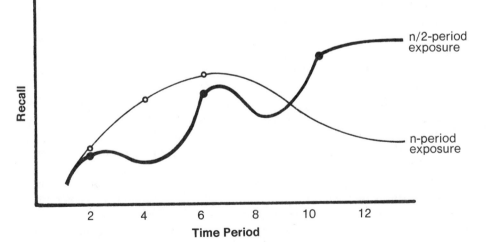

commercial was exposed six times within a half-hour simulated television show, interest and attention, as measured by the CONPAAD technique (a procedure that measures the extent to which a receiver is willing to "work" in order to see an advertisement or commercial, by pumping a foot pedal that keeps the advertising in view), declined after second or third exposure. When two different commercials were alternately exposed, in effect doubling the length of time between exposure, decay in interest was slowed.

This line of thinking raises a number of questions as to just exactly what the satiation effect is of multiple exposures to a persuasive communication over a period of time. In a significant experiment reported by Grass and Wallace (1969), attention, comprehension, and attitude levels were measured for five of eight commercials which comprised a consumer-directed advertising campaign running from April through October of 1968, during daytime and evening television programming. Subjects were recruited for the study who claimed to average at least one and one-half hours of television vewing per evening, and groups of ten were processed through the CONPAAD equipment for each of the five commercials studied—at the beginning of the campaign in April, at the middle of the campaign in July, and at the end in October. In addition, 24 hour recall measures were gathered in April and October, along with a measure of message comprehension. Of the five commercials studied, three were then removed from the air, while two continued to be aired through March of 1969 at a minimum weight level during daytime programming. Final measurements were then taken for each of the five commercials studied. Their conclusion found that, as the number of cumulative exposures increase, attention to the commercial is generated up to a maximum level, followed by a satiation effect or decline. For three of the five commercials studied, a satiation point was realized in the July measure at the middle of the campaign; for the other two, satiation was reached in October for one, but unexpectedly not reached until the March 1969 measure for the final one. An eventual equilibrium value was found for attention, which appeared to be a function of the campaign exposure frequency. The measures of commercial message comprehension were found to parallel the decay in attention, but attitude was found to be persistent and continued to increase (albeit slightly) after the satiation point in attention and comprehension had been reached. These general findings are illustrated in Figure 6.2. Grass and Wallace conclude with the observation that a regeneration of commercial attention and retained message comprehension may be possible in future exposures if the advertising is first removed from the air at the point of satiation for some period of time.

Essentially, the same results have been reported from a series of studies by Craig, Sternthal, and Leavitt (1976). They suggest that wearout is attributable to receiver inattention and lost recall motivation when there are numerous repetitions of an advertisement or commercial. This implies that there is some optimum level of repetition for advertising (or a satiation point), and that subse-

FIGURE 6.2

General Predictions of "Wearout" Functions

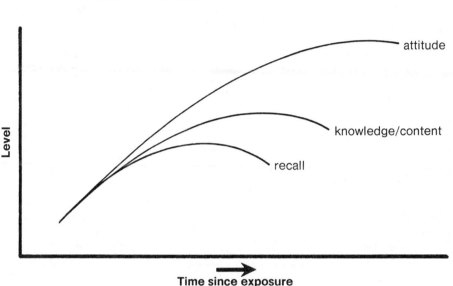

quent repetition beyond that point may cause a cognitive response that could inhibit learning. They, too, feel that the problems of wearout can be initiated by varying the execution of a particular message.

Interaction Effects

In addressing the general question of repetition and forgetting, one notes that a satiation point appears to be reached after a limited level of exposure, following which recall of persuasive communication declines (although actual attitude change does not seem to decay, or at least not so rapidly). It is now important to consider some of the interacting variables that could mediate the effects of repetition on wearout. The fact is that the shape of the curve reflecting these effects will depend not only on whether one is measuring recall or attitude, but also on such factors in the advertising situation as: the product being advertised, the target receiver, the competitive communication's environment, message variables, and even the media strategy employed. Unfortunately, not a lot of work has been done in the area of developing decay functions conditioned upon outside mediating variables, although a certain amount of exploratory analysis has been reported.

In a study by Ray and Sawyer (1971) of repeated advertising for different types of products (convenience goods versus shopping goods), they hypothesized that the satiation point, or the point at which wearout begins, should occur sooner for shopping goods advertising than for convenience goods, and be more pronounced for persuasion as opposed to reception measures. Their thinking was that, while repetition should have very little effect on measures of conative response, it should have almost no effect for shopping goods advertising, because only a handful of the receivers would be expected to be in the market for a particular product at a particular time. The results supported this hypothesis, finding that repetition of the advertising for convenience goods resulted in a significantly greater increase in both recall of the advertising and the expressed purchase intention for the advertised product after satiation of the shopping goods advertising occurred. While the satiation point for shopping goods advertising was reached after four exposures, the impact of the convenience goods advertising continued past six exposures.

Another product variable found by Ray and Sawyer to have influenced the effect of repetition on wearout is the extent of initial receiver familiarity with the product or brand advertised. They noted that advertising for well-known brands tended to benefit more from multiple exposures than did advertising for lesser known brands. In a study by Lucas and Britt (1963), it was found that increases in effectiveness measures after two exposures were, on average, twice as great for well-known brands, when compared with the gains found for the less familiar products. Sawyer (1972) also found significant differences in the effect of multiple exposures, depending upon whether the receiver claimed usage of the advertised product. Other experiments by Lo Scuito (1968) also report a correlation between product usage and brand-name recall from advertising, after one, four, and seven exposures. Using tobacco advertising, he found that brand-name recall was significantly lower among nonsmokers than among smokers at low exposure levels, but that this difference disappeared after seven exposures. His conclusion was that while infrequent or low levels of exposure may be sufficient to retain current users of a product, it is not sufficient to attract new users.

Returning to the Ray and Sawyer (1971) study, it was shown there that specific message variables could also influence the impact of repetition on eventual advertising wearout. Specifically, they looked at four message characteristics: (1) color versus black and white; (2) long versus short copy; (3) brand emphasis; and (4) whether or not the advertising was considered (by three judges associated with the study) to be different enough in format to attract attention and accomplish the bulk of its potential communication's effectiveness with a single exposure. Only this last characteristic proved to provide a significant interaction effect with repetition. It was found that this so-called "grabber" advertising declined in effectiveness almost immediately following its initial exposure. In other words, after a single exposure, the satiation was reached and the advertising was considered wornout. They suggest that this distinction might be compared to the hard-sell versus soft-sell approach so often discussed in advertising. To the extent that this surmise follows, one should be extremely careful in the use of intrusively unique advertising when seeking long-run efficiencies.

One other consideration in the effect of outside mediators on repetition or wearout is the positioning of the advertising within an overall campaign. As already suggested by the work of Grass and Wallace (1969) and Wallace (1970), variety in the advertising presented for a brand should increase the overall effectiveness of the individual pieces of advertising. An early study by Adams (1916) found that four exposures of the same print advertisements were less effective in increasing recall of the advertising than were four variations. Maddi (1961) found that, with a moderate level of variation in a set of presented stimuli, positive disposition toward the stimuli was greater than that noted for either no variety in the repeated stimuli presented, or a very high level of variety in the stimuli presented. These findings seem to suggest that when one of the desired is to generate a positive attitudinal response and to remain effective over a long period of time, to minimize wearout, one should pool that execution with at least one other within the allotted media schedule.

When considering pooling commercials or print executions, however, there is some indication that attention must also be paid to the affects of information processing. Calder and Sternthal (1977) have found that when receivers are repeatedly exposed to a pool of commercials over a period of time, they eventually evidence negative evaluations, both to a commercial that is part of the pool and to the product being advertised. Redundancy seems to affect the evaluation of commercials within a pool. To the extent that the advertising pool is reduced, lowering redundancy, evaluative reaction (which they find the central factor in a receiver's reaction to a product or advertising) is less positive; but, if the advertising environment is more redundant, the evaluation of the advertiser's commercial will tend to be more positive. While this might suggest that increasing a pool size, and, hence, lowering redundancy, should provide more positive evaluations and help prevent wearout, they caution that this is not necessarily the case. Although evaluative reactions were found to be the most crucial for wearout, these evaluations may vary with other mediating variables, such as flight length.

In summary, wearout of advertising appears to be a function of more than merely the number of repetitions. First, one must determine whether it is recall of the advertising or the attitude level sustained that will describe the satiation point. Then, the type of product or service advertised will bear on when wearout begins; the familiarity of the receiver with the advertised product or service will interact with when the satiation point is reached; and of course, the message itself, and whether it is mixed with other advertising for the brand, will mediate how long a particular execution remains efficient in its persuasive communication impact. Finally, there is evidence that wearout itself should be viewed as an active cognitive process, heavily dependent on receiver evaluative reactions to not only the advertising, but to the product itself.

SCHEDULING MEDIA

Once a workable set of cost-efficient media vehicles has been selected, it becomes necessary to decide how much or how many of each vehicle to buy, and how these buys should be distributed over a period of time. The most common way of doing this is to schedule the media and vehicles involved in such a way that the exposures occur at equal intervals, such as once every week in broadcast or every four weeks in print. But frequently it becomes necessary or advisable to "pulse," when advertising is scheduled in specific concentrations between irregular hiatus periods. Any number of reasons could occasion calling for pulsing in the media objectives and strategy. Much of the reasoning behind pulsing has already been discussed in the section on media objectives and strategy in the last chapter. For example, seasonal fluctuations in product sales would be matched correspondingly by the media schedule; special promotions might call for heavier expenditures at certain times; and, it is quite common for a new product introduction to be accompanied by a heavy introductory period of advertising, followed by lower sustaining levels. It is also not unusual to find media schedules exhibiting irregular pulses built around hypothesized purchase cycles and flighting, in order to remain within the omnipresent budget constraints. If a purchase cycle is thought to be four weeks, a schedule in which four week flights at alternating higher and lower expenditure levels, with two or three week hiatus periods would be typical.

Number of Exposures

Consideration of the number of exposures needed as outlined by one's media objectives and strategy is an important part of scheduling media. While Zajonc (1968) has suggested that even repeated "mere exposure" (by which he means nothing more than the accessibility of a stimulus to a receiver's perception) of a receiver to a stimulus is sufficient condition for the enhancement of the receiver's attitude toward it, others are not that certain (cf. Simon 1969). However, there is little disagreement that repetition is a very effective means of preventing message decay; a number of experiments in the behavioral sciences report findings that support this notion (Cook and Insko 1968; Wilson and Miller 1968; Insko 1964). Generally speaking, with repetition, the probability of immediately increasing the reception stages of the buyer response hierarchy is quite high. Sawyer (1974) points out that persuasion and attitude change are also positively affected by repetition, but to a somewhat lesser degree. In fact, it would seem reasonable to conclude that, in terms of advertising response, the reason for this may not be so much a function of repetition increasing persuasibility as such, but rather of retarding retention decay.

A study by McCullough and Ostrom (1974) illustrates how repetition of advertising exposure actually helps change attitude. Subjects were shown five executions of one of two advertising campaigns, one execution immediately following another. While viewing each of the commercials, cognitive elicitations were gathered. It was found that the net number of positive cognitions elicited significantly increased with the repetition of the advertising, while the net number of negative cognitions decreased. Overall, the total number of responses remained pretty much the same for each commercial. These results suggest that after a receiver's initial negative defenses have been elicited during early exposures, more positive cognitive reactions occur with later repetitions. It would then follow that, as positive responses increase, so too does the probability of a positive attitude change.

In a study of print advertisements and exposure, Politz (1960) investigated the effect of repeated advertising page exposure upon delayed measures of top-of-mind brand recall, aided brand recall, brand claim believability, and willingness to buy. Subjects were hand delivered copies of the *Saturday Evening Post* two days apart and were asked to read through the magazine and return it by mail. Four control advertisements were not used in either magazine (although questions about each were asked), four test advertisements were exposed in only one issue, and four more test advertisements were included in both magazines. Pages containing the test advertisements were inconspicuously sealed with a tiny spot of glue. When the magazines were returned, if the glue spot was not broken, that particular advertisement was not considered as being exposed to that subject. Call-back interviews were made three days after the delivery of the second magazine. Results from this study indicated an approximately two-fold increase in both top-of-mind and aided recall, as well as a two-fold increase in willingness to buy the advertised brand, among those exposed to the advertising twice as compared to once. Belief in the message claims showed a three-fold increase.

While the evidence clearly points to the positive benefit of repetition (or frequency) in scheduling media, more exposure does not always mean greater communication effectiveness. After some level, the effect of exposure becomes less with additional frequency. Craig, Sternthal, and Olshan (1972) studied the effects of 7, 14, and 21 exposures of 12 print advertisements and found that after about one month those exposed 14 times were able to recall more advertised brands than those exposed 21 times; both groups, however, showed higher brand recall than those exposed only 7 times. They concluded that this inverted U-shaped effect on the number of brand names recalled could have resulted from an offsetting of increased retention and irritation, corresponding to decreasing motivation to retrieve the brand name from long-term memory.

Zajonc (1968) has suggested that attitude is a linear function of the loga-

FIGURE 6.3

Attitude as a Log Function of Frequency

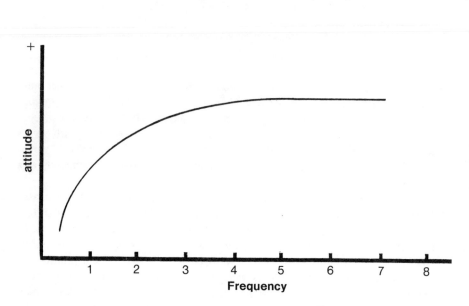

rithm of frequency that would result in an attitude-to-exposure relationship, similar to that shown in Figure 6.3. He has also remarked that this relationship is, to some extent, mediated by the familiarity of the stimulus. Although a small number of exposures may greatly increase the evaluation of a new or novel stimulus (such as a new product or brand), the more familiar the stimulus, the greater the number of additional exposures necessary to produce the same result. So, although repetition is critical to a successful media schedule, there seems to be only broad general guidelines, rather than known rules, for frequency levels available to guide the media planner. Nevertheless, attention to these guidelines is essential to efficient use of the media and media vehicles selected.

Compounding this problem of no established rules, as we have mentioned before, is that very few methods have been developed that can directly measure the actual reach and frequency of a media schedule. Media planners usually rely on some form of estimating system, based either on a simulation of media habits or probability function. DISRI, a simulation routine developed in Europe (and described in the *Proceedings* of the I.R.E.P. Annual Conference, Paris: Institut de Récherche et Études Publicités, 1966) is probably the most widely used estimating system based on simulation (Longman 1971). The most widely used system for print advertising, though, relies on probability estimates, based on the beta distribution in a formulation due to Metheringham (1964), generally considered the best because of the efficient utilization of the computer.

Following Metheringham, for example, estimates can be made of the net reach (or so-called "unduplicated reach") of a given print schedule, when insertions are used in several vehicles. Assuming first that only one insertion is placed in a given vehicle, an overall average of those receivers not reached (k_n) is calculated from an average of those not reached by each vehicle (k_1) and those not reached by any pair of vehicles in the schedule (k_2). The net reach for the entire schedule is then given by $1 - k_n$. When more than one insertion is used per vehicle, the same equation is applied, only each insertion is treated as a one-time exposure (or reach). This will then require estimates of the net cumulative reach of any two issues of the same vehicle, rather than the pair-wise estimates between vehicles originally assumed. All such net reach estimates for pairs of vehicles or multiple issue combinations are available for the media practitioner through various syndicated media research services.

As we know from our discussion of media, estimating reach is not sufficient; one must estimate the frequency distribution as well—the number of receivers reached one plus times, two plus times, and so on. Based upon the same estimates and probability functions used for reach, the Metheringham system projects the proportion of receivers reading exactly r out of n vehicles (or issues). While this method of calculating net reach and frequency has been found to provide reasonably accurate estimates, their usefulness must still be qualified.

The resulting average frequency figures from any estimating procedure are themselves no longer considered adequate measures of the concentration of exposure. The frequency distribution of media schedules tend to be asymmetrical, and consequently the majority of those exposed to a particular media vehicle are exposed less frequently than the average would seem to indicate (see Figure 6.4). This occurs because a small number of receivers are heavily exposed to any one vehicle, forcing the average frequency significantly above the median. The problem is even more difficult to control because the skewness of any one frequency distribution varies with the nature of the media schedule (Longman 1971).

Timing of Exposure

A second important consideration in the development of a media schedule is the spacing of the advertising exposures. Since a certain amount of forgetting will occur between exposures, it is important to build a schedule that seeks to maximize the probability of retention with efficient spacing of the message exposure over the length of the schedule. At present there are systems capable of estimating inter-exposure time intervals, but few are practical or commonly used. Instead, media planners, along with the advertiser and others working on a par-

FIGURE 6.4

Median versus Average Exposure from Frequency Distributions

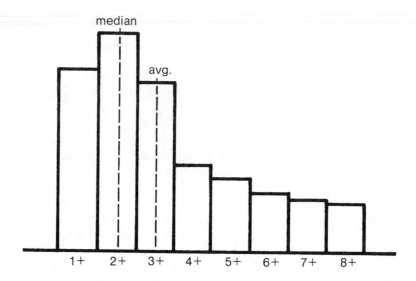

ticular account, apply their own subjective judgments of what is required for efficient timing of message exposure.

Research from the behavioral sciences can offer some guidance to media planners in selecting the most appropriate timing pattern for media exposure. Within this general area, two subfactors are identified: (1) the spacing of repeated exposures for one's own advertising; and (2) the degree of isolation one's exposures enjoy from those of competition. Considering the first, Strong (1916) varied the interval between exposure of advertising in four dummy magazines, then measured the level of advertising recognition one month after the final exposure. He found that a weekly interval was superior to monthly or daily intervals. Zielske (1959) compared a weekly schedule of 1 to 13 exposures with a four week interval schedule using direct mail. He found that with both schedules repetition was quite effective in increasing recall of the advertising, but that the four week schedule was more effective than the weekly schedule for 13 exposures, when awareness was averaged over a one year period. After 13 weekly exposures, awareness reached a level of 63 percent, but forgetting was rapid, decaying in an Ebbinghaus-like fashion to about 30 percent after four weeks and about 20 percent after six weeks. Over the entire year, the average level of awareness worked out to be about 21 percent. The four week schedule, on the other hand, built awareness much more slowly, finishing at a high of 48 percent after a full year. It then decayed to 37 percent four weeks after the final exposure, but averaged 29 percent a week for the entire year. Although the rate of forgetting may decrease as the number of exposures increases, one is rarely afforded the luxury of all but unlimited exposure opportunity, so the timing of a schedule remains critical to the effectiveness of an advertising campaign. If rapid awareness is critical, a shorter heavy-up schedule would be desirable, building awareness quickly at the expense of long-term awareness; if continued awareness is important over a longer period, a steady, more evenly timed schedule will be more effective.

Strong (1974) provides further evidence to support this generalization. In combining recall data from the Zielske study, as well as some of his own work that replicated, in part, the Zielske study, he ran simulations of various schedules based on derived regression equations. His results indicated that the most effective schedule in generating recall would be a schedule of four flights of four, three, and three biweekly exposures, with each flight starting at the beginning of each quarter of the year (with an average weekly recall of 32.2 percent), followed by a schedule of thirteen consecutive monthly exposures (30.1 percent), a biweekly schedule running 26 weeks (29.7 percent), and finally a schedule of 13 weekly exposures (26.5 percent). One may conclude from these findings that, in general, schedules with spaced individual exposures, or spaced groups of exposures, tend to be more effective than schedules that mass exposures, if one's objective is to measure the average level of communication over a specific period of time.

Turning now to the relationship of one's exposures to those of the competitors, evidence from research in the area of order effects suggests that usually there is an advantage to being "last heard." When the goal of a persuasive communication is immediate, then a recency effect operates and it is desirable to be scheduled as near to the actual behavior consequence as possible, after any communication effort by one's competition. However, if one's goal is more long term, and there is available budget for saturation level exposure, providing the message is highly persuasive, there could be advantages to preempting competitive communication. Unfortunately, true as these principles may be in theory, in practice consumers are constantly in the marketplace, making it difficult, if not impossible, to position one's advertising messages "after" a competitor's. But, it is possible to isolate one's advertising from competitors in terms of both the timing of exposures and the media and media vehicles selected for a schedule. McGuire (1964), for example, has noted that the closer competing messages occur in time, the greater the potential for counter-arguing with a lesser potential for positive attitude change. Other research has suggested similar dissonance reactions when competing messages are in close temporal proximity, suggesting the desirability of uniquely scheduling media to isolate one's message as much as possible from competitive activity.

Models for Scheduling

In an effort to cut down on the amount of guess work that is tied to the development of a media schedule, a number of scheduling models have been developed. These models range from simple routines designed to allocate parts of the day in broadcast media, through ambitious models that attempt to cover all facets of media selection and scheduling. While most of these models tend to be developed by proprietary interests (several of which are discussed by Longman [1971]), a few are publicly available through commercial media resource companies and from the advertising research literature. For example, UNITEL (1975) is a series of programs, commercially available through on-line computer access designed for analyzing television media data. The programs predict cumulative reach and frequency distributions for a broad range of audience definitions and for any given group of schedules, based upon a specific exponential function. Further, given a weekly budget and a frequency distribution objective, one of the system's subroutines will find the optimum combination of parts of the day to fulfill that particular set of objectives.

MEDIAC represents a more wide-ranging planning model (Little and Lodish 1966, 1969), based on a simplified view of how the advertising communication process works. It hypothesizes a set of market segments with unique sales potential and media habits. Exposures are sought from a media schedule consisting of insertions in various media vehicles, mediated by the timing of those insertions to minimize decay between exposures. It also allows for the introduction of seasonal patterns in the exposure to vehicles. The model realizes (as noted above) that anticipated response increases with exposure level, but with diminishing return.

More specifically, the model assumes that the market is divided into segments in which the receivers in each exhibit their own media behavior patterns and are assumed to have a given sales potential. One's media schedule provides the media and vehicles to be considered, where insertions or commercials permit exposure of the advertising to receivers in each market segment. Note that this is in contrast to the notion of the receiver presenting himself to the media, although Little and Lodish (1969) define exposure of an individual receiver to an insertion or commercial as meaning the receiver has perceived the presence of the advertising. These "exposures" then tend to raise the level of exposure (or probability of presentation) for individual receivers as they accumulate, while a lack of exposure will bring on "forgetting," or a decay in the exposure level. The importance of this concept of exposure level to the model is underscored by its assumed relationship to potential sales: the higher the exposure level, the greater the expected sales (although it is assumed to increase at a decreasing rate).

The flow of the important components in the MEDIAC model of media selection may be considered as follows:

1. Exposure or nonexposure of an individual receiver to an insertion or commercial in the media schedule is taken to be a random variable. For any particular receiver in a market segment, the probability distribution of exposure is taken to be a function of media exposure probabilities and whether or not an insertion or commercial occurs. Specific media or vehicle exposure may be weighted to account for subjective evaluations of a media's appropriateness to strategy, message, and so on.

2. Exposure (as described in point 1) is assumed to increase something called exposure level, which represents the weighted sum of the exposures resulting from implementation of the media schedule, mediated by forgetting between exposures. As a result, exposure level at any point in time is a weighted sum of past exposures, with weights decreasing in value over time.

3. Finally, exposure level is thought to influence something called market response. Market response assumes that each receiver has a sales potential, and that this sales potential varies according to market segment or other mediating market variables (such as seasonality). As a result, total market response becomes a function of individual receiver exposure levels within segments. The specific response curve representing this relationship is left somewhat up to the media planner's judgment, although it is generally considered to reflect a diminishing return at higher exposure levels (as shown in Figure 6.5).

FIGURE 6.5

Typical Response Curve Assumption

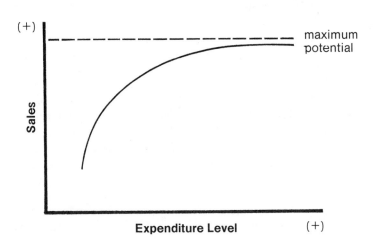

In summary, the model deals with weighted exposures that create exposure levels for aggregated receivers; a level that decays as advertising is forgotten. Sales are considered a function of the exposure level generated among the receivers within a particular market segment and defined within a specific period of time. Utilizing specific cost information, the model is then able to proceed in optimizing through a heuristic routine that media schedule which is best (or nearly best) in terms of expected advertising response.

Some of the advantages of the model commented on by FitzRoy (1976) include the fact that it has proven useful in actual practice, primarily because it approaches the problem in a realistic way. Additionally, the data required by the model is generally available and most of the estimates reasonably subjective. On the other hand, both of these operational benefits have their conceptual limitations. A model based upon a series of subjective estimations of vehicle worth and other constraints necessarily relies heavily upon the correctness of those estimates. And, as Aaker and Myer (1975) point out, the exposures are accumulated and forgotten only in an aggregate sense, which could hide bimodel distributions (or other multi-model distributions) of exposures in a particular market segment for a particular schedule.

Whereas MEDIAC assumes a model of communication that suggests an advertisement or commercial creates an exposure, which, in turn, stimulates buyer response, other models, such as ADMOD (Aaker 1975), focus on certain cognitive change in the receiver that a persuasive message is designed to effect through specific postcommunication response. For example, the response desired may be an advertising or subsequent buyer response, such as extended usage which, in the long run, will realize particular returns for the advertiser. The value of a certain schedule, in this case, is evaluated against the probability that, over the length of the schedule, buyer response will reflect the effect of the desired postcommunication response.

Another aspect of media scheduling concerns the value of pulsing (or several concentrated "bursts" of advertising) versus spacing. Moran (1976) has suggested a model for media scheduling analysis called ADEFF, based upon a simulation from 240,000 advertising impressions for 38 brands. The model itself was derived from awareness of television advertising for specific brands in four consumer packaged goods categories. Measures of awareness and purchase preference were taken at the beginning and end of a four week period, during which housewives in three television areas recorded their program viewing. At the same time, monitors recorded every commercial for the specific brands studied that were transmitted over each channel in those markets. From these data, it was possible to match program viewing with the commercial messages transmitted.

Response functions were then developed that described what happened to awareness of a brand's advertising when a message is described as being "received," how awareness decays over a period of time, and so on. Then these measures were projected over a period of time and the values of various schedules compared. The model thus offers an opportunity to simulate an expected awareness and purchase preference for one's product, given a specific media schedule.

Several limitations, however, attach themselves to this model. First, if a viewer recorded viewing television during any 15 minute segment in which a commercial was transmitted, the viewer was counted as having received the message. As we know, this only ensures the opportunity to present the viewer to the message, neglecting the additional steps of decoding and subsequent encoding involved in message processing. Second, the measures of awareness were keyed to advertising awareness, and this could tend to minimize the expected result for highly affective brands or for products for which the desired postcommunication effect is attitude related. Third, although the model is developed from heavily advertised products, extrapolation of annual schedules from a single four week period could be dangerous. Finally, and most important (perhaps because of the third point), patterns of pulsing versus spacing generated no effect on the buyer response measures of consumer attitude toward the test brand or the receiver's intention to buy.

There are, of course, numerous other models developed for use in media scheduling. FitzRoy (1976) and Aaker and Myer (1975) review some of the mathematical equations involved in several of the more common (including MEDIAC); Gensch (1973) reviews a number of additional models from both a historical and comparative viewpoint; and Little and Lodish (1969) review the many models available at the time they developed MEDIAC.

Comprehensive as these models may appear, none of the scheduling models are able to consider every problem in media selection and scheduling. There continues a large element of trial and error in the scheduling of media. Perhaps the most useful application of any of these models, from the simplest to the most complex, is as a discipline for planning. By inputting several alternatives, a good starting point may be determined for an efficient schedule, along with estimates of how each candidate schedule would be affected by the different assumptions necessary to the media planning function.

REVIEWING VARIABLE 5: SCHEDULING STRATEGY

The overall objective of this chapter has been to provide an understanding of how postcommunications effects mediate media scheduling strategy, and the impact on response to advertising. Specifically, one should be able to:

1. Illustrate the general patterns involved in the decay of message retention

2. Contrast the effects of proactive versus retroactive interference on buyer response to advertising

3. Appreciate the difficulties involved in attempting to determine the "wearout" of specific advertising

4. Distinguish between the persistence of advertising recall, comprehension, and attitude change

5. Recognize the inherent difficulties in advertising "recall" testing

6. Compare the advantages and disadvantages of specific advertising schedules in light of their effect on response to advertising

7. Understand the limitation of models in scheduling

KEY CONCEPTS

Interference Theory
  of Forgetting
Proactive Interference
Retroactive Interference
Decayed Impact over Time
Persistence Effects
Cognitive Response Retention
Recall Testing

Increased Impact over Time
Satiation
Wearout
Interaction Effects
Scheduling Media
Exposure Value
Timing
Scheduling Models

7

SUMMARY

Throughout this book, an effort has been made to present the reader with the yeast necessary for leavening advertising strategy. This required more than a description of the mechanisms of advertising or "how" advertising works. In fact, in the main, these more general discussions were ignored. Rather, an outline of the goals one should set for advertising was presented, along with an explanation of how these communication goals differ from the more direct marketing or buyer response objective. Advertising's task is more than "selling" a product or service, and the formulation of effective advertising strategy must acknowledge this difference.

We learned that mediating advertising response are five communication variables: the receiver of the communication, its source characteristics, the message itself, the media by which it is transmitted, and the schedule of its presentation. The discussion of these variables constituted the bulk of the book's instruction, because these are the variables an advertiser can control in developing and affecting an advertising strategy. Understanding these variables was found to be anything but a simple matter, but that is the reality of communication: it is not a simple matter. A great deal of theory and background research was presented, which, on the surface, may have appeared to strain any relation to advertising strategy. But, it is precisely this theoretical background that is necessary for a complete understanding and appreciation of advertising strategy; and the more an advertiser knows and understands of the tools available for effective communication, the greater the likelihood of achieving the sought-after response to advertising.

This summary chapter offers a final review of these communication variables and their impact upon response to advertising. And, in conclusion, two brief examples are presented that offer a practical look at applying advertising strategy.

RECEIVER SELECTION

Perhaps more than any other independent variable, the receiver as a variable in the communication process would seem to be most likely to influence an attitudinal response to advertising (at least the affective and conative response). After all, it is the receiver whose attitudes and behavior are affected by a persuasive communication. In a sense, any variable that affects attitude or behavior change could be thought of as a receiver variable in some fashion, since it must certainly operate within the receiver in order to produce any affect. But, we should continue to bear in mind that it is the particular state of the receiver when the receiver receives the advertising message that one speaks of, when discussing receiver selection as a variable influencing advertising response. Certain aspects of the receiver considered in the chapter, "Source Factors," involve the effect of source-receiver similarity on persuasibility—particularly those involving the original attitudes of the receiver compared with those of the source.

Receiver variables mediate advertising effectiveness through media exposure and message processing. As we have learned, media exposure should involve more than just buying media that apparently reaches the desired target receivers. Presentation by the receiver to the persuasive communication involves two important considerations: a priori selectivity on the part of the advertiser (for example, through attitudinally based market segmentation) and possible selective-avoidance on the part of the receiver (an effect that carries over into the attention stage of message processing). In the case of advertising communication, a great deal of care is taken to establish a so-called "target audience," made up of receivers characterized attitudinally, behaviorally, or demographically as compatible with the advertiser's product or service. Media are then selected to maximize the inclusion of certain kinds of receivers, to the neglect of others. To the extent that a particular set of receiver characteristics (including attitudes) is perceived as desirable, receivers matching these characteristics are afforded a greater likelihood of potential exposure to the advertising communication. Other receivers are excluded on an a priori basis owing to their initial attitudes or special individual difference characteristics.

Considering the possibility that receivers may selectively choose supportive communications, while avoiding nonsupportive messages, to the extent that such a selective-avoidance may operate, it is reasonable to assume it could affect media exposure of the message. Newcomb (1967) has suggested that, whenever possible, people tend to select their environment so it will be compatible with their attitudes. Further support for this notion is offered by the evidence of de facto selectivity: people do seem to avoid situations in which their values will be challenged and tend to make themselves available for communications with which they agree. To this extent, the receiver affects the probability of being exposed to a persuasive communication. But, as we pointed out earlier, any motivated selectivity of exposure on the part of the receiver seems doubtful (McGuire 1968c).

Turning to message processing, and the likelihood that any presented message will be attended to, this question of selective-avoidance must again be addressed. If it does, in fact, operate, either in a supportive or nonsupportive fashion, then it would affect a receiver's attention to the communication: a receiver would either attend to a persuasive communication (such as advertising), because the receiver expected it to be supportive of the receiver's position; or, the receiver expected it to be nonsupportive, because the receiver sought discrepant information. Regardless of which process is operating, it would affect attention.

Other factors important to attention would include the personality traits of the receiver. For example, a receiver with low self-esteem may feel unsure that the receiver is afraid of not comprehending a particular message, and, as a result, will ignore it. On the other hand, particularly in the case of advertising; a receiver with very high self-esteem may also completely ignore all persuasive messages, because of the receiver's feeling of knowing everything important about the subject of the advertising. As a result, perhaps those of intermediate self-esteem would be most likely to attend to a persuasive communication. Studies by Harvey (1965) and others (reviewed by Triandis, 1971) offer additional evidence of a receiver's personality traits affecting the likelihood of attending to particular communication.

In decoding a message, such obvious individualistic characteristics as intelligence or personality could affect the extent to which a persuasive message is comprehended by the receiver. Classic studies by Cooper and Jahoda (1947) and Kendall and Wolf (1949) indicated that a receiver's defensiveness could be a primary factor inhibiting message comprehension. When encoding a message, a receiver's initial attitude becomes important. As we saw in our discussion of discrepancy, assimilation and contrast affects may occur, depending on how discrepant a receiver's position is from that advocated by the advertising. A receiver will tend to evaluate a message more positively if it lies within the receiver's latitude of acceptance, and will tend to evaluate any position within the latitude of rejection as being even more discrepant from the receiver's original position than it actually is. As was pointed out at the time, implications are significant for advertising communication.

Responding to advertising objectives (for example, learning new beliefs or changing an evaluation of the advertised product or service) is less affected by demographic characteristics than by the other characteristics of a receiver, such as personality traits, ability levels, and initial attitudes. However, all contribute significantly to the probability that a receiver will yield to a persuasive communication message. Triandis (1971) suggests that there are three basic influences that cause a receiver to respond to a message: (a) the perceived power of the source, or the perceived reward-punishment effects of responding; (b) the attractiveness of the source; and (c) the extent to which the message fits with the existing values and cognitions of the receiver. This interaction of communication variables in impacting advertising response should by now be familiar to the reader. One can appreciate the relevance of the receiver's state of mind when exposed to a persuasive communication and how that affects the receiver's perception of the source. For example, highly authoritarian receivers are more likely to respond to powerful sources, while those high in need affiliation might be more easily influenced by the attractiveness of the source.

The influence of a receiver's initial attitude is even more likely to effect response. Just as we noted in message processing, discrepancy is a critical factor in the likelihood of achieving a desired response. Additionally, cognitive factors, such as the receiver's perspective or tolerance for inconsistency might affect response. Ostrom and Upshaw (1968) have shown that those with a broader range of attitudinal positions tend to be more moderate in their own evaluations than people with a more narrow perspective, who will tend to reject positions that are only mildly discrepant from their own. The importance of this in the selection of a target audience for advertising is clear: one should attempt to exclude receivers with a narrow understanding of the product category or service addressed in the persuasive communication. This would be even more important for the introduction of a new product or when a significant departure from usual behavior is advocated. On the other hand, Rosenberg (1965) has shown that some people tend to be troubled more than others when confronted with discrepancies, responding more readily when these discrepancies are made salient. The trick, of course, is discriminating between the two, and identifying their presence in a target market.

An additional critical consideration, from a purely pragmatic standpoint, results from a receiver's ability level—specifically, memory capacity. If a receiver has a poor memory, it will be more difficult for the receiver to retrieve the encoded message, and his initial response to the message. In advertising, this supports the need for so-called reminder advertising scheduled to reinforce a decision to purchase or to use at times when shopping or usage is likely, as well as point-of-purchase reminders; both interact with the scheduling variable. At the final point of a choice decision, a number of receiver variables are important: attitudes, existing behavioral patterns, expectancies of reinforcement, and group norms. Triandis (1971) reviews a number of studies supporting the notion that behavioral change is more likely if the cognitive and affective components of attitude are consistent with adoption. Again, this underscores the need for the proper attitudinal information from a segmentation study. Also, we have seen how important personality traits of a receiver effect the probability of behavioral change.

As one by now must certainly understand, any one receiver variable may be positively related to persuasive impact via some mediating steps in the communication process, and negatively related by others. The importance of this confounding to advertising, and the need to clearly understand the communication task prior to selecting means, has frequently been stressed. The interactions of certain receiver variables (for example, personality traits as considered by Mc-Guire [1968a], in his theory of personality-persuasibility) compound this problem. There are interactions not only between receiver variables, but frequently among specific characteristics, each affecting media exposure, message processing, and eventual response, in a unique fashion. To illustrate the complexity of a receiver's involvement in this process, we shall consider ability levels and personality traits and how they affect message reception and response.

In our earlier discussion of intelligence in the section in chapter 2 on ability levels, we remarked on the rather commonsense notion that somehow there should be a negative relationship between persuasibility and intelligence. It seemed reasonable to feel that, the more intelligent a receiver, the more difficult it should be to persuade that receiver. However, this conjecture focused only on particular responses to advertising and ignored all the others. It would be equally likely to suggest that a positive relationship of intelligence with the message processing stages of attention and decoding should exist, since the more intelligent the receiver, the more likely it is that the receiver will adequately and correctly comprehend the message points of the advertising and the arguments used. Once again, we are confronted with a situation in which the relation between intelligence and persuasibility tend in opposite directions, suggesting that, for a wide range of conditions the net relationship between the two will be a nonmonotonic function, the by now familiar inverted-U. This being the case, receivers with medium levels of intelligence would be most susceptible to attitude change, while those with higher or lower levels would be more difficult to persuade: the lower because they would be less likely to be receptive; the higher because they would be less likely to respond.

Of course, in practice there is more to the equation than this. One would not direct, in the case of advertising, all efforts against receivers of average intelligence. Rather, in message construction and consideration of the other communication variables, attention would be paid to the mediating effects of all influences on advertising strategy. For example, if the objective of an advertising campaign was awareness of a new product introduction, one would wish to captalize on the greater likelihood of intelligent receivers to attend to and comprehend the message. Attitudinal responses, at that point, are less important. If these were important, and the message itself detailed or complex, again higher ability levels would be desirable. The important point is to appreciate the probabilities of various interactions, and to account for them in your strategic advertising planning.

Considering receiver personality traits, McGuire (1968a) has suggested that any personality trait that exhibits a positive relationship to message processing will tend to be negatively related to attitudinal advertising responses (for example, self-esteem), while those negatively related to message processing will generally be positively related to these responses (for example, anxiety). This is of particular note in the creation of advertising, but results can be doubly confounding: both inter-variable and intravariable effects are present. The net effect of a personality trait, such as self-esteem, on advertising strategy predicts a negative relationship when the message is easy to understand, an inverted-U relationship in moderately difficult communication (in other words, as the receiver's self-esteem increases, there is more change up to some optimal point, after which the amount of change decreases), and no relationship at all when the advertising message tends to be quite difficult. These predictions, supported by Nisbett and Gordon (1967), indicate that, as difficulty of reception increases, the level of self-esteem at which maximum persuasion occurs also increases. In addition, the more difficult it is to respond to the message, the lower the level of self-esteem will be at which maximum persuasion occurs. This suggests that in creating advertising designed to evoke a significant attitudinal or behavioral change on the part of the receiver, to the greatest extent possible, one should avoid a target audience with high self-esteem. The problem, of course, will be to isolate those receivers.

In attempting to isolate those receivers, a communication oriented attitudinal segmentation is necessary. This approach to segmenting a market differs from the more traditional methods in that it first asks the question: What can I say that will offer the greatest potential for advertising response, and then profile those whom will be most likely to respond. Traditional segmentation approaches first ask the question: Who would seem most likely to behaviorally respond (such groups as heavy category users, older people, up-scale families, those with "favorable" attitudes); then, what should I say to them to stimulate an advertising response that will lead to that buyer response?

Many of these complex interactions have been implied throughout this book. Once again we are reminded that the mediating effects of receiver variables on the communication process are not simple or easily predicted. Yet, an understanding of the reality of these many effects, in the case of advertising communication, helps the advertiser better understand how the message will be received by the target receivers, and within what constraints the advertiser may be able to maximize the persuasive efforts.

SOURCE FACTORS AND MESSAGE STRATEGY

The source may have an ultimate effect on attitude or behavior change by affecting any or all phases of the communication process. The persuasive impact attributed to the source in affecting message processing and advertising response may vary considerably, depending upon the source characteristic involved. For example, suppose an advertiser was unsure whether to use a source perceived similar to the receivers in the target audience (for example, in a "slice of life" presentation) or a source clearly perceived as an expert authority figure. It would be possible to determine how both sources would affect this probability of achieving the desired advertising response. Since both sources would be presented through the same media to the same target audience, the probability of a receiver being exposed to the message should be the same for both sources. In processing the message, considering the likelihood that any presented message will be attended to, we might predict that the expert source would receive more attention because such things as the expert's novelty, and authoritative status would have more attention-provoking potential than the comments of someone perceived similar to the receiver. However, in decoding or comprehending, the similar source might have the advantage, since its way of presenting the material would be easily recognized and understood by the receiver.

Next, suppose a cognitive response objective were set for the advertising. The expert source may be considered better because of higher status, while the similar source is evaluated equal to the receiver. The expert source should also have an advantage if an affective or conative response objective were set, again because high prestige status and perceived knowledgeability should constitute a more compelling force on the receiver to agree with such material in the message as was understood. One might expect the message delivered by the expert source to be retained and behavior result if the opportunity to behave occurs within a short time of message exposure, because of this greater probability of response. However, because the similar source is more readily comprehended, if the desired response is achieved, it should persist over a longer period of time.

It should be clear from this example that two alternative source characteristics may be positively related to persuasive impact in some cases, while negatively related by others. As a result, the immediate goals of one's advertising strategy assume an important role in the source selection. When setting response objectives, one must consider McGuire's (1972) observation that the net relationship source variables and eventual attitude or behavior change can be either positive or negative, depending upon whether the particular social influence situation with which one is dealing allows for more variance in one mediator or the other. For example, if the message was quite simple and repetitious—one most normal people would understand regardless of the source to which it is attributed—then it could be assumed that extensive message processing would play little role in determining the net relationship between the source variable and the desired advertising response. In other situations, in which the message is much more complicated and one would expect a great deal of variance among receivers in the extent to which they understand a message, message processing considerations would assume more importance in determining the net relationship between the source variable and the desired response. This suggests the importance of clearly understanding the strategic task before the selection of a source.

The basic components of advertising strategy as we have presented them, albeit in somewhat different form, have received a great deal of attention in the literature. Triandis (1971) has found that the more confident a source appears to the receiver, the greater attention is paid to the communication. McGuire (1969a) remarks on the existence of a large-scale "testimonial" industry, devoted to securing endorsements of products by celebrities, suggesting this seems to attest to the faith of advertising and marketing practitioners in the attention-eliciting impact of certain sources. Having a beautiful actress deliver a message for diesel trucks can be justified by assuming her appearance will attract attention to the advertisement rather than generate any confidence in the receiver as to the credibility of the message.

McGuire (1969a) has also suggested that, in terms of message comprehension, there is some indication that messages from unknown sources may be better learned than messages from sources known to be high or low in credibility. In terms of the effects of beliefs about the source, or attitudes toward the source, Fishbein and Ajzen (1975) report the evidence overwhelmingly indicates that neither beliefs about the source's credibility nor attitudes toward the source communicator have any appreciable effects on the receiver's recognition or recall of the contents of the communication. They review a study by Johnson and Scileppi (1969) in which subjects read a communication attributed to one of two very different sources: a medical expert versus a quack. Even this extreme manipulation of source credibility had no significant effects on a measure of recall of message content. McGuire's (1969a) reasoning on this and other experiments demonstrating a general lack of source recall (comprehension) relationship is to suggest a receiver can be regarded as a lazy organism who tries to master message content only when absolutely necessary to make a decision. When the perceived source is clearly positively or negatively valenced, the receiver uses this information as a cue to accept or reject the message's conclusion, based solely upon the perception of the source, without really absorbing the arguments used. Only when the source is not easily categorized as positive or negative (in terms of one of the source characteristics) will a receiver really find it necessary to learn and absorb the arguments used, and thus exhibit a higher recall-of-content score.

This underscores one of the serious indictments of recall-score-evaluations of advertising. There is no particular reason for an advertising communication to be well learned if the source is perceived as either highly credible or attractive. Reaction to the communication message may be merely a reinforcement of an already favorable evaluation of the product or service being advertised. As a result, an advertisement that does a fine job in enhancing an image and propensity to consume may find itself scoring poorly on message-related recall measurements.

Triandis (1971), in several studies of the "cognitive similarity" of the source and the message, found that the greater the similarity, the more likely it was to lead to better understanding of the message; comprehension was maximized when the source categorizes experience the same way as the receiver. Source credibility, on the other hand, is thought to have less affect on message processing per se, little affect on an awareness response, but significant affect upon attitudinal responses. For example, if the receiver is very sure that a source is objective, the receiver may not pay much attention to the argument because the receiver is sure the source is knowledgeable about the subject, or is reluctant to take issue with an "acknowledged" expert. On the other hand, if the source comes right out and warns the receiver that the source is out to persuade (as with a refutational message strategy), the receiver may be more likely to pay attention to the message. McGuire (1973) suggests that while the source credibility effect tends to show up in ultimate change, the source variables tend not to be manifested in detectable differences in the extent of learning the message contents, at least not in a rectilinear way. A framework for evaluating source factors, of course, was provided by the VisCAP model of source effectiveness.

Thus, we see that the source variable seems to affect overall advertising response less by encouraging the receiver to learn the arguments of a highly perceived source than by making the source's arguments appear better merely because they are attributed to a more credible source. One final point on the effects of positively versus negatively perceived sources and likely advertising responses should be made. Any persuasive message, if well argued, should move the receiver in the direction of the desired conclusion, regardless of source perception. If the source is perceived poorly, this should only have the effect on lessening this natural pull toward a positive response. Only when one is dealing with a largely contentless message from a source purportedly endorsing conclusions without applicable arguments, does one actually get a negative boomerang effect due to a negative source's endorsement (Tannenbaum 1956). Unfortunately, this is often the case with advertising.

The impact of message variables in advertising strategy is probably more generally interrelated with other mediating communication variables than one finds with source, receiver, media, or scheduling variables. After all, it is the message itself that is the vehicle for the arguments contained in advertising. Nevertheless, perception of the source of these arguments, their compatibility with the attitudes and behavior of the receiver, how they are transmitted to the receiver, and toward what end, obviously mediate the effects of a message on response to that advertising.

The probability of a particular message being presented to a receiver, as well as the receiver's attending to it, has a great deal to do with a certain level of de facto selectivity. While it has been pointed out in earlier chapters that evidence for a conscious selective exposure theory is weak (cf. McGuire 1973), there is overwhelming evidence to support the notion that, whenever possible, a receiver will tend to select the environment so that it will be compatible with the receiver's attitudes (Newcomb 1967). To the extent that a message is compatible with a receiver's environment, one should expect a greater or lesser probability of media exposure and attention. Further, Lowenthal (1969) has found that receivers tend to have a preference for messages that are strong consonant or weak dissonant, as opposed to weak consonant or strong dissonant. In other words, one should expect greater attention to messages that are strongly compatible with a receiver's attitudes; hence our emphasis on attitudinally based segmentation in receiver selection. When the message is not compatible (for example, advertising for a product not used by the receiver), one would expect more attention when the differences are cognitively negative.

The functional approach to message reception would predict that if the subject of an advertisement or commercial is not ego-involving, the usefulness of the information provided in the message will probably become the primary mediator of attention. In this case, whether the information is supportive or not supportive of the receiver's attitudes would be largely irrelevant, since there is low involvement on the part of the receiver. While it is true that most people in everyday life are exposed de facto to disproportionate amounts of supportive messages, there is no support for the notion they prefer to be exposed to supportive as opposed to nonsupportive messages. It is only when a receiver's attitudes are challenged on an ego-involving issue (or when arguments have little actual utility) that the receiver will prefer supportive communication. Other factors too, although less prominent in the literature, seem quite likely to enhance message attention (Triandis 1971): messages attributed to unusual, exotic, loud, or prestigious sources; and messages containing controversial, interesting, or surprising elements.

Message processing obviously requires that a message be understandable to the receiver. The clearer a message is and the less likely a message is to place the receiver on the defensive, the greater the likelihood it will be comprehended. Message differences affect encoding and response to the extent that they fit with the existing beliefs and values of the receiver. For example, a message that makes it clear that there will be some form of positive reinforcement following acceptance of the message's argument will stand a greater chance of positive evaluation and a subsequent attitudinal response than one in which a positive inference is more difficult.

The more frequently a message is repeated or presented to the receiver, the longer it is likely to be retained. In addition, Jones and Kohler (1958) have found that implausible dissonant and believable consonant messages tend to be better remembered than unbelievable consonant or plausible dissonant messages. They suggest that this may be because messages that are implausible or inconsistent with the receiver's attitudes would tend to be difficult to refute or painful, and hence forgotten more readily. On the other hand, messages compatible with existing beliefs are reinforcing and useful to remember for future reference, while those messages generally consistent with the receiver's attitudes, but not believable (for example, advertising extolling the virtues of using a product category, but suggesting only one worthwhile brand), are useless and as a result more easily forgotten.

It should be clear from this discussion that an understanding of the environment in which a receiver behaves, along with a thorough understanding of the receiver's attitudes, is necessary for the successful implementation of a persuasive message; and that these understandings help one maximize advertising response. Adoption of the argument contained in a persuasive message, a positive cognitive, affective, or conative response, is in the end most likely if the cognitive and affective components of the receiver's attitude are consistent with that message.

But, in addition to this notion of message-attitude compatibility, we have also seen the importance of how a message is written, not in terms of the creative content of the advertising, but the grammatical structure, plus the importance of visual imagery. While these considerations may seem to have little to do with the development of strategic advertising plans, they have everything to do with the probable success of that strategy. It is for this reason that these aspects of the message variable in advertising received so much attention.

The impact of words, and how they are put together in sentences, must be addressed when evaluating advertising, if one is to be certain one is maximizing the opportunity for the desired advertising response. Word meaning must be clear, and, as a rule, this means avoiding such semantic components as synonyms, homonyms, and antonyms, unless their meanings are unambiguous. Word usage also affects comprehension: higher frequency words are more likely to be heard or read, and understood, by the receiver; concrete words stimulate visual imagery and, as a result, generate a more favorable affective response.

Moving from words to sentences, we have also learned the length of sentences used in advertising copy must coincide with the natural way in which a receiver will "break up" the sentence for processing. This means that one must beware of content ambiguity. Overall comprehension, too, is more likely if negative and passive forms are avoided, even though, under the right circumstances, if a habitual comprehension strategy is involved, they could be appropriate. Sticking to conventional meanings of words and avoiding ambiguity increases the likelihood of memorability, and hence retention of the desired response. This, too, seems to be a function of the "difficulty" of a sentence, following an active, passive, negative, passive-negative ordering. The more difficult a sentence, the more likely it will be misunderstood or ignored altogether.

Finally, it was pointed out in the discussion of the work by Rossiter and Percy (1978) that visual content can potentially affect advertising response as affectively as verbal content. In certain instances, a visual rather than verbal orientation to advertising can have significant impact on cognitive and affective response. The notion of visual reinforcement resulting from visual imagery was also introduced, and hypothesized as a possible explanation of the superior learning produced by television over comparable print advertising.

We have seen how the development of a persuasive message requires more than following the creative outline of an advertising strategy. The way in which a creative strategy is executed, the actual words and visual affects used, will significantly affect the way in which a receiver understands your message.

MEDIA SELECTION AND SCHEDULING

Throughout the chapters, "Media Selection" and "Scheduling Strategy," examples were given of how variations in mass media variables can effect response to advertising. It should also be clear to the reader at this point, recalling the chapter on source factors, that a medium or media vehicle may itself assume the role of a source in the communication process, and as such attach to it all of the characteristics and effects of a source. This section will provide a brief overview of the effects of mass media variables in strategy advertising planning, considering, however, only intrinsic media differences and not possible source attribution effects.

Thinking first of the probability of exposure or presentation given a particular medium, outdoor and transit advertising (and to a certain extent point-of-purchase material) tend to be the most intrusive, followed by broadcast media, and finally print, which tends to be quite easily avoided. Attention is probably maximal for television, followed by other broadcast and print media, with outdoor and transit advertising least likely to attract attention (again we are referring only to the media without consideration of the possible stopping power of any particular advertisement or commercial). Triandis (1971) has suggested that, while this affect may obtain generally for non-ego-involving attitude objects, such as soap, when the issue is more ego-involving, influence will follow the two-step communication model of Katz (1957); mass media will first influence the so-called opinion leaders, who will in turn influence a greater audience through personal communication. A review of several studies supporting this notion is offered by Schramm (1963). In terms of message processing, those media that allow a receiver to proceed at the receiver's own pace tend to be more likely to maximize comprehension. The more difficult a message, the more important this becomes. It is obvious that print media hold a distinct advantage when the persuasive message is either complex or there are many beliefs to be assimilated. If the message is simple, comprehension through broadcast media would tend to be reinforced by greater attention, compensating in part for the lack of self-pacing.

Specific advertising response should, in some measure, reflect the prestige and belief affects associated with a media (for example, the high level of news reporting believability associated with television versus newspaper); the carryover from more prestigious media would be likely to enhance the evaluation of a product or brand being advertised. Attitudinal responses (cognitive, affective, and conative) are perhaps most effected by the unique characteristics of a particular medium or media vehicle. The more specialized a media, the greater the chance for group identification and attending motivation to comply; the better the quality of reproduction, the more likely the full impact of a message will not be distorted; the fewer the competitive advertisements or commercials (or other noise), the higher the probability of the desired response (again only from a media effects standpoint). More than any other phase of advertising strategy, the effects on response from mass media variables tend to be more a function of the media being perceived as a source variable.

While a knowledge of media characteristics is certainly essential to strategic advertising planning, the key to a successful implementation of media strategy is the proper selection of media vehicles. Although this could be thought of as rather straightforward, as we have seen, it is actually quite complicated, and rarely affected properly. The framework for media vehicle selection presented in the "Media Selection" chapter offers a paradigm for efficient vehicle selection.

It was pointed out that, although each media vehicle one may consider has a certain reported audience size, the exposure value, or number of people it actually delivers for an advertisement, is somewhat less than this figure, and varies from media to media and vehicle to vehicle. As a result, one must first determine the exposure value of each candidate, and estimate the probable size of the exposed audience. Next, this exposed audience is evaluated for its probable effect on the desired advertising response (awareness, cognitive, affective, or conative). A weighted probability must be attached to the exposed audience, reducing it to what one might call a "persuasible" audience, or the number of receivers likely to change their response to the advertising as a result of exposure in this vehicle to a persuasive message for the advertised product or service.

Once established, a profile of these receivers is developed and their characteristics compared with those of the desired target receivers (remembering that, although we have just qualified this audience as highly persuasible, this is only from a media vehicle standpoint, not potential use of the advertised product or service). This will indicate how many receivers within the persuasible audience are also likely to have the characteristics of the desired target receivers. Yet, as we have seen, this is still no guarantee of target receiver delivery. Only a proportion of those with the desired characteristics will actually be probable target receivers. This would be especially true if all one had available were the usual demographic or usage information. The more detailed correlates one has with media behavior, (as a result of, for example, a communication based attitudinal segmentation), of course, the better position one will be in to establish the correctness of the audience or probable target receivers.

Dividing the cost per thousand of delivered audience by the probable target receivers will provide a relative measure of a media vehicle's efficiency in delivering the desired receivers with a maximum probability of effecting the desired advertising response. Those media vehicles with high cost efficiencies should then be selected for inclusion in the media schedule. This analysis requires a great deal of effort, but it is critical in maximizing your potential for reaching the desired target receivers and effecting the hoped-for response indicated by the advertising strategy.

Having selected the appropriate media vehicles, one must schedule them.

Retention of any advertising response will be, perforce, a function of its exposure, and particularly the repetition of exposure: the concepts of reach and frequency. In a restricted time period, broadcast media, as a rule, will provide a better opportunity for maximizing retention of a response, since it offers more opportunity for repetition. But, as we learned from the chapter on scheduling strategy, rarely is the strategic question so simple.

Once a workable set of cost-efficient media vehicles has been selected, it becomes necessary to decide how much or how many of each vehicle to buy, and how these buys should be distributed over a period of time. A common way of doing this is to schedule the media and vehicles involved in such a way that the exposures occur at equal intervals, such as once every week in broadcast or every four weeks in print. On the other hand, often advertising is scheduled in specific concentrations between irregular hiatus periods, something called "pulsing." Any number of reasons could occasion calling for pulsing in the media objectives associated with an advertising strategy. Much of the reasoning behind pulsing was discussed in the section on media objectives and strategy in the "Media Selection" chapter. For example, seasonal fluctuations in product sales would be matched correspondingly by the media schedule; special promotions might call for heavier expenditures at certain times; and it is quite common for a new product introduction to be accompanied by a heavy introductory period of advertising, followed by lower sustaining levels. It is also not unusual to find media schedules exhibiting irregular pulses built around hypothesized purchase cycles and flighting, in order to remain within the omnipresent budget constraints. If a purchase cycle is thought to be four weeks, a schedule of four flights at alternating higher and lower expenditure levels, with two or three week hiatus periods, would be typical.

Yet, the question of when and how to schedule "pulsing" is subject to much debate. The available simulations of Strong (1974, 1977) would suggest that something other than evenly distributed "pulses" will optimize average recall over a period of time. Unfortunately, the dependent variable in these, as in the original Zielski (1959) work, is advertising recall. But, this limitation not withstanding, the logic is sound in establishing a schedule that packs media pressure in such a way as to build response over a period of time by arresting attrition with a new "pulse," before the desired response effect has dropped to a level that requires a significant effort to achieve the earlier levels.

Postcommunication effects, the retention of an advertising response, are in large measure dependent upon the initial response desired. What may be a proper scheduling strategy for one advertising response is not for another. It has been pointed out, for example, that an awareness response tends to be short-lived (if advertising associated), while cognitive responses are more long-lasting; and indications are that retention of an affective or intention response tends to be independent of persistence in response to advertising. There also tends to be some evidence that when a receiver's initial thoughts are negative (for example, in counter-arguing, or source derogation) they may restrict initial positive response, but over a period of time these negative thoughts are discounted and a more positive attitude change develops.

One of the most persistent questions, and one of the most difficult to answer associated with scheduling strategy is "wearout." One must initially determine whether the advertising response is to be measured by recall of the advertising itself or the response level sustained which will establish the satiation point. The type of product or service advertised has a significant affect on when wearout begins; the familiarity of the receiver with the advertised product or service will interact with when the satiation point is reached, and of course, the message itself and whether it is mixed with other advertising for the product or service, will mediate how long a particular execution remains efficient in its persuasive communication impact. Also, there is evidence that wearout itself should be viewed as an active cognitive process, heavily dependent on receiver evaluative reactions to not only the advertising, but the advertised product or service itself. Clearly, wearout of advertising appears to be a function of more than merely the number of repetitions.

Media expenditures are the largest component of the advertising budget, yet media scheduling is the strategic input we know least about. All other aspects of advertising strategy will be wasted, unless the message reaches the target receivers with sufficient frequency and continuity to attain the necessary advertising response and thus stimulate buyer behavior.

APPLIED ADVERTISING STRATEGY

With the guidance provided by the discussion in this book, the reader should now be in a strong position to not only develop effective advertising strategy, but also to evaluate the expected impact of those strategies upon advertising response. It has been pointed out that when beliefs are known to be strongly held by a group of receivers, advertising messages directed toward those receivers should, if possible, be compatible and designed to reinforce those beliefs. On the other hand, when beliefs are weak or must be changed, a refutational appeal designed to stimulate counter-arguing would be more likely. Two situations are presented and reviewed from the perspective of an advertiser developing and evaluating message strategy based upon a specific advertising response strategy.

Suppose a brand manager for new products was interested in introducing a new cooking oil. A large scale communication based segmentation study is conducted, and indicates that beliefs about cooking oils were categorized as either functional or usage beliefs by those consumers whose attitudes toward cooking oil suggest they should comprise the target receivers. Figure 7.1 shows a joint plot of cooking oil brands and functional beliefs. The closer together any two

FIGURE 7.1

Two-Dimensional Plot of Brand-Feature Functional Beliefs and Ideal-Features Associations from Prefmap Phase III Analysis

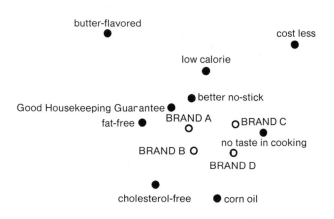

beliefs, the more likely receivers would be to believe a cooking oil containing one feature would also contain another. For example, a "low calorie" cooking oil could provide "better no-stick," but could not be "cholesterol-free" or have "corn oil." The fact that all the brands (with the exception of brand E, a butter-flavored cooking oil) tend to cluster together in the midst of the functional beliefs would indicate that there is very little perceived differentiation among these brands on the functional features. Looking next at Figure 7.2, we find a great deal of uniqueness among the usage belief congruence, but more important, the brands are thought to differ in terms of usage features among the target receivers. In other words, while brands A and B are thought to be "clear," brands C and D are more likely to be perceived as "lightly coats surface."

Those findings have important implications for developing an advertising strategy leading to a desired advertising response. Because the cognitive or belief

FIGURE 7.2

Two-Dimensional Plot of Brand-Feature Usage Beliefs and Ideal-Features Associations from Prefmap Phase III Analysis

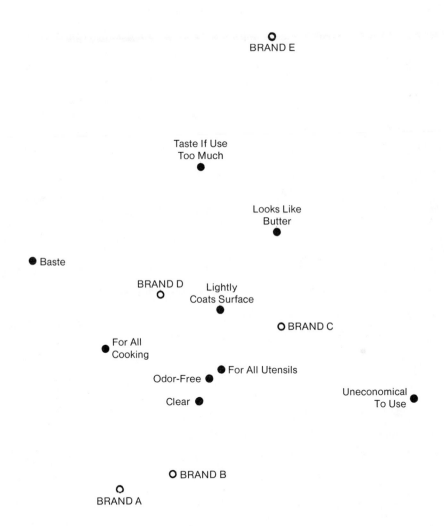

space of the target receivers is so involved with brand identification, beyond creating awareness for the new cooking oil, a cognitive response associating the new oil with unique positive beliefs should be sought. Assuming this cognitive advertising response, one would only wish to feature usage beliefs. While receivers may feel some functional beliefs are important, they are ascribed equally to all brands and would offer no unique association with the new product. On the other hand, by capitalizing on important usage beliefs a more unique position can be created for your brand. For example, if the rank order of importance among these usage beliefs were as shown in Table 7.1, the brand manager seeking to introduce a new cooking oil would want the advertising message points to create an image of the product being "for all cooking" and "basting." These are the most important beliefs to the target receivers, and importantly, they believe certain brands could differ in their ability to deliver these features. As such, they would form the communication basis of an advertising strategy seeking a cognitive advertising response. Advertising that effectively associates these positive discriminating usage beliefs with the advertiser's product will tend to maximize the potential for the desired response. The advertiser with this understanding clearly has a competitive edge.

But what of the advertiser who conducts basic attitudinal segmentation research and discovers a situation in which a large number of consumers hold

TABLE 7.1

Rank Importance of Cooking Oil Usage Beliefs

Beliefs	Rank
for all cooking	1st
baste	2nd
lightly coats surface	3rd
odor-free	4th
clear	5th
for all utensils	6th
looks like butter	7th
taste if use too much	8th
uneconomical to use	9th

negative beliefs toward the product—so many that it becomes inefficient to address advertising and marketing strategies to the few who retain a positive attitude? This could occur in spite of some residual positive feelings, as happened with the consumer attitude toward potatoes in the late 1960s and early 1970s. During that period potato growers and processors experienced a steady decline in potato consumption, along with an increasing belief that potatoes lacked much food value and were fattening. This occurred despite the fact that homemakers continued to believe potatoes tasted good and that their families enjoyed them. As we have learned, however, regardless of the positive characteristics attributed to something, a single highly negative salience subjectively outweighs the positive in determining overall attitude, and, except for awareness, advertising response.

If one were the advertising account manager charged with developing an advertising strategy designed to reverse this downward trend in potato consumption and to correct the "fattening" image of potatoes, one should realize a refutational strategy would be in order, with two options available. One has the choice of either ignoring counter-arguments and using a one-sided argument or refuting them with a two-sided argument. The ignoring strategy, we have learned, would perhaps work if the receiver's counter-arguments (that is, negative beliefs) were either weak or nonsalient; but, in the potato problem, they were found to be neither. In fact, any attempt at persuasion along these lines would fail to generate the necessary belief congruence required with the existing beliefs of the target receivers, since those beliefs would be at variance with the message. Rather, the advertiser should opt for a two-sided argument, acknowledging the receiver's beliefs, but refuting them. This permits the advertiser an opportunity to break down the existing beliefs and replace them with new beliefs that may be subsequently associated in a positive fashion with potato usage. Clearly, we are seeking a cognitive response initially, and, once beliefs are changed, an affective response.

The general refutation format available in developing the message strategy is as follows:

1. *Forewarn the receiver of the intended conclusion.* This places the source bias out in the open at the very beginning, maximizing potential reception of the message's point. It is, however, no guarantee of persuasion.

2. *Present receiver beliefs first.* This has the effect of preventing an early tune-out of the message; and importantly, tends to reduce the likelihood of the receiver raising those same beliefs in counter-arguments after the advertiser's side of the message.

3. *Present message points that refute receiver's negative beliefs and support advertiser.* This is the heart of the advertiser's message.

4. *Draw the conclusion explicitly.* This serves three functions: (a) it overcomes any receiver reluctance to draw the conclusion himself; (b) it provides a

sense of closure and completeness; and (c) it underscores the confidence of the advertiser in the position.

An actual execution following this format featured a headline reading "Lies, lies, lies," over a picture of a large baked potato, surrounded by captions reflecting the receiver's negative beliefs (for example, "fattening," "no real food value," "too many calories," "few vitamins"). Body copy then refuted those beliefs, pointing out the true value of eating potatoes and their generally lower calorie content, closing with a tag line that drew the conclusion explicitly: "The Potato. Something good that's good for you." The reader should recognize such an execution as carefully following the refutational strategy outlined, as reviewed in Table 7.2.

TABLE 7.2

Application of Refutation Strategy to Reduce Highly Salient Negative Beliefs about Potatoes

Refutation Steps	Execution
1. Forewarn the receiver of the intended conclusion	Headline: "Lies, lies, lies"
2. Present receiver-beliefs first	Visual: picture of large baked potato surrounded by captions reflecting negative beliefs
3. Present message points which refute receiver's negative beliefs and support advertiser	Copy: refutes misconceptions, underscores positive health benefits
4. Draw the conclusion explicitly	Tag: "The Potato, something good that's good for you"

In fact, a campaign based upon this advertising strategy for potatoes was actually used, affecting a significant cognitive response over a two-year period. As reported in the *Marketing News* (1976), the general level of attitude toward potatoes changed from a "not-very-nutritious, fattening substance, to a nutritious vegetable that isn't too fattening." They report data from a research study that show the number of people who believe potatoes have too many calories dropped from 1/3 to 1/4, while the percent who believe potatoes basically nutritious grew from 55 percent to 81 percent. And most important, this cognitive response led to positive market behavior. Consumption of fresh potatoes by the average household rose 17.7 percent, the first major rise in usage in almost 25 years.

As these examples illustrate, the more one knows about the communication variables available to the advertiser, the easier it becomes to develop advertising strategy. But beyond better knowledge of receiver, source, message, media, and scheduling variables, it is the understanding of the many potential affects these variables may have upon a specific advertising response that this book has addressed. With this understanding as a foundation, the reader should now be in a position to positively affect the development and implementation of effective advertising strategy.

BIBLIOGRAPHY

Aaker, D. A. 1975. ADMOD: "An Advertising Decision Model." *Journal of Marketing Research*, February, 37–45.

Aaker, D. A., and Myers, John G. 1975. *Advertising Management*. Englewood Cliffs, New Jersey: Prentice Hall.

Abelson, R. P. 1973. "The Structure of Beliefs Systems." In *Computer Simulation of Thought and Language*, edited by K. Colby and R. Schank, San Francisco: W. H. Freeman.

Abelson, R. P., Aronson, E., McGuire, W. J., Newcomb, T. M., Rosenberg, M. J., and Tannenbaum, P. H. (eds.). 1968. *Theories of Cognitive Consistency: A Sourcebook*. Chicago: Rand McNally & Co.

Abelson, R. P., and Kanouse, D. E. 1966. "Subjective Acceptance of Verbal Generalization." In *Cognitive Consistency: Motivational Antecedents and Behavioral Consegments*, edited by S. Feldman, New York: Academic Press.

Abelson, R. P., and Reich, C. M. 1969. "Implicational Metecubes: A Method for Extracting Meaning from Input Sentences." Paper presented at International Joint Conference on Artificial Intelligence, Bedford, Mass.

Adams, H. F. 1916. *Advertising and Its Mental Laws*. New York: Macmillan.

Alpert, M. I. 1972. "Personality and the Determinant of Product Choice." *Journal of Marketing Research*, 9: 89–92.

Anderson, N. H. 1959. "Test of Model of Opinion Change." *Journal of Abnormal Social Psychology*, 371–81.

Anderson, R. C., and Carter, J. F. 1972. "Retroactive Inhibition of Meaningful-Learned Sentences." *American Educational Research Journal*, 9: 443–48.

Anisfeld, N., and Knapp, N. E. "Association, Synonymity, and Directionality in False Recognition." *Journal of Experimental Psychology* 1968. 77: 171–79.

Arndt, Johan. 1967. *Word of Mouth Advertising*. New York: Advertising Research Foundation.

Aronson, E. 1968. "Dissonance Theory: Progress and Problems." In *Theories of Cognitive Consistency: A Sourcebook*, edited by R. P. Abelson et al., Chicago: Rand McNally.

Aronson, E., and Carlsmith, J. M. 1962. "Performance Expectancy as a Determinant of Actual Performance." *Journal of Abnormal Social Psychology* 65: 182.

Aronson, E., and Golden, B. W. 1962. "The Effect of Relevant and Irrelevant Aspects of Communication Credibility on Attitude Change." *Journal of Personality* 30: 135-46.

Aronson, E.; Willerman, B.; and Floyd, Joanne. 1966. "The Effect of a Pratfall on Increasing Interpersonal Attraction." *Psychomic Science* 4: 227-28.

Baner, B. A. 1964. "The Obstinate Audience: The Influence Process from the Point of View of Social Communication." *American Psychologist* 319-28.

Barber, T. X., and Calverley, D. S. 1964. "Hypnotizability, Suggestibility and Personality: IV. A Study with the Leary Interpersonal Checklist." *British Journal of Social Clinical Psychology* 3: 149-50.

Bartlett, F. C. 1932. *Remembering.* Cambridge, Eng.: Cambridge Univ. Press.

Bauer, R. A. 1960. "Consumer Behavior as Risk Taking." In *Dynamic Marketing for a Changing World, Proceedings of the 43rd Conference of the American Marketing Association*, edited by R. S. Hancock, 389-400.

——. 1964. "The Obstinate Audience." *American Psychologist* 19 May; 319-28.

——. 1965. *A Revised Model of Source Effect.* Presidential Address of the Division of Consumer Psychology, American Psychological Association Annual Meeting, Chicago.

——. 1973. "The Audience." In *Handbook of Communication*, edited by I. DeSona Pool et al. Chicago: Rand McNally.

Belson, W. A. 1956. "Learning and Attitude Change Resulting from Viewing a Television Series, 'Bon Voyage '." *British Journal of Educational Psychology* 26: 31-38.

Bem, D. J. 1968. "Dissonance Reduction in the Behaviorist." In *Theories of Cognitive Consistency: A Sourcebook*, edited by R. P. Abelson et al. Chicago: Rand McNally.

Bennet, Edith. 1955. "Discussion, Decision, Commitment and Consensus in Group Decisions." *Human Relations*, 8: 251-74.

Bennis, W. G., and Peabody, D. 1962. "The Conceptualization of Two Personality Orientations and Sociometric Choice." *Journal of Social Psychology* 57: 203-15.

Berelson, B. 1942. "The Effect of Print upon Public Opinion." In *Print, Radio, and Film in a Democracy*, edited by D. Waples, pp. 41-65. Chicago: University of Chicago Press.

Berlyne, D. E. 1968. "The Motivational Significance of Collative Variables and Conflict." In *Theories of Cognitive Consistency: A Sourcebook*, edited by R. P. Abelson et al. Chicago: Rand McNally.

Bettinghaus, E. P. 1973. *Persuasive Communication.* New York: Holt, Rinehart and Winston.

Blumer, Herbert. 1946. "The Crowd, the Public and the Mass." In *New Outline of the Principles of Society*, edited by Alfred McCluinglee, Jr., New York: Barnes and Noble.

Boucher, Jr., and Osgood, C. W. 1969. "The Pollyanna Hypothesis." *Journal of Verbal Learning and Verbal Behavior* 8: 1-8.

Broadbent, D. E. 1958. *Perception and Communication*. New York: Pergamon Press.

Bugelski, B. P. 1970. "Words and Things and Images." *American Psychologist* 25: 1001-12.

———. 1977. "Imagery and Verbal Behavior." *Journal of Mental Imagery* 1: 39-52.

Bull, B. L., and Wittrock, M. C. 1973. "Imagery in the Learning of Verbal Definitions." *British Journal of Educational Psychology* 43: 289-93.

Burke, D. 1962. *A Grammar of Motives and a Rhetoric of Motives*. Cleveland: Would.

Calder, B. J. and Sternthal, B. 1977. "Television Commercial Wearout: An Information Processing View." Unpublished Working Paper, Northwestern University.

Calder, B. J.; Insko, C. A.; and Yandel B. 1974. "The Relation of Cognitive and Memorial Processes to Persuasion in a Simulated Jury Trial." *Journal of Applied Social Psychology* 4: 62-93.

Cantril, H. and Allport, G. W. 1935. *The Psychology of Radio*. New York: Harper.

Carlson, E. G. 1956. "Attitude Change through Modification of Attitude Structure." *Journal of Abnormal Social Psychology* 52: 256-61.

Carroll, J. B. 1971. "Measurement Properties of Subjective Magnitude Estimates of Word Frequency." *Journal of Verbal Learning and Verbal Behavior* 10: 722-69.

Carter, R. F. and Greenberg, B. A. 1965. "Newspaper or Television: Which Do You Believe?" *Journalism Quarterly* 42: 29-34.

Chalmers, D. K. 1969. "Meanings, Impressions, and Attitudes: A Model of the Evaluation Process." *Psychological Review* 76: 450-60.

Chase, L. J. and Kelly, C. W. 1976. "Language Intensity and Resistance to Persuasion: A Research Note." *Human Communication Research* 3: 83-85.

Clark, H. H. 1969. "Linguistic Processes in Deductive Reasoning." *Psychological Review* 76: 387-404.

Coffin, T. 1975. "Some Notes Regarding the Design of an ARF Study of the Automated Checkstand as a Tool for Advertising Research." Mimeographed.

Cohen, A. R. 1957. "Need for Cognition and Order of Communication as a Determinant of Opinion Change." In *Order of Presentation in Persuasion*, edited by C. I. Hovland, pp. 79-97. New Haven: Yale Univ. Press.

Cohen, B. P.; Berger, J. B.; and Zelditch, M. 1972. "Status Conceptions and Interaction: A Case Study of the Problem of Developing Cumulative Knowledge." In *Experimental Social Psychology*, edited by C. G. McClintock. New York: Holt, Rinehart, and Winston.

Coleman, E. B. 1962. "Sequential Interference Demonstrated by Serial Reconstruction." *Journal of Experimental Psychology* 64: 46-51.

Conrad, C. 1974. "Context Effects in Sentence Comprehension—A Study of the Subjective Lexicon." *Meaning and Cognition* 2: 130-38.

Cook. T. D. and Insko, C. A. 1968. "Resistance of Induced Attitude Changes as a Function of Conclusion Re-exposure: A Laboratory-Field Experiment." *Journal of Personality and Social Psychology* 9: 322-28.

Cook, T. D., and Wadsworth, A. 1972. "Persistence of Induced Attitude Changes as a Function of Overlearned Conclusions and Supportive Attributions." *Journal of Personality* 40: 50-61.

Cooper, E., and Jahoda, M. 1947. "The Evasion of Propaganda: How Prejudiced People Respond to Anti-prejudice Propaganda." *Journal of Psychology* 23: 15-25.

Cox, D. F., Ed. 1967. *Risk Taking and Information Handling in Consumer Behavior.* Cambridge, Massachusetts. Graduate School of Business Administration, Harvard University.

Cox, D. F., and Bauer, R. A. 1964. "Self-confidence and Persuasibility in Women." *Public Opinion Quarterly* 28: 453-66.

Craig, C. S.; Sternthal, B.; and Leavitt, C. 1976. "Advertising Wearout: An Experimental Analysis." *Journal of Marketing Research* 13: 365-72.

Craig, C. S.; Sternthal, B.; and Olshan, K. 1972. "The Effect of Overlearning on Retention." *Journal of General Psychology* 87: 85-94.

Craik, F. I. M. and Lockart, R. S. 1972. "Levels of Processing: A Framework for Memory Research." *Journal of Verbal Learning and Verbal Behavior* 11: 671-84.

Crane, E. 1972. *Marketing Communications.* New York: John Wiley & Sons.

Crespi, L. P. 1942. "Quantitative Variation of Incentive and Performance in the White Rat." *American Journal of Psychology* 55: 467-517.

DeLozier, M. W. 1976. *The Marketing Communication Process.* New York: McGraw-Hill.

Deutschmann, P. J. 1957. "The Sign-situation Classification of Human Communication." *Journal of Communication* 7: 63-73.

Dixon, T. R. and Dixon, J. F., 1964. "The Impression Value of Verbs." *Journal of Verbal Learning and Verbal Behavior* 3: 161-65.

Ebbinghaus, H. 1885. *Grundzuge der Psychologie* (Leipzig, Germany: Veit), Translated by H. A. Ruger and C. E. Bussenius in *Memory.* New York: Dover, 1964.

Eberhard, J. C. and Bauer, R. A. 1941. "An Analysis of the Influence on Recall of a Controversial Event." *Journal of Social Psychology*, 14: 211-28.

Ehrenberg, A. S. C. 1974. "Repetitive Advertising and the Consumer." *Journal of Advertising Research* 14: (No. 2), 25-34.

Eldersveld, S. J. 1956. "Experimental Propaganda Techniques and Voting Behavior." *American Political Science Review* 50: 154-65.

Engle, J. F., Kollat, D. T., and Blackwell, R. D., 1973. *Consumer Behavior* 2nd ed. New York: Holt, Rinehart & Winston.

Evans, J. St. B. T. 1972. "Reasoning with Negatives." *British Journal of Psychology* 63.

Evans, R. I.; Rozelle, R. M.; Lasater, T. M.; Deubroski, T. M.; and B. P. Allen. 1970. "Fear Arousal, Persuasion and Actual Versus Implied Behavioral Change: New perspective utilizing a real-life dental hygiene program." *Journal of Personality and Social Psychology* 1: 220-227.

Feather, N. T. 1963. "Cognitive Dissonance, Sensitivity, and Evaluation." *Journal of Abnormal and Social Psychology* 66: 157-63.

Feldman, S. 1966. "Motivational Aspects of Attitudinal Elements and Their Place in Cognitive Interaction." In *Cognitive Consistency: Motivational Antecedents and Behavioral Consequents*, edited by S. Feldman, New York: Acadeure Press.

Festinger, L. 1957. *A Theory of Cognitive Dissonance*. Stanford: Stanford University Press.

Festinger, L. and Maccoby, E. 1964. "On Resistance of Persuasive Communications." *Journal of Abnormal and Social Psychology* 68: 359-66.

Fishbein, M. 1967. "A Behavioral Theory Approach to the Relations between Beliefs about an Objective and the Attitude toward the Object." In *Readings in Attitude Theory and Measurement*, edited by M. Fishbein. New York: Wiley.

Fishbein, M. and Ajzen, I. 1975. *Belief, Attitude, Intention and Behavior: An Introduction to Theory and Research*. Reading, Mass.: Addison-Wesley.

FitzRoy, P. T. 1976. *Analytical Methods for Marketing Management.* London: McGraw-Hill.

Fodor, J. A.; Bever, T. G.; and M. F. Garrett. 1974. *The Psychology of Language.* New York: McGraw-Hill.

Foss, D. J.; Bever, T. G.; and Silver, M. 1968. "The Comprehension and Verification of Ambiguous Sentences." *Perception and Psychophysics* 4: 304-06.

Frank, R. E. 1968. "Market Segmentation Research: Findings and Implications." In *Applications of the Services in Marketing Management*, edited by F. Bass et al. New York: Wiley.

Frank. R. W.; Massy, W. F.; and Wind, Y. 1972. *Market Segmentation*. Englewood Cliffs: Prentice-Hall.

Freedman, J. L., and Sears, D. O., 1965. "Warning, Distraction and Resistance to Influence." *Journal of Personality and Social Psychology* 1: 262-66.

Freidson, E. 1953. "Communications Research and the Concept of the Mass." *American Sociological Review* 18: 313-17.

Frey, Frederick W. 1966. "The Mass Media and Rural Development in Turkey." Rural Development Report 3. Cambridge: Massachusetts Institute of Technology Center for International Studies.

Furbay, A. L. 1965. "The Influence of Scattered Versus Compact Seating on Audience Response." *Speech Monograph* 32: 144–48.

Garrod, S., and Trabasso, T. 1973. "A Dual-memory Information Processing Interpretation of Sentence Comprehension." *Journal of Verbal Learning and Verbal Behavior* 12: 155–67.

Gewirtz, J. L., and Baer, D. M. 1958. "Deprivation and Satiation of Social Reinforcers as a Drive Condition." *Journal of Abnormal and Social Psychology* 57: 165–72.

Gensch, Dennis. 1973. *Advertising Planning*. New York: Elsvier.

Gillig, P. M., and Greenwald, A. G. 1974. "Is it Time to Lay the Sleeper Effect to Rest." *Journal of Personality and Social Psychology* 29: 132–39.

Gilson, C. and Abelson, R. P. 1965. "The Subjective Use of Inductive Evidence." *Journal of Personality and Social Psychology* 2: 301–10.

Glanzer, M., and Clark, Wilt. 1969. "Accuracy of Perceptual Recall: An Analysis of Organization." *Journal of Verbal Learning and Verbal Behavior.* 5: 289–99.

Glucksberg, S. and Danks, J. H. 1975. *Experimental Psycholinguistics*. Hillsdale, N.J.: Lawrence Erlbaum Associates.

Glucksberg, S.; Trabasso, T.; and Wald J. 1973. "Linguistic Structures and Mental Operations." *Cognitive Psychology*, 5: 338–370.

Gough, P. B. 1965. "Grammatical Transformations and Speed of Understanding." *Journal of Verbal Learning and Verbal Behavior* 4: 107–11.

——. 1966. "The Verification of Sentences: The Effects of Delay of Evidence and Sentence Length." *Journal of Verbal Learning and Verbal Behavior* 5: 492–96.

Grass, R. C. and Wallace, W. H. 1969. "Satiation Effects of TV Commercials." *Journal of Advertising Research* 9: 3–9.

——. 1974. "Advertising Communication: Print vs. TV." *Journal of Advertising Research* 14: 19–23.

Greeno, J. G., James, C. T., Da Polito, F., and Polson, P. G. 1978. *Associative Learning: A Cognitive Analysis*. Englewood Cliffs, New Jersey: Prentice-Hall.

Greenwald, A. G. 1968. "Cognitive Learning, Cognitive Response to Persuasion, and Attitude Change." In *Psychological Foundations of Attitudes*, edited by A. G. Greenwald, T. C. Brock, and T. M. Ostran. New York: Academic Press.

Grossman, L. and Eagle, M. 1970. "Synonymity, Antonymity, and Association in False Recognition Responses." *Journal of Experimental Psychology*, 83: 244–48.

Gruner, C. R. 1965. "An Experimental Study of Satire as Persuasion." *Speech Monographs* 43: 288–97.

——. 1967. "Effects of Humor on Speaker Ethos and Audience Information Gain." *Journal of Communication* 17: 228–33.

——. 1970. "The Effect of Humor in Dull and Interesting Information Speeches." *Central States Speech Journal* 21: 160–66.

Guthrie, E. R. 1952. *The Psychology of Learning*. rev. ed. New York: Harper & Row.

Haaland, C. and Venkatesan, M. 1968. "Resistance to Persuasive Communications: An Examination of the Distraction Hypothesis." *Journal of Personality and Social Psychology* 9: 167–70.

Haley, R. J. 1968. "Benefit Segmentation: A Decision-directed Research Tool." *Journal of Marketing* 30–35.

Hall, E. T. 1959. *The Silent Language*. Garden City, N.Y.: Doubleday.

——. 1966. *The Hidden Dimension*. Garden City, N.Y.: Doubleday.

Hall, W. 1938. "The Effect of Defined Social Stimulus Material upon the Stability of Attitudes towards Labor Unions, Capital Punishment, Social Insurance and Negroes." *Purdue University Studies in Higher Education* 34: 7–19.

Hartmann, G. W. 1936. "A Field Experiment on the Comparative Effectiveness of "Emotional" and "Rational" Political Leaflets in Determining Election Results." *Journal of Abnormal Social Psychology* 31: 99–114.

Hartman, F. R. 1961. "Single and Multiple Channel Communicator: A Review of Research and a Proposed Model." *A. V. Communication Review* 9: 235–62.

Harvey, O. J. 1965. "Some Situational and Cognitive Determinants of Dissonance Resolution." *Journal of Personality and Social Psychology* 1: 349–55.

Haskins, J. B. 1964. "Factual Recall as a Measure of Advertising Effectiveness." *Journal of Advertising Research* 4: 2–8.

Hediger, H. 1961. "The Evolution of Territorial Behavior." In *Social Life of Early Man*, edited by S. L. Washburn. Viking Fund Publications in Anthropology, no. 31.

Heider, F. 1946. "Attitudes and Cognitive Organization." *Journal of Psychology* 21: 107–12.

Helmreich, R.; Aronson, E.; and LeFan, J. 1970. "To Err is Humanizing—Sometimes: Effects of Self-Esteem, Corruptence, and a Pratfall on Interpersonal Attraction." *Journal of Personality and Social Psychology* 16: 259–64.

Hendon, D. W. 1973. "How Mechanical Factors Affect Ad Perception." *Journal of Advertising Research* (August), 39–45.

Hilgard, E. R., and Bower, G. H. 1975. *Theories of Learning*. Englewood Cliffs, N.J.: Prentice-Hall.

Hilgard, E. R.; Lauer, L. W.; and Melei, J. P. 1965. "Acquiescence, Hypnotic Susceptibility and the MMPI." *Journal of Consulting Psychology*.

Holt, L. E. 1970. "Resistance to Persuasion on Explicit Beliefs as a Function of Commitment to, and Desirability of, Logically Related Beliefs." *Journal of Reasonality and Social Psychology*.

Holt, L. E. and Watts, W. A. 1973. Immediate and Delayed Effects of Forewarning of Persuasive Intent. *Proceedings of the 81st Annual Convention*, American Psychological Association, 361–362.

Hovland, C. I. 1954. "Effects of the Mass Media of Communication." In *Handbook of Social Psychology*, edited by G. Lindzey, vol. 2. Cambridge, Mass.: Addison-Wesley.

——. 1957. *The Order of Presentation in Persuasion*. New Haven: Yale University Press.

——. 1959. "Reconciling Conflicting Results Derived from Experimental and Survey Studies of Attitude Change." *American Psychologist* 14: 8–17.

Hovland, C. I., and Janis, I. L. eds. 1959. *Personality and Persuasibility*. New Haven: Yale University Press.

Hovland, C. I., and Mandel, W. 1952. "An Experimental Comparison of Conclusion-Drawing by the Communicator and by the Audience." *Journal of Abnormal Social Psychology* 47: 581–88.

Hovland, C. I., and Weiss, W. 1951. "The Influence of Source Credibility on Communication Effectiveness." *Public Opinion Quarterly*, 15: 635–50.

Hovland, C. I.; Janis, I. L.; and Kelley, H. H. 1953. *Communication and Persuasion*. New Haven: Yale University Press.

Hovland, C. I.; Lumsdaine, A. A.; and Sheffield, F. D. 1949. *Experiments and Mass Communications*. Princeton: Princeton University Press.

Howard, J. H., and Sheth, J. H. 1969. *The Theory of Buyer Behavior*. New York: John Wiley & Sons.

Hsia, H. 1968. "On Channel Effectiveness." *AV Communication Review* 16: 245–67.

Hull, C. L. 1933. *Hypnosis and Suggestibility*. New York: Appleton-Century-Crofts.

Hulse, S. H.; Deese, J.; and Egeth, H. 1975. *Psychology of Learning*. 4th ed. New York: McGraw-Hill.

Insko, C. A. 1964. "Primary versus Recency in Persuasion as a Function of the Timing of Arguments and Measures." *Journal of Personality and Social Psychology* 69: 381–91.

——. 1967. *Theories of Attitude Change*. New York: Appleton-Century-Crofts.

Insko, C. A.; Arkoff, C. A.; and Insko, V. M. 1965. "Effects of High and Low Fear-arousing Communicating upon Opinions toward Smoking." *Journal of Experimental Social Psychology* 1: 256–66.

Jacobson, H. 1950. "The Information Capacity of the Human Ear." *Science* 112: 143-44.

——. 1951. "The Information Capacity of the Human Eye." *Science* 113: 292–93.

Janis, I. L. 1955. "Anxiety Indices Related to Susceptibility to Persuasion." *Journal of Abnormal and Social Psychology* 51: 663-67.

——. 1958. *Psychological Stress*. New York: Wiley.

——. 1969. *The Contours of Fear*. New York: Wiley & Sons.

Janis, I. L., and Feirabend, R. L. 1957. "Effects of Alternative Ways of Ordering Pro and Con Arguments in Persuasive Communication." In *Order of Presentation in Persuasion*, edited by C. I. Hovland, pp. 125–57. New Haven: Yale University Press.

Janis, I. L., and Feshbach, S. 1953. "Effects of Fear Arousing Communications." *Journal of Abnormal Social Psychology* 48: 78-92.

Janis, I. L., and Hovland, C. I. 1959. "An Overview of Persuasibility Research." In *Personality and Persuasibility*, edited by C. I. Hovland and I. L. Janis. New Haven: Yale University Press.

Janis, I. L., and Rife, D. 1959. "Persuasibility and Emotional Disorder." In *Personality and Persuasibility*, edited by C. I. Hovland, and I. L. Janis, pp. 121-40. New Haven: Yale University Press.

Janis, I. L.; Kaye, D.; and Kirschner, P. 1965. "Facilitating Effects of "Eating-while Reading" and Responsiveness to Persuasive Communications." *Journal of Personality and Social Psychology* 1: 181–86.

Janis, I. L., and Mann, L. 1965. "Effectiveness of Emotional Role Playing in Modifying Smoking Habits and Attitudes." *Journal of Experimental Research in Personality*, 1: 84-90.

Johnson, H. H., and Scileppi, J. A. 1969. "Effects of Ego-Involvement Conditions on Attitude Change to High and Low Credibility Communications." *Journal of Personality and Social Psychology* 13: 31-36.

Johnson-Laird, P. N. and Tagart, J. 1969. "How Implication is Understood." *American Journal of Psychology* 82: 367-73.

Jones, E. E. and Kohler, R. 1958. "The Effects of Plausibility on the Learning of Controversial Statements." *Journal of Abnormal Social Psychology* 57: 315-20.

Kanouse, D. E. 1968. "The Effects of Verb Type on the Cognitive Processing of English Sentences." Ph.D. dissertation, Yale University.

———. 1972. "Language, Labeling, and Attribution." In *Attribution: Perceiving the Causes of Behavior*, edited by E. E. Jones et al., 121–36. Morristown, N.J.: General Learning Press.

Karlins, M. and Abelson, H. I. 1970. *Persuasion*. New York: Springer Publishing.

Katz, D. 1960. "The Functional Approach to the Study of Attitudes." *Public Opinion Quarterly* 24: 163–204.

Katz, D.; Sarnoff, I.; and McClintock, C. 1956. "Ego-defense and Attitude Change." *Human Relations* 9: 27–45.

Katz, D., and Stotland, E. 1959. "A Preliminary Statement of a Theory of Attitude Structure and Change." In *Psychology: Study of Science*, vol. 3, edited by S. Kock, pp. 423–75. New York: McGraw-Hill.

Katz, E. 1957. "The Two-step of Communication; An up-to-date Report on a Hypothesis. *Public Opinion Quarterly* 21: 61–78.

———. 1968. "On Reopening the Question of Selectivity in Exposure to Mass Communications." In *Theories of Cognitive Connitive Consistency; A Sourcebook*, edited by R. P. Abelson. Chicago: Rand McNally.

Katz, E., and Lazarsfield, P. F. 1955. *Personal Influence*. Glencoe, Ill.: Free Press.

Katz, J. J. 1972. *Semantic Theory*. New York: Harper & Row.

Kausler, D. H. and Settle, A. J. 1973. "Associated Relatedness vs. Synonymity in the False Recognition Effect." *Bulletin of the Psychomonic Society* 2: 129–31.

Kelman, H. C. 1958. "Compliance, Identification, and Internalization, Three Processes of Opinion Change." *Journal of Conflict Resolution* 2: 51–60.

———. 1961. "Processes of Opinion Change." *Public Opinion Quarterly* 25: 57–78.

Kelman, H. C. and Hovland, C. I. 1953. "'Reinstatement' of the Communicator in Delayed Measurement of Opinion Change." *Journal of Abnominal and Social Psychology*, 48, 327–35.

Kendall, P. L., and Wolf, K. M. 1949. "The Analysis of Deviant Cases in Communication Research." In *Communications Research*, edited by P. F. Lazersfield and F. N. Stanton. New York: Harper.

Keppel, G.; Postman, L.; and Zavortink, B. 1968. "Studies of Learning to Learn: VIII. The Influence of Massive Amounts of Training upon the Learning and Retention of Paired-Associate Lists." *Journal of Verbal Learning and Verbal Behavior*, 7: 790–96.

Klare, G. R. 1968. "The Role of Word Frequency in Readability." In *Readability, National Conference on Research in English*, edited by J. R. Bormuth, pp. 7–17. New York.

Knepprath, E. and Clevenger, T. 1965. "Reasoned Discourse and Motive Appeals in Selected Political Speeches." *Quarterly Journal of Speech* 51: 152–156.

Knower, F. H. 1935. "Experimental Studies of Change in Attitude: I. A Study of the Effect of Oral Arguments on Changes of Attitudes." *Journal of Social Psychology* 6: 315–47.

Kotler, P. 1976. *Marketing Management*. 3rd ed. Englewood Cliffs, N.J.: Prentice Hall.

Kresler, C. A. and Sakumura, J. 1966. "A Test of a Model for Commitment." *Journal of Personality and Social Psychology* 3: 458–67.

Krugman, H. E. 1962. "An Application of Learning Theory to TV Copy Testing." *Public Opinion Quarterly*, 26: 626–34.

———. 1967. "The Measurement of Advertising Involvement." *Public Opinion Quarterly* 30, 583–96.

———. 1972. "Why Three Exposures May be Enough." *Journal of Advertising Research*, December, 11.

Laming, D. 1973. *Mathematical Psychology*. London: Academic Press.

Lasswell, H. D. 1948. "The Structure and Function of Communication in Society." *Communication of Ideas*, edited by L. Bryson. New York: Harper.

Lautman, M. R.; Percy, L. H.; and Kordish, G. R. 1978. "Campaign from Multidimensional Scaling." *Journal of Advertising Research*, 18: 35–40.

Lazarsfeld, P. E. 1940. *Radio and the Printed Page*. New York: Onell, Sloan and Pearce.

———. 1963. "Trends in Broadcasting Research." In *Studies of Broadcasting*, edited by A. Katagiri and K. Motona, pp. 49–64. Radio and TV Culture Research Institute, Japan Broadcasting Corp.

Lazarsfeld, P. E., and Merton, R. K. 1948. "Mass Communication, Popular Task and Organized Social Action." In *Communication of Ideas*, edited by L. Bryson. New York: Harper.

Leaf, W. A. 1969. "Subjective Processes in the Acceptance of Verbal Generalizations." Unpublished Ph.D. dissertation, Yale University.

Lehmann, S. 1970. "Personality and Compliance: A Study of Anxiety and Self-esteem in Opinion and Behavior Change." *Journal of Personality and Social Psychology* 15: 76–86.

Leventhal, H. 1970. "Findings and Theory in the Study of Fear Communication." In *Advances in Experimental Social Psychology*, vol. 5, edited by L. Berkowitz. New York: Academic Press.

Leventhal, H., and Perloe, S. I. 1962. "A Relationship between Self-esteem and Persuasibility." *Journal of Abnormal and Social Psychology* 64: 385–88.

Leventhal, H., and Watts, J. C. 1966. "Sources of Resistance to Fear-arousing Communications on Smoking and Lung Cancer." *Journal of Personality* 34: 155–75.

Leventhal, H.; Watts, J. C.; and Pagano, F. 1967. "Effects of Fear and Specificity of Recommendations on Smoking Behavior." New Haven: Department of Psychology, Yale University. Mimeographed.

Little, D. C. and Lodish, L. M. 1966. "A Media Selection Model and its Optimization by Dynamic Programming." *Industrial Management Review* 8: 15–23.

———. 1969. "A Media Planning Calculus." *Operating Research* 17: 1–35.

Loftus, G. R. and Loftus, E. F. 1976. *Human Memory: The Processing of Information.* Hillsdale, New Jersey: Lawrence Erlbaum Associates.

Longman, K. A. 1971. *Advertising.* New York: Harcourt, Brace, Jovanovich.

Lo Scuito, L. A. 1968. "Effects of Advertising Frequency and Product Usage on Recall: A Laboratory Simulation." *Proceedings of the 76th Annual Convention, American Psychological Association,* 679–80.

Lowenthal, K. 1969. "Semantic Features and Communicability of Words of Different Classes." *Psychonomic Science* 17: 79–80.

Lowin, A. 1969. "Further Evidence of an Approach-Avoidance Interpretation of Selective Exposure." *Journal of Experimental Social Psychology* 5: 265–71.

Lucas, D. B. and S. H. Britt, 1963. *Measuring Advertising Effectiveness.* New York: McGraw-Hill.

Lull, P. E. 1940. "The Effectiveness of Humor in Persuasive Speeches." *Speech Monographs* 7: 26–40.

Lyons, J. 1963. *Structural Semantics,* Oxford: Blackwell.

MacLean, M. S. 1954. "Mass Communication of Public Affairs News." Ph.D. dissertation, University of Wisconsin.

McCullough, J. L. and Ostrom, T. M. 1974. "Repetition of Highly Similar Messages and Attitude Change." *Journal of Applied Psychology* 59: 395–97.

McGaugh, J. A. 1932. "Forgetting and the Law of Disuse." *Psychological Review* 39: 352–70.

McGuire, W. J. 1957. "Order of Presentation as a Factor in "Conditioning" Persuasiveness." In *Order of Presentation in Persuasion,* edited by C. I. Hovland, pp. 98–114. New Haven: Yale University Press.

———. 1960a. "Direct and Indirect Persuasive Effects of Dissonance-producing Messages." *Journal of Abnormal and Social Psychology* 60: 354–58.

———. 1960b. "A Syllogistic Analysis of Cognitive Relationships." In *Attitude Organization and Change,* edited by C. I. Hovland and M. J. Rosenberg, pp. 65–111. New Haven: Yale University Press.

———. 1961. "Resistance to Persuasion Confirmed by Active and Passive Prior Refutation of the Same and Alternative Counter-arguments." *Journal of Abnormal and Social Psychology* 63: 326-32.

———. 1962. "Persistence of the Resistance to Persuasion Induced by Various Types of Prior Belief Defenses." *Journal of Abnormal and Social Psychology* 64: 241-48.

———. 1963. "Innovation against Persuasion." New York: Department of Social Psychology, Columbia University. Mimeographed.

———. 1964. "Inducing Resistance Persuasion: Some Contemporary Approaches." In *Advances in Experimental Social Psychology*, vol. 1, edited by L. Berkowtiz, pp. 191-229. New York: Academic Press.

———. 1966. "Attitudes and Opinions." *Annual Review of Psychology* 17: 475-514.

———. 1968a. "Personality and Susceptibility to Social Influence." In *Handbook of Personality Theory and Research*, edited by E. F. Borgatta and W. W. Lambert. Chicago: Rand McNally.

———. 1968b. "Personality and Attitude Change: An Information-processing Theory." In *Psychological Foundations of Attitudes*, edited by A. G. Greenwald et al. New York: Academic Press.

———. 1968c. "Selective Exposure: A Summing Up." In *Theories of Cognitive Consistency: A Sourcebook*, edited by R. P. Abelson et al. Chicago: Rand McNally.

———. 1969a. "The Nature of Attitudes and Attitude Change." In *The Handbook of Social Psychology*, vol. 3, edited by G. Lindzey and E. Aronson, pp. 136-314. Reading, Mass.: Addison-Wesley Publishing.

———. 1969b. "Personality and Susceptibility to Social Influence." In *Handbook of Personality Theory and Research*, edited by E. F. Borgatta and W. W. Lambert. New York: Academic Press.

———. 1972. "Attitude Change: The Information-Processing Paradigm." In *Experimental Social Psychology*, edited by C. G. McClintock. New York: Holt, Rinehart and Winston.

———. 1973. "Persuasion, Resistance, and Attitude Change." In *Handbook of Communication*, edited by I. deSala Pool et al., pp. 216-52. Chicago: Rand McNally.

McGuire, W. J., and Millman, S. 1965. "Anticipatory Belief Lowering Following a Forewarning of a Persuasive Attack." *Journal of Personality and Social Psychology* 2: 471-79.

McGuire, W. J., and Papegeorgis, D. 1962. "Effectiveness of Forewarning in Developing Resistance to Persuasion." *Public Opinion Quarterly* 26: 24-34.

McGuire, W. J., and Ryan, J. 1955. "Receptivity as a Mediator of Personality-persuasibility Relationships." Minneapolis: University of Minnesota. Mimeographed.

McLuhan, M. 1964. *Understanding Media*. New York: McGraw-Hill.

McLuhan, M., and Fiore, Q. 1967. *The Medium is the Massage*. New York: Bantam.

McMahon, L. E. 1963. "Grammatical Analysis as Part of Understanding a Sentence." Ph.D. dissertation, Harvard University.

McPhee, W. N., ed. 1952. "The 1950 Congressional Election Study." New York: Columbia University, Bureau of Applied Social Research. Mimeographed.

Maddi, S. R. 1961. "Affective Tone during Environmental Regularity and Change." *Journal of Abnormal and Social Psychology* 52: 338–45.

——. 1968. "The Pursuit of Consistency and Variety." In *Theories of Cognitive Consistency: A Sourcebook*, edited by R. P. Abelson et al. Chicago: Rand McNally.

Mann, L. 1967. "The Effects of Emotional Role Playing on Smoking Attitudes and Behavior." *Journal of Experimental Psychology* 3: 334–48.

Mann, L., and Janis, I. L. 1968. "A Follow-up of the Long-term Effects of Emotional Role Playing." *Journal of Personality and Social Psychology* 8: 339–42.

Mansuer, B. 1954. "The Effect of Prior Reinforcement on the Interaction of Observed Pairs." *Journal of Abnormal and Social Psychology* 49: 65–68.

Mansuer, B., and Block, B. L. 1957. "A Study of the Additivity of Variables Affecting Social Interaction." *Journal of Abnormal and Social Psychology* 54: 250–56.

Marcel, A. J. and Steel, R. G. 1973. "Symantic Cueing in Recognition and Recall." *Quarterly Journal of Experimental Psychology* 25: 368–77.

Matthews, J. 1947. "The Effect of Loaded Language on Audience Comprehension of Speeches." *Speech Monographs* 14: 176–87.

May, M. A. 1965. *World-picture relationships in audio-visual presentation*. Report to the U.S. Office of Education (July). Washington, D.C.: Office of Education, Dept. of Health, Education, and Welfare.

Mehrabian, A., and Wiener, M. 1967. "Decoding of Inconsistent Communications." *Journal of Personality and Social Psychology* 6: 109–14.

Metheringham, R. 1964. "Measuring the Net Cumulative Coverage of a Print Campaign." *Journal of Advertising Research* 4.

Miller, N. E. and Campbell, D. T. 1959. "Recency and Primacy in Persuasion as a Function of the Timing of Speeches and Measurements." *Journal of Abnormal and Social Psychology* 59: 1–9.

Millman, S. 1965. "The Relationship between Anxiety, Learning, and Opinion Change." Ph.D. dissertation, Columbia University.

——. 1968. "Anxiety, Comprehension and Susceptibility to Social Influence." *Journal of Personality and Social Psychology* 9: 251–56.

Mitchell, A. and Olson, J. 1977. "Cognitive Effects of Advertising Repetition." In *Advances in Consumer Research*, vol. 4, edited by W. D. Perrault, Jr., pp. 213–220. Atlanta, Georgia: Association for Consumer Research.

Moran, W. T. 1976. Does Flighting Pay. Paper presented at the 22nd Annual Advertising Research Foundation meeting. New York, New York.

Murphy, G., Murphy, L. B., and Newcomb, T. N. 1937. *Experimental Social Psychology* (revised edition) New York: Harper.

Neisser, V. 1967. *Cognitive Psychology*. Englewood Cliffs, N.J.: Prentice-Hall.

Nelson, C. E. 1968. "Anchoring to Accepted Values as a Technique for Immunizing Beliefs against Persuasion." *Journal of Personality and Social Psychology* 9: 329–34.

Newcomb, T. M. 1961. *The Acquaintance Process*. New York: Holt, Rinehart and Winston.

———. 1967. *Persistence and Change: Bennington College and its Students after 25 Years*. New York: John Wiley & Sons.

Nisbett, R. E., and Gordon, A. 1967. "Self-esteem and Susceptibility to Social Influence." *Journal of Personality and Social Psychology* 5: 268–76.

Olson, D. R. and Filby, N. 1972. "On the Comprehension of Active and Passive Sentences." *Cognitive Psychology* 3: 361–81.

Osgood, C. E.; Succi, F.; and Tannenbaum, P. H. 1957. *The Measurement of Meaning*. Urbana, Illinois: Univeristy of Illinois Press.

Osterhouse, R. A. and Brock, I. C. 1970. "Distraction Increases Yielding to Propaganda by Inhibiting Counter-arguing." *Journal of Personality and Social Psychology* 15: 344–58.

Ostrom, T. M., and Upshaw, H. S. 1968. "Psychological Perspective and Attitude Change." In *Psychological Foundations of Attitudes*, edited by A. C. Greenwald et al. New York: Academic Press.

Papageorgis, D. 1963. "Bartlett Effect and the Persistence of Induced Opinion Change." *Journal of Personality and Social Psychology* 67: 61–67.

———. 1967. "Anticipation of Exposure to Persuasive Messages and Belief Change." *Journal of Personality and Social Psychology* 5: 490–96.

Papageorgis, D., and McGuire, W. J. 1961. "The Generality of Immunity to Persuasion Produced by Pre-exposure to Weakened Counter-arguments." *Journal of Abnormal and Social Psychology* 62: 475–81.

Paivio, A. 1969. "Mental Imagery in Associative Learning and Memory." *Psychological Review* 76: 241–63.

———. 1971. *Imagery and Verbal Processes*. New York: Holt, Rinehart, and Winston.

————. 1979. "A Dual Coding Approach to Perception and Cognition." In *Modes of Perceiving and Processing Information*, edited by A. L. Pick, Jr., and E. Saltzman, pp. 39–51. Hillsdale, New Jersey: Lawrence Erlbaum Associates.

Paivio, A., and O'Neil, B. J. 1970. "Visual Recognition Thresholds and Dimensions of Word Meaning." *Perception & Psychophysics* 273–75.

Paivio, A.; Yuille, J. C.; and Madigan, S. 1968. "Concreteness, Imagery, and Meaningfulness Values for 925 Words." *Journal of Experimental Psychology Monograph Supplement* 86: 1, pt. 2.

Peckham, J. O. 1975. *Wheel of Marketing*. Unpublished monograph.

Percy, L. 1975. "Relating Personality Profiles and Consumer Behavior via Underlying Attitude and Perceived Behavior." Paper presented at the American Psychological Association 83rd Annual Convention, Division 23.

————. 1976a. "How Market Segmentation Guides Advertising Strategy." *Journal of Advertising Research* 16: 11–22.

————. 1976b. "A Look at Personality Profiles and the Personality-Attitude-Behavior Link in Predicting Consumer Behavior." *Advances in Consumer Research, vol. 3, Proceedings of the Sixth Annual Conference of the Association for Consumer Research.*

Perrin, P. G. 1965. *Writers Guide and Index to English*. Glenview: Scott, Foresman.

Peterson, M. J. and McGee, S. H. 1974. "Effects of Imagery Instructions, Imagery Ratings and Number of Dictionary Meanings upon Recognition and Recall." *Journal of Experimental Psychology* 102: 1007–14.

Peterson, R. C. and Thurstone, L. L. 1933. *The Effect of Motion Picutres on the Social Attitudes of High School Children*. Chicago: University of Chicago Press.

Pierce, J. R. and Karlin, J. E. 1957. "Reading Rates and the Information Rate of a Human Channel." *Bell System Technical Journal* 36: 497–516.

Politz Media Studies. 1960. *The Rochester Study*. New York: Saturday Evening Post.

Postman, L. 1970. "Effects of Word Frequency on Acquisition and Retention under Conditions of Free-recall Learning." *Quarterly Journal of Experimental Psychology* 22: 185–95.

————. 1971. "Transfer, Interference, and Forgetting." In *Woodworth and Schlosberg's Experimental Psychology* 3rd. ed., edited by J. W. Kling and L. A. Riggs. New York: Holt, Rinehart and Winston.

Preston, I. L. 1967. "Logic and Illogic in the Advertising Process." *Journalism Quarterly* 44: 231–39.

Ray, M. L. 1973. "Marketing Communication and the Hierarchy of Effects." In *New Models for Communication Research*, edited by P. Clarke, pp. 147–76. Beverly Hills: Sage Publications.

Ray, M. L., and Sawyer, A. G. 1971. "A Laboratory Technique for Estimating the Repetition Function for Advertising Media Models." *Journal of Marketing Research* 8: 20-29.

Ray, M. L., and Wilkie, W. L. 1970. "Fear: The Potential of an Appeal Neglected by Marketing." *Journal of Marketing* 34: 54-62.

Regan, D. T., and Cheng, J. 1973. "Distraction and Attitude Change: A Resolution." *Journal of Experimental Social Psychology* 9: 138-47.

Reynolds, F. D., and Wells, W. D. 1977. *Consumer Behavior*. New York: McGraw-Hill.

Richardson, A. 1977. "Verbalizer-Visualizer: A Cognitive Style Dimension." *Journal of Mental Imagery* 1: 96-110.

Robertson, T. S. 1971. *Innovative Behavior and Communication*. New York: Holt, Rinehart, and Winston.

——. 1976. "Low Commitment Consumer Behavior." *Journal of Advertising Research* 16: 19-23.

Robinson, E. S. 1932. *Man as Psychology Sees Him*. New York: Macmillan.

Rogers, Everet M. 1962. *Diffusion of Innovations*. New York: Free Press of Glencoe.

——. 1973. Mass Media and Interpersonal Communicator. In *Handbook of Communication*, edited by Ithrei de Sola Pod, et al. Chicago: Rand McNally.

Rosenberg, M. J. 1965. "Some Content Determinants of Intolerance for Attitudinal Inconsistency." In *Affect, Cognition and Personality*, edited by S. S. Tomkins and C. E. Izard. New York: Springer.

Rosenthal, P. I. 1966. "Concept of Ethos and the Structure of Persuasive Speech." *Speech Memographs* 33: 114-26.

Rosenthal, R. 1967. "Covert Communication is the Psychological Experiment." *Psychological Bulletin* 67: 356-67.

Rosnow, R. L. 1965. "A Delay-of-Reinforcement Effect in Persuasive Communication?" *Journal of Social Psychology* 67: 39-43.

Rossiter, J. R. and Percy, L. 1978. "Visual Imaging Ability as a Mediator of Advertising Response." In *Advances in Consumer Research*, vol. 5, edited by H. K. Hunt, pp. 621-29. Ann Arbor, Michigan: Association for Consumer Research.

Salter, D. and Haycock, V. 1972. "Two Studies on the Process of Negative Modification." *Journal of Psycholinguistic Research* 1: 337-48.

Samelson, F. 1957. "Conforming Behavior under Two Conditions of Conflict in the Cognitive Field." *Journal of Abnormal and Social Psychology* 35: 181-87.

Savin, H. and Perchonock, E. 1965. "Grammatical Structure and the Immediate Recall of English Sentences." *Journal of Verbal Learning and Verbal Behavior*. 4, 348–353.

Sawyer, A. G. 1972. "Demand Characteristics, Familiarity, and the Attitudinal Effects of Mere Exposure." Unpublished working paper, University of Massachusetts.

———. 1974. "The Effects of Repetition: Conclusions and Suggestions about Laboratory Research." In *Buyer/Consumer Information Processing*, edited by G. D. Hughes and M. I. Ray, pp. 190–219. Chapel Hill, North Carolina: University of North Carolina Press.

Schramm, W. 1963. *The Science of Human Communicators*. New York: Basic Books.

———. 1973. "Channels and Audiences." In *Handbook of Communicators*, edited by Ithrel de Sola Pod et al. Chicago: Rand McNally.

Sears, D. O. 1968. "The Paradox of De Facto Selective Exposure without Preferences for Supportive Information." In *Theories of Cognitive Consistency*, edited by R. P. Abelson et al. Chicago: Rand McNally.

Sears, D. O., and Freedman, J. L. 1967. "Selective Exposure to Information a Critical Review." *Public Opinion Quarterly* 31: 194–213.

Shannon, C. E. 1949. "The Mathematical Theory of Communications." In *The Mathematical Theory of Communication*, edited by C. E. Shannon and W. Weaver, pp. 1–91. Urbana, Ill: University of Illinois Press.

Shepard, R. N. 1967. "Recognition Memory for Words, Sentences, and Pictures." *Journal of Verbal Learning and Verbal Pictures* 6: 156–63.

———. 1978. "The Mental Image." *American Psychologist*, 33, No. 2, February, 125–137.

Sherif, M. 1935. "A Study of Some Social Factors in Perception." *Archives of Psychology* New York, No. 187.

Sherif, M., and Hovland, C. I. 1961. *Social Judgment*. New Haven: Yale University Press.

Sherif, C. W.; Sherif, M.; and Nebergall, R. E. 1965. *Attitude and Attitude Change*. Philadelphia: Saunders.

Sherman, M. A. 1973. "Bound to be Easier: The Negative Prefix and Sentence Comprehension." *Journal of Verbal Learning and Verbal Behavior* 12: 76–84.

Silk, A. J., and Vavra, T. G. 1974. "The Influence of Advertising Effective Qualities on Consumer Response." In *Buyer/Consumer Information Processing*, edited by G. D. Hughes and M. L. Ray, pp. 157–86. Chapel Hill, N.C.: University of North Carolina Press.

Silverman, I. 1964. "Differential Effects of Ego Threat upon Persuasibility for High and Low Self-esteem Subjects." *Journal of Abnormal and Social Psychology* 69: 567–72.

Simon, J. L. 1969. "New Evidence for No Effect of Scale in Advertising." *Journal of Advertising Research* 9: 38-41.

Sims, V. M. 1938. "Factors Influencing Attitude toward the TVA." *Journal of Abnormal Social Psychology* 33: 34-56.

Sissors, J. Z. and Petray, R. 1976. *Advertising Media Planning*. Chicago, Crain Books.

Slobin, D. I. 1966. "Grammatical Transformations and Sentence Comprehension in Childhood and Adulthood." *Journal of Verbal Learning and Verbal Behavior* 5: 219-27.

———. 1971. *Psycholinguistics*. Glenview, Ill.: Scott Foresman.

Smith, F. T. 1943. "An Experiment in Modifying Attitudes toward the Negro." *Teach. Coll. Contribution to Education* no. 887.

Sorguist, J. A. and Morgan, J. 1969. "The Detection of Interaction Effects—A Report on Computer Programs for the Selection of Optimal Combinations of Exploratory Variables." Monograph No. 35. Ann Arbor: University of Michigan, Institute for Social Research, Survey Research Center.

Sparks, D. L. and Tucker, W. T. 1971. "A Multivariate Analysis of Personality and Product Use." *Journal of Marketing Research*, 8, 68-70.

Spielberger, C. D.; Lushene, R. E.; and McAdoo, W. O. 1977. "Theory and Measurement of Anxiety States." In *Handbook of Modern Personality Theory*, edited by R. B. Cattell and R. M. Dreger, pp. 239-53. New York: Hemisphere Publishing.

Staats, C. K. and Staats, A. W. 1957. "Meaning Established by Classical Conditioning." *Journal of Experimental Psychology* 54: 74-80.

Sternthal, B. and Craig, C. S. 1973. "Humor in Advertising." *Journal of Marketing* 37: 12-18.

Stewart, J. B. 1964. *Repetitive Advertising in Newspapers: A Study in Two New Products*. Boston: Harvard University Division of Research.

Stoke, S. M. 1929. "Memory for Onomatopes." *Journal of Genetic Psychology* 3: 594-96.

Stotland, E.; Katz, D.; and Patchen, M. 1959. "The Reduction of Prejudice through the Arousal of Self-Insight." *Journal of Personality* 27: 507-31.

Strong, E. C. 1974. "The Use of Field Experimental Observations in Estimating Advertising Recall." *Journal of Marketing Research* 11: 369-78.

———. 1977. "Space and Timing of Advertising." *Journal of Advertising Research*, December, 25-31.

Strong, E. K. 1912. "The Effect of Length of Series upon Recognition." *Psychological Review* 19: 44-47.

———. 1916. "The Factors Affecting a Permanent Impression Developed through Repetition." *Journal of Experimental Psychology* 1: 319-38.

Stukát, K. G. 1958. *Suggestibility: A Factorial and Experimental Study*. Stockholm: Almgvist and Wiksell.

Szybillo, G. J. and Heslin, R. 1973. "Resistance to Persuasion: Innoculation Theory in a Marketing Context." *Journal of Marketing Research* 10: 369–403.

Tannenbaum, P. H. 1966. "Mediated Generalization of Attitude Change the Principle of Congruity." *Journal of Personality and Social Psychology* 3: 493–99.

———. 1967. "The Congruity Principle Revisisted—Studies in the Reduction, Induction, and Generalization of Presentation." In *Advances in Experimented Social Psychology*, vol. 3, edited by L. Berkowitz, pp. 271–320. New York: Academic Press.

———. 1968. "The Congruity Principle: Retrospective Reflections and Recent Research." In *Theories of Cognitive Consistency: A Sourcebook*. R. P. Abelson et al. Chicago: Rand McNally.

Thorndike, E. L. 1932. *The Fundamentals of Learning*. New York: Teachers College.

Thorne, F. C. 1966. "Theory of the Psychological State." *Journal of Clinical Psychology* 22: 127–235.

Travers, R. M. W. 1964. "The Transmission of Interaction to Human Receivers." *AV Communication Review* 12: 373–85.

Triandis, H. C. 1971. *Attitude and Attitude Change*. New York: John Wiley & Sons.

Underwood, B. J. 1957. "Interference and Forgetting." *Psychological Review* 64: 49–60.

Underwood, B. J., and Postman, L. 1960. "Extra-Experimental Sources of Interference in Forgetting." *Psychological Review* 67: 73–95.

UNITEL 1975. Television Analysis System. Paper presented at 10th Annual Advertising Age Media Workshop, Chicago, Illinois.

Vidale, M. L. and Wolfe, H. B. 1957. "An Operations Research Study of Sales Response to Advertising." *Operations Research* 370–381.

Wallace, W. H. 1970. "Predicting and Measuring the Wearout of Commercials." Speech to Kansas City American Marketing Association.

Wason, P. C. 1961. "Response to Affirmative and Negative Binary Statements." *British Journal of Psychology* 52: 133–42.

———. 1965. "The Contexts of Plausible Denial." *Journal of Verbal Learning and Verbal Behavior* 4: 7–11.

———. 1972. *Psychology of Reasoning: Structure and Content*. Cambridge, Harvard University Press.

Wason, P. C., and Johnson-Laird, P. N. 1972. *Psychology of Reasoning*. Cambridge: Harvard University Press.

Wason, P. C., and Jones, S. 1963. "Negatives: Denotation and Connotation." *British Journal of Psychology* 54: 229–307.

Watts, W. A. 1967. "Relative Persistence of Opinion Change Induced by Active Compared to Passive Participation." *Journal of Personality and Social Psychology* 5: 4–15.

Watts, W. A., and McGuire, W. J. 1964. "Persistence of Induced Opinion Change and Retention of Induced Message Content." *Journal of Abnormal and Social Psychology* 68: 233–41.

Wearing, A. J. 1973. "The Recall of Sentences of Varying Length." *Australian Journal of Psychology* 12: 156–61.

Weber, S. J. 1972. "Source Primary-Recency Effects and the Sleeper Effect." Paper presented at the Annual Meeting of the American Psychological Association, Washington, D.C.

Weiss, W. 1953. "A Sleeper Effect in Opinion Change." *Journal of Abnormal and Social Psychology* 48: 173–80.

———. 1969. "Effects of the Mass Media of Communication." In *The Handbook of Social Psychology*, edited by G. Lindzey and E. Aronson Wiley. Reading, Mass.: Addison-Wesley.

Weitzenhoffer, A. M. 1953. *Hypnotism: An Objective Study in Suggestibility.* New York: Wiley.

Wells, W. D., and Tigert, D. J. 1971. "Activities, Interests, and Opinions." *Journal of Advertising Research* 11: 27–35.

Whittaker, J. O., and Meade, R. D. 1967. "Sex of the Communicator as a Variable in Source Credibility." *Journal of Social Psychology* 72: 27–34.

Wilson, W., and Miller, H. 1968. "Repetition, Order of Presentation, and Timing of Arguments and Measures as Determinants of Opinion Change." *Journal of Personality and Social Psychology* 9: 184–88.

Winograd, E., and Geis, N. F. 1974. "Symantic Encoding and Recognition Memory—A Test of Encoding Variability Theory." *Journal of Experimental Psychology* 102: 1061–68.

Wright, P. 1969. "Transformations and the Understanding of Sentences." *Language and Speech* 12: 156–66.

———. 1972. "Some Observations on how People Answer Questions about Sentences." *Journal of Verbal Learning and Verbal Behavior* 11: 188–95.

———. 1973. "The Cognitive Processes Mediating Acceptance of Advertising." *Journal of Marketing Research* 10: 53–62.

——. 1974a. "On the Direct Monitoring of Cognitive Response to Advertising." In *Consumer Buyer Information Processing*, edited by E. D. Hughes and N. L. Ray. Chapel Hill, North Carolina: University of North Carolina Press.

——. 1974b. "Analyzing Media Effects on Advertising Responses." *Public Opinion Quarterly* 38: 192–205.

——. 1976. "Conditional Consumer Choice Processor and Advertising Strategy." Paper presented at 7th Annual Attitude Research Conference, American Marketing Association, Hilton Head, South Carolina.

Wyer, R. S. 1973. "The Effects of Information Inconsistency and Grammatical Context upon Evaluations of Persons." *Journal of Personality and Social Psychology* 25: 45–49.

——. 1974. *Cognitive Organization and Change: An Information Processing Approach*. Potomac, Maryland: Lawrence Erlbaum Associates.

Wyer, R. S., and Schwartz, S. 1969. "Some Contingencies in the Effects of the Source of a Communication upon the Evaluation of the Communication." *Journal of Personality and Social Psychology* 11: 1–9.

Zajonc, R. B. 1968. "The Attitudinal Effects of Mere Exposure." *Journal of Personality and Social Psychology Monograph Supplement* 9: 1–27.

Zielske, H. A. 1959. "The Remembering and Forgetting of Advertising." *Journal of Marketing* 23: 239–43.

Zimbardo, P. G. 1960. "Involvement and Communication Discrepancy as Determinants of Opinion Conformity." *Journal of Abnormal and Social Psychology* 60: 86–94.

Zimbardo, P. G.; Weisenberg, M.; Firestone, I.; and Levy, B. 1965. "Communicator Effectiveness in Producing Public Conformity and Private Attitude Change." *Journal of Personality* 33: 233–55.

INDEX

Note: Certain terms in this index are so general to the discussion and are repeated so frequently throughout the text that specific page references for these terms would not be very helpful to the reader. In such cases, page numbers are used only to indicate where the definition or discussion relevant to understanding the term can be found.

ABOUT THE AUTHORS

LARRY PERCY is Vice President and Corporate Research Director of CREAMER INC, and has extensive experience in the practical application of communication and information processing theory to strategic marketing and advertising decisions. Prior to joining CREAMER INC in 1978, he spent over 14 years with three other advertising agencies: Gardner Advertising, Ketchum MacLeod & Grove, and Young and Rubicam.

Publications of Mr. Percy have appeared in many journals, including the *Journal of Marketing Research*, and *Journal of Advertising Research*. He has contributed chapters to several marketing and communication textbooks, has regularly contributed papers to professional conferences and is a frequent invited participant at both professional and academic seminars. He also serves on the Editorial Board of the *Journal of Marketing Research* and the Editorial Review Board of *Current Issues and Research in Advertising*.

Mr. Percy received a B.S. in mathematics from Marietta College in 1965.

JOHN R. ROSSITER is associate professor of business at the Graduate School of Business, Columbia University. He has taught previously at The Wharton School, University of Pennsylvania.

Publications by Dr. Rossiter have appeared in many business and behavioral science journals, including the *Journal of Consumer Research, Journal of Marketing Research, Journal of Advertising Research, Journal of Genetic Psychology,* and *Sociometry*. He is coauthor of *Televised Medicine Advertising and Children* (Praeger Special Studies, 1979). He has delivered management seminars in the U.S. and Australia on communication theory applied to advertising and promotion.

Dr. Rossiter received his Ph.D. in communications from the University of Pennsylvania in 1974, after spending a number of years in the marketing research industry. He has an M.S. in marketing from UCLA and an undergraduate honors degree in psychology from the University of Western Australia.